BLACK TELEVISION TRAVELS

CRITICAL CULTURAL COMMUNICATION
General Editors: Sarah Banet-Weiser and Kent A. Ono

Black Television Travels

African American Media around the Globe

Timothy Havens

NEW YORK UNIVERSITY PRESS

New York and London

NEW YORK UNIVERSITY PRESS
New York and London
www.nyupress.org

References to Internet Websites (URLs) were accurate at the time of writing. Neither the author nor New York University Press is responsible for URLs that may have expired or changed since the manuscript was prepared.

An earlier version of chapter 4 was published as Timothy Havens, "The Biggest Show on Earth: *The Cosby Show* and the Ascent of American Situation Comedies in the International Market," in *The Columbia History of American Television*, by Gary Edgerton (New York: Columbia University Press, 2007), 390–409.

Library of Congress Cataloging-in-Publication Data
Havens, Timothy.
Black television travels : African American media around the globe / Timothy Havens.
pages   cm. — (Critical cultural communication)
Includes bibliographical references and index.
ISBN 978-0-8147-3720-0 (cl : alk. paper) — ISBN 978-0-8147-3721-7 (pb : alk. paper) — ISBN 978-0-8147-6076-5 (e-book) — ISBN 978-0-8147-5944-8 (e-book)
1. African Americans on television. 2. Television programs—Social aspects—United States. 3. Foreign television programs—History and criticism.   I. Title.
PN1992.8.A34H38 2013
791.45'08996073—dc23   2012042160

New York University Press books are printed on acid-free paper, and their binding materials are chosen for strength and durability. We strive to use environmentally responsible suppliers and materials to the greatest extent possible in publishing our books.

Manufactured in the United States of America

c   10 9 8 7 6 5 4 3 2 1
p   10 9 8 7 6 5 4 3 2 1

For Rita, Robi, and Reni
who are my very world

Contents

Acknowledgments

In one guise or another, I've been working on this book for the past fifteen years, during which time I've received encouragement, advice, critique, and assistance from more people and institutions than I can remember. I have received funding from the Indiana University Center for International Business Education and Research, the Institute of International Education's Fulbright Program, the Old Dominion University Research Foundation, the Office of the Vice President of Research at the University of Iowa, the University of Iowa's International Programs, the College of Liberal Arts and Sciences at the University of Iowa, and the National Association of Television Program Executives.

Several television professionals have graciously shared with me their time, ideas, and access to industry materials and gatherings. Without their assistance, this book could never have come together. Bruce Johansen and Pam Smithard of NATPE served as my initial industry informants and introduced me to most of the television professionals I interviewed for the book. Gary Marenzi patiently explained to me how the business of trade works over the course of several conversations. Peggy Refford of Reed-Midem and Patrick Jucaud of NATPE-DISCOP kindly permitted me to attend their trade markets when I had no official business there. Finally, dozens of television merchants, programmers, and producers have been willing to speak frankly with me about subject matter that is oftentimes controversial. I am grateful for their candor. I would also like to acknowledge the assistance of the curators of the David Wolper Archives at the University of Southern California.

As with all intellectual undertakings of this scope, this project benefited from the input of many people: Christopher Anderson, Michael Curtin, John Lucaites, Roopail Mukherjee, and Radhika Parameswaran all provided valuable feedback on the early stages of this project, and have continued to encourage and enlighten me as it has progressed. Mark Andrejevic, Bruce Gronbeck, Kembrew McLeod, John Peters, Deborah Whaley, and Rita Zajácz at the University of Iowa, and Gary Edgerton, Dana Heller, and Avi Santo at Old Dominion University have been invaluable colleagues and collaborators on the ideas contained herein, as have Mary Beth Haralovich and Barbara Selznick at the University of Arizona, David Hesmondhalgh at the

University of Leeds, Aniko Imre at USC, Shanti Kumar at the University of Texas, Amanda Lotz at the University of Michigan, Serra Tinic at the University of Alberta, Martin Botha at the University of Cape Town, and John Downing. In addition, numerous current and former graduate students and research assistants contributed immensely to the thinking and research in this book, in particular Deirdre Egan, Daniel Faltesek, Gina Giotta, Sangeet Kumar, Cate Lagueux, David Morris, and Daniel Munksgaard.

Finally, I want to thank my wife, Rita, my son, Robi, and my daughter, Reni, for the intellectual and emotional nourishment they provide me on a daily basis. Writing a book is like running a marathon—the end always seems so far off—and without support and sustenance, a runner will fade and collapse.

Preface

The metaphor of commercial cultural exchange that informs this book is travel. I propose thinking of exchanges of television, film, music, and other forms of popular culture through the heuristic metaphor of travel because of the connotations of change, power, effort, and uncertainty that the word bears. To travel is to make a conscious choice to leave one's familiar, everyday surroundings and, in some manner, be changed. Through travel, no matter how touristic, one agglomerates the traces of the people and places that one encounters. Travel is reserved for the privileged of the world, or at minimum, for those of moderate privilege who have the disposable income and time to plan and execute a trip. We have other words to describe the temporary or permanent relocations of the oppressed—exile, immigration, guest worker programs, the Middle Passage.

The word "travel" shares a root with "travail" and continues to bear the traces of the struggles and uncertainties associated with that term. For me, this makes travel a more accurate way of describing the dangers, miscommunications—even surprises—that attend African American television as it journeys the world than other contemporary ways of characterizing global television: flows, circulation, exchange, trade, export.

When cultural products such as television travel abroad, they likewise exhibit the changes, privileges, efforts, and uncertainties that mark human travel. When non-U.S. broadcasters air imported African American television programs, their actions and perceptions can alter the way those programs are thought of domestically, as well as the ways African Americans are portrayed. Cultures, like people, agglomerate the traces of their travels —something that the metaphor of travel foregrounds much more directly than other metaphors. Moreover, not all forms of culture "flow" or "circulate" equally; instead, it is the cultures of the privileged or moderately privileged that travel most frequently and widely. This is even the case for Nigerian videofilms, which enjoy wide distribution across Africa, the Black Atlantic, and beyond, and which address the abjection of life lived at the periphery of modern capitalism. Still, Nollywood is among the more privileged of the underprivileged media industries in the Global South, capable of exploiting a range of domestic and foreign markets to generate revenues.

Cultural travel, like human travel, is both exciting and dangerous. What happens, both culturally and politically, when, say, viewers abroad watch *Amos 'n' Andy*, *Chappelle's Show*, or even *The Cosby Show*? Chance encounters and unexpected affinities lie around every corner, as do devious hucksters, strange customs, and simple, utter confusion. Indeed, in my opinion, these excitements and dangers are precisely what make the study of cultural globalization so compelling. I hope that this volume helps spark, renew, or enlarge a similar commitment in some of its readers.

Introduction

African American Television Trade

On December 8, 2005, the Museum of Television and Radio in New York broadcast an interactive panel discussion where television writers, actors, programming executives, and viewers at colleges across the country discussed new opportunities for women in dramatic television series. I called in with a question about why dramas featuring women of color have not enjoyed the same success as those with white leads. Susanne Daniels, president of entertainment for Lifetime Entertainment Services, fielded the question:

> It is my understanding . . . this is . . . how I've been educated . . . that one of the ways we make money from these shows is selling them internationally, and that the international marketplace will pay less for shows with certain ethnic leads than they will for white leads. . . . When I've asked that question before, I've heard that answer.

Daniels's comments are not idiosyncratic. I have heard similar assessments from more than a dozen television executives, demonstrating just how widespread the assumption is, and how much perceptions of international salability influence domestic portrayals of African Americans and their potential to circulate transnationally.[1] In this instance, globalization places limits on which genres are and are not likely to feature African Americans. As we shall see throughout this volume, globalization also shapes the characterizations, narratives, settings, themes, and cultural politics of African American and black television programs in more complex and ambivalent ways.[2]

In the pages that follow, I view media globalization not as a restrictive or liberating force, but as productive of certain kinds of representational outcomes rather than others. In some ways globalization has expanded the diversity of African American television, while in other ways it has severely restricted that diversity. With respect to genre, for instance, globalization has helped expand innovations in African American situation comedy, sketch comedy, animation, and even, to a much smaller degree, drama. Globalization has also resulted in more diverse portrayals of African American men, especially young men, in terms of class, politics, and professions. For African American women, by contrast, globalization has helped narrow the diversity of portrayals or eliminate them altogether, in large part because African American characters and cultural allusions are most frequently used to attract young male demographics across multiple racial and national boundaries.

The Production of Racial Discourse in the Cultural Industries

The institutional changes associated with global television—selling to and acquiring from international program markets, buying or starting channels in multiple territories, developing global channel brands, and designing programs with foreign viewers in mind—have influenced U.S. television for a long time, and African American television series have been at the forefront of several worldwide trends. However, American television executives have frequently been slow or unwilling to recognize the importance of black characters and themes in facilitating the globalization of those series. One of the main aims of this book, then, is to reclaim the history of African American television travels in an effort to correct and counteract this predominant industry lore.

A second aim of this book is to understand in detail how the globalization of the media industries shapes the representational politics of African American television. Media globalization entails identifying, developing, and exploiting popular culture trends over as wide a geographic area as possible. It is an attempt to exert corporate control over both producers and consumers of popular culture—to predict and control viewers' tastes and behaviors, to initiate and manage cultural trends. As such, media globalization is unequivocally an exercise in corporate capitalist power.

My approach to corporate power draws on Michel Foucault's perspective that power produces both social realities and available forms of resistance:

> We must cease once and for all to describe the effects of power in negative terms: it "excludes," it "represses," it "censors," it "abstracts," it "masks," it "conceals." In fact, power produces; it produces reality; it produces domains of objects and rituals of truth. (1979, 194)

When it comes to African American television, the power of transnational media conglomerates creates the conditions within which particular African American portrayals are and are not thinkable. Furthermore, as we shall see in several cases throughout this volume, the efforts of these corporations to shape African American programming in particular ways also produce the dominant forms against and within which creative workers strive to tell different kinds of stories about African American life and culture.

As I will argue, the power of the global cultural industries to produce reality operates on both popular and institutional levels, through distinct yet interwoven discursive practices. My main interest lies with the institutionalized discourses, why they activate certain popular trends rather than others, and how they form, circulate, and change. While I certainly attend to the popular reception of African American television abroad and some of the enlightening and inspiring purposes it can serve, these popular uses are not my primary focus. Indeed, I consider the production of reality *within* the industry generally more powerful than the production of popular realities, given that institutional perceptions determine in the first instance whether and how to represent African Americans, how and where those representations will be seen, and how the preferences and priorities of minority and majority groups around the world filter back into the television industry's representational practices.

Industry Lore in Global Television

In examining institutional discourses about race and the globalization of African American television, I focus predominantly on industry intermediaries who work at three main moments in the value-chain of commercial global television: the moment of broadcast abroad, the moment of program exchange, and the moment of program production. These moments of interface serve as locations where cultural values like pleasure and popularity get transcoded into commercial values like profit, market share, and business strategies (Lampel, 2011). For example, foreign broadcasters work to integrate the tastes and interests of viewers with self-produced or acquired programming, all the while operating within the institutional priorities of their organizations (whether those priorities are commercial, cultural, democratic, etc.). The global programming markets, meanwhile, involve such obvious institutional considerations as the price and fit of imported programs. At the same time, program trade is an act of cross-cultural interaction and imagination that requires executives to envision the possible resonances and dislocations between foreign programs and local audiences—again, within the institutional demands of their organizations (Bielby and Harrington, 2008; Havens, 2006). Finally, television production serves as an interface between the creative visions of those involved in making television and the institutions that shape, direct, limit, and encourage their efforts (Newcomb and Alley, 1983).

The intermediaries I study serve as organizational "linking pins" (Turow, 1996) between different divisions and firms, bearing intelligence as well as interpretations of popular trends from one field of business activity to another. As such, media industry intermediaries are members of overlapping interpretive communities who actively work to decipher viewers' tastes, textual meanings and pleasures, and industry priorities and trends, and to spread those perceptions as widely as possible. While these interpretive communities operate primarily at the domestic and local levels, they increasingly intersect with executive interpretive communities elsewhere, including the wealthy and powerful Hollywood executives who still tend to reign over global television.

Despite the differential power relationships among executives and firms in global television, however, institutionalized discourses—or what I term "industry lore" throughout—are not monolithic. Indeed, industry lore is inherently characterized by a good deal of disagreement because definitions of what can and cannot travel well internationally help determine such practical business realities as program prices, demographic slant, and sales revenues. Consequently, different firms and executives compete to shape industry lore in ways that benefit them and their organizations.

Industry lore functions essentially as a carrier discourse; its main function is to carry the discourses encoded into television programming, which I refer to as *televisual* discourses (or, more frequently, televisual representations), from one location to another, much as carrier waves in radio communication do not possess broadcast content, but transport that content from the source to the receiver. Industry lore similarly moves television programming between nations; it is a way of talking and thinking about audiences and programming that permits television insiders to imagine connections between audience members and television programming from around the world.

As a carrier discourse, industry lore operates within distinct fields of knowledge and serves quite different functions than televisual discourse. Industry lore is parasitic on televisual discourse, seizing only on those elements and insights that are useful for institutional goals and discarding all else. This "institutional point of view," as Ien Ang (1991) calls it, "[allows] these institutions to realize their ambitions to govern and control the formal frameworks of television's place in contemporary life" (2). While industry lore does not determine either television content or the meanings that television carries for real viewers, it does shape what gets produced as well as how, where, and when productions get watched. Industry lore provides the conduit through which the economic demands of the cultural industries get transcoded into concrete representational practices. Despite its real power to produce markets, representations, and subjectivity, however, rarely does industry lore become visible to the general public.

Industry lore, then, is a distinct form of power/knowledge (Ang, 1991; Foucault, 1979). When it comes to industry lore about blackness and race in general, the particular forms, functions, and cultural manifestations of power/knowledge within the global cultural industries differ significantly from the power/knowledge of the state, where cultural representations of race traditionally resided. For the state, race acts as a form of "biopower" that helps manage perceived internal threats to bourgeois rule by ensuring the purity, legitimacy, and longevity of the bourgeoisie (Foucault, 1980; Goldberg, 2002; Stoler, 1995). For the cultural industries, by contrast, race acts as a potential transnational conduit for connecting consumers and commercial culture: a global market.

Obviously, the commercial cultural industries are primarily interested not in the continuation of bourgeois or elite rule, but in profits. In their focus on economic power rather than biopower, the cultural industries follow quite different logics than the state in producing and circulating racial discourses. Because their measure is popularity, not political efficacy, the cultural industries rely on the aforementioned, two-pronged discursive strategy, where televisual discourses travel widely and serve a range of institutional labors, while industry lore constantly scavenges for profitable, reproducible practices and trends to exploit on a global scale. Televisual discourse, then, is centrifugal, while industry lore is centripetal (Curtin, 2008). Such an arrangement works to maximize the diversity of uses for programming itself to enhance profitability, while ensuring that commercially viable, local trends get reproduced in as many places as possible. Moreover, as mentioned above, because commercial cultural industries, unlike branches of state, are competitive rather than cooperative, the motivation to innovate in representational practices, institutional labors for imported programming, and industry lore is strong.

Industry lore arises from and influences the myriad institutional labors that imported television programs—including African American series— perform for broadcasters around the world. While such uses may appear at first blush to be little more than business decisions, they shape the ideologies and representations that circulate through popular television, the audience makeup for specific shows and channels, and the shared cultural experiences and sympathies among segments of the viewing public. These decisions are neither accidental nor arbitrary, but are rather calculated efforts to press imports into the service of domestic institutional goals, a fact that the term "labor" is intended to signify. Institutional labor, then, refers to various forms of encoding, or the process that media professionals go through to create meaningful programs and program lineups that intersect with viewers' lifestyles and cultural sensibilities (Hall, 1993b).[3]

Blackness in Industry Lore

What I offer in these pages is a chronicle of the various institutional labors that African American television has performed in different historical eras, as well as a reading of the dominant racial cartography of the world among television industry insiders, which those labors have given rise to. This institutionalized racial cartography has become more organized over the decades examined in *Black Television Travels* as the global markets themselves have become more organized, predictable, and important for television producers and broadcasters everywhere. What were once mostly sporadic and idiosyncratic uses of African American imports became conventionalized in the late 1980s around an industry lore about the "universal" appeal of some television shows, which supposedly tapped into shared human themes that audiences everywhere could relate to. African American programs fared poorly under this discursive regime for several reasons: (a) a good deal of African American popular culture tries to distinguish itself from mainstream white culture, making it unlikely that white executives would recognize such anti-mainstream representations as universal; (b) the television industries were organized as national markets, endorsing the perception that nationality was the primary organizer of human identity and blinding executives to the possibility for transnational forms of identity such as race to bind audiences together; and (c) nationwide European broadcasters serving predominantly white, middle-class family audiences were the most lucrative markets for American distributors.

Due to changes in delivery technologies, government policies, funding sources, politics, and the unexpected success of some African American shows on the world markets, industry lore in the mid-1990s began to accommodate the potential appeal of some African American themes and characters for certain transnational audience groups, specifically youth. However, while these newer uses of African American imports made it clear that the discourse of universals did not cover all instances of successful export, a formalized industry lore did not cohere until the middle of the first decade of the twenty-first century. Today the idea that viewers who watch imported television are on a "cultural journey" has begun to seep into industry lore. Though by no means dominant, the nascent lore of cultural journeys has begun to take hold in certain sectors of the global television industries. The discourse of cultural journeys and the discourse of universals work today to anchor four distinct representational regimes of blackness in television: integrated workplace dramas, multicultural domestic comedies, hyperreal "quality" serials, and satirical travesties.

A Note on Terminology and Method

For the purposes of this study I use the phrase "African American television" to refer to series that make consistent reference to African American political, thematic, or cultural concerns. I make this definition intentionally broad in order to allow us to explore the widest possible diversity of trade routes suggested by the history of U.S. exports. Because the global trade in African American television has been intermittent and often limited to shows produced primarily for middle-class white viewers in the United States, I hesitate to limit my analysis to shows that meet only particular standards for fear of overlooking important examples due to an overly narrow initial definition. In other words, I take the history of African American television trade as an index of potential routes, rather than the last word on the kinds of programs that are capable of worldwide travel and their possible uses. Consequently, I include integrated series such as *Benson* (1979–1986) and *Diff'rent Strokes* (1978–1986) that might arguably be said to focus on white concerns about integration and fantasies of egalitarian white folks. Nevertheless, integration was an issue facing a growing number of African Americans in the seventies and eighties, and shows such as these were not wholly absent of African American concerns. In some respects, integrated programs offered fantasized depictions of black and white cooperation in personal and professional arenas that had the potential to serve as momentary escapes from the realities of everyday discrimination for black viewers from the United States to South Africa, much the same as *The Cosby Show* (1984–1992) did later in the decade (Downing, 1988; Havens, 2000). For these reasons, I cast a wide net when looking at the worldwide circulation of U.S. programs that depict aspects of African American life.

The Globalization and Commercialization of Black Popular Culture

The globalization of African American television raises two related concerns: the impact of commercialism on the content, relevance, and politics of African American popular culture *and* the impact of globalization. Given the countercultural ethos of many black communities and their general exploitation by modern capitalism, it is tempting to assume that those forms of culture that are most intimately tied to global commerce, such as television, are inherently less relevant for black communities than less commodified forms such as dance or poetry. Karen Ross (1996), for instance, suggests that the globalization of the media industries increases "[t]he potential for negative media stereotypes to circulate internationally" (172) and relegates "less popular and more challenging oppositional work to the margins" (175). This argument, however, is accurate only if we assume several things: first, that stereotypes are somehow universal, while other forms of televisual expression are not; second, that globalization leads to a mainstreaming of expression, which ignores the fact that globalization and commercial audience fragmentation go hand in hand, leading to complex centrifugal and centripetal cultural and institutional configurations; and third, that the global audience is somehow a white audience that prefers negative black stereotypes over other kinds of black characters and stories.

In the pages that follow, I reject the idea that the relevance of African American cultural forms is inversely proportional to their sales revenues. While a relationship between economic goals and cultural forms surely exists, it is a complex and ambivalent one, where competing and sometimes conflicting cultural, political, historical, and institutional priorities put their stamps on the final cultural product. For some contemporary critics, the poet Langston Hughes's collection *Fine Clothes to the Jew* (1927) was largely irrelevant for African American readers, while for many television critics, *Roc* (1991–1994) and *Frank's Place* (1987–1988) were quite relevant (Gray, 1995; Jackson, 2005, 16; Zook, 1999), despite the fact that the latter were decidedly commercial ventures. The point here is that the cultural consequences of African American television trade cannot simply be inferred from sales records and balance sheets; they need to be examined in specific cases.

Notwithstanding commercial television's potential for connecting with black communities around the world, we still need a way to analyze and interpret the cultural politics of transnationally circulated African American television programs. This may seem like an easy task of identifying which shows contain negative stereotypes and which do not, but such identification is far from an exact science. Nor does the presence or absence of recognizable stereotypes exhaust the cultural politics of a television program.

In a particularly stark example of the inexactness of defining what is and is not a negative portrayal, Alvin Poussaint in his foreword to Robin R. Means Coleman's (1998) book *African American Viewers and the Black Situation Comedy* praises *The Fresh Prince of Bel-Air* (1990–1996) as one of the only programs in the late nineties that was not a throwback to "old-style Black sitcoms" that "affirm White superiority and Black inferiority" (xii). A few pages later, however, Coleman herself refers to the same show as "contemporary minstrelsy" (115), drawing a direct connection between racist stereotypes and *The Fresh Prince of Bel-Air*.

The approach I take to stereotypes here is central to my analysis of the global trade in African American television. However, I want to distinguish my understanding of television stereotypes and their functions from some dominant forms of stereotype analysis popular among scholars who implicitly or explicitly adopt a cognitive psychological model. Such a model sees stereotypes as trans-historical, transcultural characterizations that give audiences either "positive" or "negative" attitudes toward African Americans (Dixon, 2000; Gandy, 1998; cf. Goldberg, 1993, 121–33). The limitations of this view have been debated in a variety of other places (Acham, 2004; Torres, 2003; Zook, 1995), so I do not discuss them at length here. Suffice it to say that stereotype analysis deflects attention from other features of the televisual text, including narrative, visual, and audio elements, which work with and against character elements to complicate the text's meanings and cultural politics. In addition, such analyses rely on an oversimplified idea of positive and negative "images" that does not do justice to the range of emotional and intellectual responses that television viewers have to characters. Most importantly, for our purposes, the model of media and society that underlies stereotype analysis tends to isolate viewers and programs from their cultural surroundings, assuming that stereotypes feed directly into deep cognitive structures of the viewer, which is what causes them to operate in the same way in all historical periods and cultures. By contrast, I would argue that stereotypes derive their power precisely because they are embedded in specific cultures and eras. Hence, the Sambo stereotype, which dominated American cultural projections of African American men from the 1660s through the 1960s, served quite different functions in different places and eras: its durability owed not to the singularity of its cognitive impact, but to the flexibility of its cultural and political uses (Boskin, 1986).

Stereotype analysis can call our attention to how similar character types recur throughout history and serve a variety of racist ends, and in my opinion this is when the method is at its strongest. Stereotype analysis is at its weakest when it prescribes certain types of programs or representational practices as inherently superior or inferior to others. In these instances, the method can restrict rather than expand the diversity of African American cultural expression in television. Let me be clear here that my critique of the excesses of some forms of stereotype *analysis* is not an endorsement of those stereotypes in any way. There can be no doubt that brutal stereotypes of African Americans have been integral to justifications of extreme forms of physical, psychological, cultural, and economic violence. Unfortunately, the animus behind those stereotypes cannot be done away with simply by replacing them with positive images. As Ella Shohat and Robert Stam (1994) observe regarding film stereotypes, "A cinema in which all the characters resembled

Sidney Poitier might be as much a cause for alarm as one in which they all resembled Step'n Fetchit" (204). Thus, rather than ask whether the world-wide traffic in African American television is filled with stereotypes, we need to ask whether particular series, portrayals, and uses of African American television serve oppressive or liberating racial projects at home and abroad.

For the reasons just outlined, I do not use positive and negative stereotypes as a way to evaluate the cultural politics of African American television exports. Instead, I understand all televisual representations of African Americans as inherently dialectical, exhibiting oppression and liberation, assimilation and difference, capitulation and resistance. A good deal of recent scholarship in African American television studies, in fact, has sought to reclaim the more redemptive dimensions of this dialectic, even of long-disgraced television series that are, for some, the epitome of racist representation, such as *Amos 'n' Andy* (Ely, 1991; Watkins, 1994) and *Sanford and Son* (Acham, 2004). These studies share a commitment to the historicity of television, its embeddedness in the time and place of its origin, along with a recognition that popular culture is never univocal. Instead, as Stuart Hall (1993b) has written, "black popular culture [enables] the surfacing, inside the mixed and contradictory modes even of some mainstream popular culture, of elements of a discourse that is different" (111).

The method of analysis I employ throughout this volume, then, begins with the assumption that television programming is complex and dialectical, integrating a range of social and political perspectives that are drawn from contemporaneous developments in society at large. Much as with industry lore, however, this diversity of perspectives is both limited in its range and structured hierarchically by the production process, such that certain perspectives are more prevalent and more easily decoded by viewers, while other voices tend to be textually submerged and require a good deal more effort on the part of viewers to ferret them out (Fiske, 1987; Newcomb and Hirsch, 1983).

Each chapter below includes an analysis of the dominant forms of televisual representation of African Americans in the era under analysis, along with a discussion of the dominant social and political developments of the era that inform those representational practices. Next, the analysis turns to consider how programmers abroad exploited those representational practices to meet their own institutional ends, focusing especially on which perspectives and themes embedded in the programming they found useful. Thereafter, the chapter charts how these international institutional labors found—or failed to find—their way into dominant industry lore among distribution and production executives, and whether and how that lore encouraged future representational practices. Throughout, I try to attend closely to political and cultural changes, changes in technology and industry structure, changes in institutional practices and industry lore, and changes in representations of African Americans, as well as the complex determinations that exist among each of these fields.

Commercialization and Authorship in African American Television

The discussion of stereotyping and representation is closely linked to concerns about African American authorship in television. Questions of authorship among African American media scholars have been a particular concern, given the long history of objectification of African Americans at the hands of white popular culture and the intimate connections between popular portrayals and racist political projects (Nederveen Pieterse, 1992). In general, scholars have treated television as an ambivalent site for African American portrayals, at once closely linked to traditional racist stereotypes in the service of white political and economic interests, while also offering the potential for African Americans to tell new and distinct stories that can reach a multiracial audience.

Most observers have located authorship in the hands of either writer-producers or corporate owners who advance, neglect, or exploit the interests of African American communities. However, much as scholars have sought to reclaim the racially progressive dimensions of long-disparaged television series, they have also identified an ever widening scope of creative and institutional actors who contribute to authoring particular series. Much of the early work on African Americans and television originated among mass communication scholars examining the effects of television stereotypes on viewers, especially minority and children viewers. These studies almost invariably included discussions about why the commercial television industry consistently produced racial stereotypes as well, although examinations of ownership, gatekeepers, and production remained secondary and empirically thin (Poindexter and Stroman, 1981).

Beginning with Herman Gray's book *Watching Race* (1995), which offered the first sustained analysis of how the commercial television industry and African American representation interact, cultural studies scholars began to examine the production of African American representations alongside the representations themselves. Rooted in set visits and interviews with African American program producers, Gray's work demonstrated how the technological and economic changes associated with the post-network era—the introduction of cable and the VCR and the founding of the Fox Network —gave African American writer-producers more leeway to reflect the complexity of African American life than they had enjoyed during the network era. Kristal Brent Zook (1999) employs methods similar to Gray's in her investigation of the "revolutionary" African American programs produced by the Fox Broadcasting Corporation in the 1990s.

The analysis of African American authorship that Gray and Zook introduced has subsequently been expanded upon to include performers (Acham, 2004), popular critics (Acham; Harper, 1998), audiences (Bodroghkozy, 1992), and corporate owners (Smith-Shomade, 2007; Zook, 2008). All of these examinations of authorship in African American television have focused on creative (or journalistic) personnel who work above-the-line or corporate owners and strategists whose business plans set the agendas of their television operations. However, as I have already discussed, in fictional television at least, a layer of programming personnel mediates between corporate strategies and creative visions. It is these programming executives who are ultimately responsible for producing industry lore about global audience tastes, which constitutes the main vehicle whereby economic and technological globalization influences cultural representations on television.

The analysis of authorship in African American television has also tended to focus on moments of significant upheaval within the industry, which permitted African American creators, producers, and performers a good deal of leeway in trying to tell stories in their own manner. Given those extraordinary historical conditions, it is not surprising that these studies have not for the most part attempted to theorize the degree of authority and agency that various stakeholders enjoy in day-to-day production, distribution, and programming decisions under more conventional circumstances. For a study such as this, however, which aims to untangle the articulations between institutionalized and popular discourses of race in television, a theoretical understanding of such autonomy is vital.

Among scholars working from a "critical media industry studies" perspective, questions of creative authority and agency have tended to take center stage (Havens, Lotz, and Tinic, 2009). In particular, these scholars address how a range of institutional actors serve as cultural mediators who ultimately shape the representational politics of television programming. In approaching authorship, critical media industry scholars have focused on the complex articulations between production, representation, and reception as a way of conceiving of the process as more than a matter of individual expression, while retaining the crucial role of authorial intent in the creation of cultural meanings. In other words, this line of research conceives of meaning-making as an intentional activity, while retaining a critical understanding of intentionality as embedded within history, discourse, institutions, relations of power, and cultural traditions. Consequently, the hallmark of critical media industry studies is that it addresses *neither* the agency of producers and consumers *nor* the meanings of texts, but rather the interactions among these sites as a way to comprehend the impact of communications technologies and industries on contemporary culture.

Critical media industry scholarship adopts anthropological and sociological methods to examine questions of power, authority, and agency within media industries, particularly the methods of fieldwork. Among those who have focused on the television industries, at least in the United States, the writer-producer has long been the main locus of authorship (Newcomb and Alley, 1983; Newcomb and Hirsch, 1983). From this perspective, producers are understood as the visionaries behind their series and as cultural bricoleurs who translate cultural trends and industry demands into finished programming, which nevertheless varies only mildly from standard formats due to industry pressure. Early scholarship in this vein also emphasized the *production company*, as well as competition among national networks and broader cultural changes, in shaping aesthetic styles and ideological content in fictional television programming (Feuer, Kerr, and Vahimagi, 1983; Turow, 1981).

Carefully researched and argued, these studies were also, in some ways, products of an era during which independent producers flourished because of the FCC's Financial Interest and Syndication Rules, which forbade the national networks from owning or profiting from the shows they broadcast. Because the real money in U.S. television had long been the local syndication markets, the FCC's rule effectively created lucrative markets for independent television producers. After the repeal of the rule in 1993, television producers found themselves with generally smaller revenues and, in many instances, with less creative control than they had enjoyed in the seventies and eighties. In today's fragmented multimedia environment, executive producers/head writers, or "show runners," have reasserted their authorial agency within the television industry, due to their ability to convince both audiences and industry executives that they have their fingers on the pulse of contemporary cultural trends and tastes.

While most scholarship on television authorship continues to concentrate on the producer-as-author, most analysts also recognize the importance of other corporate actors, funding mechanisms, and industry practices as limitations on producerly independence. However, they tend to view the interventions of business executives (or "suits") as *limitations* on creativity, rather than as productive of programming practices, styles, and genres. Todd Gitlin's *Inside Prime Time* (1983) and John Thornton Caldwell's *Production Culture* (2008) offer two noteworthy departures from this focus on the limitations of business intermediaries, examining, among other things, the influence of executives on programming, the importance of studying the intersection between production cultures and representational strategies, and the variety of ways that executives, above-the-line talent, and below-the-line workers, not just writers and producers, exert agency over television texts as cultural bricoleurs.

Ultimately, in its focus on programming executives, *Black Television Travels* follows Gitlin's study more closely, though it also attends to the ways industry lore filters down to producers and writers, as well as how these "creatives" work with the grain of industry lore to tell the kinds of stories they want to about African American culture on television. Executive culture provides a crucial site of investigation, because it translates between technological, economic, and popular forces, as executives seek to take advantage of new media and new trends to maximize profits within the institutional and economic structures in which they work.

Global Television Basics

This volume limits its analysis to television because television offers a unique combination of words, images, and practices that distinguish it from other cultural forms, even as it draws upon, amplifies, and recirculates discourses from elsewhere. First, television has traditionally been an oral medium, which arises from and portrays everyday life, due to its small screen size, its moderate image quality, and the domestic nature of its reception in most cultures (Fiske, 1987). Television, therefore, reflects the dialects, rhythms, settings, and stories of our immediate day-to-day lives. When it comes to international trade, television's stories are more difficult to unmoor from their immediate cultural surroundings than more spectacular cultural products such as film. At the same time, it is significantly cheaper to buy television program rights than it is to produce one's own programming, and the international markets offer an attractive, low-cost option for most of the world's broadcasters. Consequently, the economics of television make international distribution and acquisition attractive options, while the cultural specificity of television confounds trade.

Second, television is distinct from other cultural forms in that it has historically included a duality of address, one encoded within the program itself, the other encoded within television's overall flow, the lineup and identity of the channels that broadcast the program, and, within multichannel environments at least, competing programs that vie for the viewer's attention in real time. Unlike film or music, which tend to retail as distinct cultural products, television primarily comes to us prepackaged with a range of cues about how we should interpret it—cues that also profoundly influence industry-wide interpretations about whether imported programs succeed in fulfilling institutional goals. For instance, foreign broadcasters of the miniseries *Roots* (1977) and the situation comedy *Benson* (1979–1986) repositioned the programs with distinct local scheduling practices to better serve their institutional goals.

Finally, television trade must navigate distinct economic and regulatory pressures that other cultural forms do not, specifically, the vagaries of the advertising industry, which often directly or indirectly funds production, and the maze of different national regulations surrounding broadcasting and communications around the world. Because my interests here are not the articulations of discourses *across* multiple cultural sites, but rather those articulations that exist *among* industrial conditions and representation, it makes most sense to focus on the operations and portrayals of a single cultural industry.

With more than 1.2 billion households owning a set in 2009, television remains the most widely used communications medium in the world and the primary way—whether we like it or not—that the world's residents gain knowledge about African American culture and people (IDATE, 2010). Commercial cultural discourses, such as those that circulate through television, are the dominant discourses of blackness and race in today's world. While popular and commercial representations of blacks and African Americans have always been central to the racial projects of Western nations, these representations traditionally operated in the service of imperialism and the exploitation of labor and raw materials (Nederveen Pieterse, 1992; Goldberg, 1993; Stoler, 1995). By contrast, popular discourses of blackness today travel in search of audiences, acceptance, and popularity in as many locations as possible. The institutional and technological forces that shape and support these flows operate relatively independently of state interests, much as the interests of capital in general have grown increasingly independent of state interests over the past few centuries (Ruggie, 1993).

The Cultural Politics of Program Exchange

The history of nationwide public service and state broadcasting, combined with the quotidian modes of reception and representation common in television, puts a premium on connecting with the most immediate viewers of a television channel, as do the typical practices of selling advertising time based upon Gross Rating Points measured every fifteen minutes or so. Practically speaking, these historical and institutional forces give the local programmer a good deal of authority when it comes to designing channel lineups and making programming decisions; perhaps more authority than music retailers or movie theatre operators abroad. Even Western-owned transnational television brands, such as MTV Germany, HBO Latin America, and Cartoon Network Poland, typically employ local programming executives who select and program a range of television shows, some identical to their U.S. sister channels, and some quite distinct.

The exceptions to this rule are low-rent transnational channels, which target large swaths of territory with little if any variation in programs, schedules, or advertisements. These channels, encompassing a wide array of channels devoted to reality TV, pornography, telenovelas, and action series, really do very little to conceptualize difference in audience tastes across national or cultural boundaries. The business model that they work from permits them to turn small, consistent profits because of the cheapness of programming and delivery costs, but they are generally not a significant presence, either in the markets where they are imported or in the construction of industry-wide discourse about programming and audiences.[4]

In most instances, then, local programmers, or acquisitions executives, make active choices about which programs to purchase, even as distributors try their utmost to influence those choices in order to increase overall sales numbers and maximize sales of particularly expensive programming. While acquisition choices are driven by economic considerations, especially pricing, cultural considerations are rarely absent. In this way, acquisition is a form of cultural interpretation; it is an effort to imagine the cultural similarities and differences between foreign programs and domestic viewers.

Acquisition and scheduling decisions work to privilege certain elements of programs over others in particular markets. These elements, in turn, are sought out or avoided in the global marketplace, depending on how a series performs. If a buyer is important for a distributor, her perception of the performance of prior purchases, as well as her interpretations of why the programming performed as it did, will shape the distributor's efforts to promote new shows. Moreover, if the distributor has influence over future production decisions, as is the case with the major Hollywood studios that produce and distribute most African American television, an important buyer's tastes can shape production practices as well. We can see this phenomenon quite clearly in Susanne Daniels's comment above that the preferences of important international buyers depress domestic production of dramas featuring African Americans.

Just how important international revenues are for domestic production financing depends on the relationship between the distributor and the producer, the genre of programming, and also the sales potential of the programming in the domestic syndication markets. Most U.S. network television series have traditionally required three seasons' worth of episodes before they can be sold in the domestic syndication market.[5] Because domestic U.S. syndication revenues far outstrip international revenues in most cases, American television series tend to be heavily reliant on international revenues in the first three season, prior to their domestic syndication; the longer they stay on the air thereafter, the larger the percentage of their revenues that comes from domestic syndication. So international syndication revenues tend to be important in the short run, but less important in the long run.[6]

Again, as we will see throughout the following chapters, both the genre of programming and the historical period in which it was produced and syndicated influence the importance of international markets and their subsequent sway over domestic production decisions. When it comes to contemporary, mainstream Hollywood productions, international sales executives from within the organization are "fully involved" in the decision-making process (Kaner, 1999), whereas independent distributors, even moderately sized ones that carry U.S. network series, only suggest "little things, or touches" to make programming more translatable to international markets (Lazarus, 1999). Still, while the level of involvement may differ, more and more television productions, both at home and abroad, attempt to account for foreign viewers' tastes. Even the producers of the animated New Zealand series *bro'Town*, a culturally distinct animated series featuring Samoan and Māori teenagers living in the Morningside suburb of Auckland, report taking the preferences of foreign viewers into consideration during production (Mitchell, 2009).

The enabling and disabling influence of global syndication markets on African American television portrayals is well captured in the case of *Soul Food* (2000–2004), a Showtime drama focused on an African American family trying to recover from the death of their mother, particularly through family cooking and gatherings. The series was adapted for television from the 1997 film of the same name and was jointly produced by Paramount Pictures and Twentieth Century Fox Television. *Soul Food* was a critical and ratings success for Showtime at a time when it aired very little original programming, but problems with its international syndication revenues were a perpetual headache for Paramount. Originally included in the company's output deal with KirchMedia, a German firm aggressively seeking program deals in the late 1990s in advance of its launch of a digital satellite service with hundreds of channels, *Soul Food* lost its international syndication revenues when KirchMedia declared bankruptcy in 2002. For the remaining seasons, *Soul Food*'s budget was in constant jeopardy, creating numerous conflicts between Paramount and the series' executive producer, Felicia D. Henderson, as well as perpetual efforts to cut production costs. While the series was able to struggle through for two more seasons, making it the longest-running television drama with a predominantly black cast to date, the case of *Soul Food* provides some crucial insights into the globalization of African American television (Henderson, 2010). First, it demonstrates how African American shows can benefit from the revenue opportunities that foreign markets represent, especially in periods of significant technological and industrial change. Second, it shows how important those revenues are for African American shows to continue on the air. Third, it shows that when there is no robust industry lore supporting them, African American television dramas are vulnerable to the vagaries of the world's television industries. That is, absent the faith of distributors and broadcasters in the appeal of African American dramas, their hold on foreign syndication revenues can only ever be tenuous.

Race, Globalization, Institutionalization

The global travels of African American television take place within a much longer history of cultural trade, racialization, and economic exploitation, even as they build upon and alter those processes. In its modern incarnations, dating from the eighteenth century, race has referred to transnational categories of identity whose members are thought to share similar physical, emotional, and cultural traits (Goldberg, 1993; Omi and Winant, 1994). Omi and Winant refer to these racial categories as racial *formations*, or "the sociohistorical process by which racial categories are created, inhabited, transformed, and destroyed" (55). Racial formations are produced by particular racial projects, which involve "an interpretation, representation, or explanation of racial dynamics, and an effort to reorganize and redistribute resources along particular racial lines" (56). The strength of Omi and Winant's conceptualization of racial projects is that it connects representational systems with economic and political structures, or cultural practices with institutional ones.

In their concentration on legal and political structures, however, Omi and Winant tend to privilege domestic racial projects, while racial formation has also been a transnational undertaking since at least the nineteenth century

(Goldberg, 1993; Stoler, 1995). Ann Laura Stoler, drawing on Michel Foucault's arguments in *The History of Sexuality* and later lectures at the Collège de France, identifies racial discourses as central components of the establishment of bourgeois rule within and beyond Europe in an era of colonialism. "Race," she writes, became

> the organizing grammar of an imperial order in which modernity, the civilizing mission, and the "measure of man" were framed. And with it, "culture" is harnessed . . . not only to mark difference, but to rationalize the hierarchies of privilege and profit, to consolidate the labor regimes of expanding capitalism, to provide the psychological scaffolding for the exploitative structure of colonial rule. (27)

In Stoler's understanding of colonial history, then, racial ascriptions and racism served to solidify the superiority of European civilization and rationalize the economic and physical exploitation of non-Europeans. Not only did race identify transnational human groupings, but, in its modern incarnations at least, it also grew out of economic and political structures.

European efforts to establish and enforce racial categories and hierarchies around the world inevitably met resistance among non-Europeans. While much of this resistance was local, historical evidence suggests that resistant cultural tactics also traveled worldwide, a phenomenon that Arjun Appadurai (1996, 10) has called "vernacular globalization." Scholars of the African diaspora have been central to efforts to demonstrate that, "despite some five hundred years of disruption and relocation, such links [between black communities in the Western world] have endured and are incontrovertible" (Gomez, 2006, 18). The links between Africa and black communities worldwide include intellectual, political, and cultural exchanges that maintain a persistent yet fluid idea of "blackness" as a utopian counterculture that seeks "to transcend both the structures of the nation state and the constraints of ethnicity and national particularity" (Gilroy, 1993, 19).

Several recent publications address the aesthetic and theoretical bases of African diaspora culture (Elam and Jackson, 2005; Gomez, 2006; Clarke and Thomas, 2008). While *Black Television Travels* owes many of its insights to such publications, I am less interested in specifying how the *content* of African American television speaks to audiences abroad or how television creators in different black communities incorporate and recirculate diasporic television culture than I am in understanding how the commercialization, institutionalization, and globalization of cultural expression work to produce certain forms of racial subjectivity while excluding others.

The main contribution of this volume to our understanding of African diaspora studies, then, lies in its exploration of how the globalizing cultural industries shape and channel the cultural products of the diaspora. Although other black cultural forms such as music, literature, and poetry may seem immune from the influences of global corporate capitalism, they still must navigate the priorities and preferences of their respective institutional gate-keepers. As the organizational sociologist Paul Hirsch (1972) has explained,

> In modern, industrial societies, the production and distribution of both fine art and popular culture entail relationships among a complex network of organizations which both facilitate and regulate the innovation process. Each object must be "discovered," sponsored, and brought to public attention by entrepreneurial organizations or nonprofit agencies before the originating artist or writer can be linked successfully to the intended audience. (640)

Most studies of black cultural traffic to date have addressed the creation, meaning, and community uptake of diaspora culture, sidelining crucial questions about how institutions and industries shape culture and communal bonds. Nevertheless, as Kennell Jackson (2005) reminds us, "[black] cultural traffic [always] involves some system of exchange or commerce" (8).

A growing number of scholars have begun to examine how institutions and industries process black culture. A collection of historical essays edited by the critical anthropologists Kamari Maxine Clarke and Deborah A. Thomas (2008) traces the long and complex "relationships among racial ideologies, trade networks, capital mobility, and governance" (5). Contributors to the volume explore the racial projects of a variety of institutions, including the church, the state, and capital, in different locales and time periods. My study takes up similar concerns, albeit from a critical cultural studies perspective that addresses the contemporary cultural industries. As I suggested above, the cultural industries are particularly significant for understanding contemporary racial discourse, given their ubiquity and the ways they simultaneously encourage and discipline difference via the twin logics of industry lore and televisual representation.

Herman Gray's (2005) *Cultural Moves*, meanwhile, comes closest to this volume in examining both the globalization of television and its significance for African American cultural politics. The book is a meditation on the changes in African American culture and cultural politics at a time when black creators have gained access to and influence over dominant U.S. cultural institutions. Arguing that cultural critics must go beyond "a conception of cultural politics that continues to privilege representation itself as the primary site of hope and critique" (2), Gray examines the multiple and complex ways African American cultural producers have come to "[occupy] and use . . . institutional cultural spaces and the politics that emanate from them." In other words, Gray sees the successful institutionalization of some forms of African American culture as a move that "complicate[s] rather than simplif[ies] the very notion of black cultural politics."

Gray examines a range of cultural practices, from classical jazz to avant garde art to computing, including the globalization of American television. Regarding television, he writes that "black shows, where they were developed at all, were and are selectively developed and deployed by major commercial networks as part of their overall marketing and branding strategy, a strategy and ideal demographic that in all likelihood does not include black people as a prime market" (84). For these reasons, he notes, few television series incorporating African American themes, concerns, and viewers get produced today, while those that "finally do make it to a network or cable schedule . . . are required . . . to speak in a universal language" (85). Going beyond a concern with writer-producers, he attributes authorial control, in particular control over whether and where African American programs appear on television, to global institutional priorities and practices, such as corporate brands.

Of course, all television series aimed at transnational audience segments have to speak a "universal language" and today, international sales executives participate in the development of almost every television series produced in the United States (Caldwell, 2008, 258; Havens, 2006). However, industry lore about what constitutes a universal language and who can and cannot speak that language changes over time and crucially depends upon the locations, channel brands, and institutional priorities of a distributor's main clients and competitors, which shape overall corporate strategies. While Gray is right to be concerned about the consolidation of institutional and discursive power within carefully branded, transnational commercial organizations, it is also the case that industry lore about universality has fragmented in recent years as general broadcasting has given way to increasingly tailored programming and channels—a process that began with the unexpected global popularity of *The Fresh Prince of Bel-Air* in the mid-1990s, which led some industry insiders to believe that African American youth culture provided a kind of adolescent lingua franca. In fact, programmers at niche cable and satellite channels, as well as publicly funded minority channels, increasingly deploy an industry lore about "cultural journeys" rather than "universal language" that, I will argue, can help sustain African American and minority programming.

Gray's book was written prior to the worldwide success of *Chappelle's Show* (2003–2006); *Grey's Anatomy* (2005–present), which features a larger African American cast than any network television drama since the short-lived *City of Angels* (2000); and HBO series such as *The Wire* (2002–2008) that have set a worldwide standard for "quality" television, which includes the representation of gritty drug scenes populated by young African American men. In other words, the evolving logic that Gray identified in *Cultural Moves* has produced specific textual tendencies that bear analysis and help clarify the influence of globalization on contemporary African American television.

African American Television Trade Routes

Beginning with the limited circulation of *Amos 'n' Andy* (1951–1953) to Kenya, Bermuda, Nigeria, England, Australia, and Guam in the early 1960s, African American programs have shown up in predictable and unexpected places, often traveling alongside or slightly behind other African American cultural forms, especially popular music and film. I have decided to periodize the history of this trade in order to examine how changes in the television industries and technologies around the world have altered the global circulation of African American television and institutional labors and industry lore that sustain those travels. Each of the following chapters concentrates on a different historical era, examining the social and political issues surrounding blackness in America at the time; how American television selected, framed, and represented those issues; where those representations traveled and were used abroad; and the ways dominant industry lore explained and tried to capitalize on those uses abroad that seemed to offer worthwhile opportunities.

Chapter 1 address the miniseries *Roots*, broadcast in 1977 in the United States, which went on to become a worldwide sensation: more than thirty years later, people from around the world can remember vivid details about watching the broadcast of *Roots* in their countries. The chapter looks at how *Roots'* portrayals of blackness, particularly black masculinity, drew on black nationalist and Black Power discourses circulating in American society at the time, and how those discourses served the quite different institutional needs of American, Western European, and Eastern European broadcasters, as well as some of the ways other features of the miniseries helped and hindered its export potential. By concentrating primarily on how lucrative Western European broadcasters programmed the miniseries, however, American television executives failed to take notice of some of the more interesting uses, as well as the opportunities for trade in African American dramatic television that *Roots* opened up. While *Roots: The Next Generations* (1979) went on to rack up impressive international syndication revenues as well, even the limited elements of black nationalism and Black Power that helped propel *Roots* around the world failed to register in the dominant industry lore of the time. Consequently, the American industry primarily focused on producing historical miniseries centered on white American and European history in the wake of *Roots'* success.

Because miniseries addressing white American history were the main beneficiaries of the international popularity of *Roots*, the generally expensive miniseries genre did not become a vehicle for African American stories in the early eighties. Instead, most recurrent African American characters were relegated to integrated situation comedies that featured one or two African American characters in an otherwise white cast and white cultural surroundings. With the racial and political turmoil of the 1960s and 1970s behind them, the television industries began to focus on color-blind characters and television series championing "assimilationist" politics (Gray, 1986). Chapter 2 addresses the acquisition and programming of these integrated sitcoms in apartheid South Africa. The majority of the chapter analyzes how the commercial South African channel Bop-TV used integrated sitcoms to construct an overtly antiapartheid program schedule and channel identity. In addition to dismantling the prevalent industry lore that programming must have "universal themes" in order to appeal to international viewers, the story of integrated situation comedies in South Africa demonstrates the variety of different institutional labors that broadcasters could make imported African American programming perform, as well as the centrality of African American themes, even in highly integrated series, in explaining the value that foreign broadcasters often find in such imports.

The sale of low-end genres such as sitcoms to less developed television markets like South Africa accounted for the majority of African American television trade through much of the eighties, but the unexpected popularity of *The Cosby Show* in dozens of markets abroad suddenly made U.S. distributors aware of the international sales potential of situation comedies. Chapter 3 addresses the worldwide phenomenon of *The Cosby Show*, in particular how the growing internationalization of U.S. syndication markets increased the variety of programs and genres traveling worldwide and industry explanations about why they failed or succeeded. *The Cosby Show* enacted a scrupulous reclamation of the African American nuclear family and its access to the American Dream at a time when rap music had begun to highlight black male poverty, criminality, and "hardness" and conservative racial discourses focused on the antisocial behaviors of street thugs and "welfare queens" (Gray, 1995). The series' global success subsequently led to a popular perception among industry insiders that African American series with "strong family themes" could overcome the supposed insularity of African American culture. As the series' distributor put it, in the minds of television executives at the time, *The Cosby Show* succeeded abroad because it was "not black." During this period, the series appeared in more than eighty markets, surpassing the international sales record of *Dallas* (1978–1991). However, much as the industry lore surrounding *Roots* downplayed the role of African American history in the miniseries' worldwide success, so did explanations of *The Cosby Show*'s popularity abroad tend to ignore the importance of distinctly African American elements of the series that are evident in viewer responses from around the world. In addition, *The Cosby Show* marks the beginning of the development of a coherent *transnational* industry lore regarding the audience appeal and proper institutional labors of African American television programs abroad.

If *The Cosby Show* blazed a trail on the global program markets for U.S. situation comedies with pro-family themes, *The Fresh Prince of Bel-Air* demonstrated that shows steeped in African American youth culture could become even more successful. Chapter 4 examines the international viability of African American youth television in the late nineties and the early part of the twenty-first century, when audiences across Europe and Latin America continued to fragment due to increased competition from commercial broadcasters and cable channels and as young viewers in non-peak hours became an appealing demographic. Many channels turned to imported U.S. sitcoms as a cheap way to lure such viewers, in particular sitcoms featuring African American pop stars, including *The Fresh Prince of Bel-Air*. During this period, black youth culture became a lingua franca of revolt, sexuality, and coolness among adolescents around the world. By 1997 *The Fresh Prince of Bel-Air* had sold into more markets than *The Cosby Show*, and in a time of greater competition among internationally syndicated series. The series' runaway popularity led global television merchants to revise their explanations about what kinds of African American television programs travel well. For the first time, international buyers began to value certain distinctly African American cultural allusions in youth-oriented sitcoms, and these preferences filtered back into the dominant industry lore and production practices of American executives. In fact, European channels pioneered the use of African American sitcoms to attract youth demographics, which practice only later appeared in U.S. schedules and production practices. Although this trend had largely passed by 2005, as European channels replaced imports with domestically produced youth series, the idea that youth-oriented shows with African American pop stars and hip-hop cultural references are globally appealing remains prevalent in industry lore, as evidenced by the recent popularity abroad of Chris Rock's situation comedy *Everybody Hates Chris* (2005–2009) and especially the ease with which its success has been accepted in dominant industry lore as unsurprising.

The preferences of program buyers from predominantly white European markets continue to shape the kinds of African American programs that get made, as well as their budgets. However, in recent years new television technologies have expanded the variety of African American television series in the United States, from sketch comedy on Comedy Central's *Chappelle's Show* (2003–2006) to the adult animation series *The Boondocks* (2005–present) on Cartoon Network to high-end dramas on HBO and Showtime. Chapter 5 examines the international circulation of these newer forms of African American television, in particular how different network organizations and audience configurations create opportunities for new kinds of African American television flows. While these new developments have altered and in some ways expanded the range of African American television series that get produced, the variety of foreign channels that purchase them, and the types of viewers they reach abroad, they continue to encourage certain kinds of representations rather than others. Specifically, the institutional priorities of premium cable channels, general entertainment broadcasters, and comedy channels abroad, combined with industry lore about "edgy" and "quality" programming, lead to a heavy reliance on black masculinity, heteronormativity, crime, violence, and frequent use of the word "nigger" in contemporary series. These same aesthetic choices tend to dominate web-based television series as well, in large part because online producers often strive to have their programs noticed by more traditional television outlets. These textual tendencies do not determine or exhaust the cultural politics of the series, as I make clear in this chapter. Instead, series creators need to navigate these institutional expectations of what African American television should include in order to get their shows on air.

Finally, chapter 6 shifts our focus beyond the United States and African American television to consider how black programming produced elsewhere navigates the circuits of contemporary commercial television and global, digital distribution platforms, as well as the interactions between the institutional labors, industry lore, and representational practices that these different trade routes exhibit. Specifically, we will look at three examples of non-American black television and video programming: the global circulation of the animated Samoan/ Māori television series *bro'Town* (2004–2009), which has enjoyed widespread international syndication on a variety of public service and commercial channels; the booming Nigerian videofilm industry known as Nollywood; and the transnational pirating of the first Belizean television drama *Noh Matta Wat* (2005–2008), which undermined DVD sales and led to funding problems serious enough to halt production. Together, these cases demonstrate several important trends in black television during an era of digitization, globalization, and marketization. First, we see an obvious increase in the variety of video and television programming featuring non-U.S. blacks circulating internationally, as well as a complexity of venues and trade routes. Second, these programs retain significant cultural specificity, again revealing the fallacy that globally popular television must possess universal themes in order to travel. Third, we can see that much black television programming travels through disorganized, parallel markets, which, while they permit a range of representational practices, make production funding highly precarious. For Nollywood video producers, who make almost all of their money from domestic markets, such parallel markets do not make the business model unworkable, though they do depress revenues. For smaller markets like Belize, however, piracy prevents commercial television producers from developing workable business models to cover production costs.

Ironically, while new technologies of television recording make it economically possible for a nation like Belize to produce television dramas in the first place, new distribution technologies make it impossible to profit sufficiently from DVD and other sales to keep the production afloat. By contrast, a series like *bro'Town* shows how a culturally specific black television series can find legitimate commercial and noncommercial buyers in today's fragmented television landscape. However, despite the unique elements and global success of this series, as a satirical adult animation hailed as "*The Simpsons* of the South Pacific" (Nippert, 2004), *bro'Town* also incorporates into its aesthetic practices a good deal of conventional industry lore about what does and does not travel well globally.

Together, these chapters demonstrate how transnationally shared industry lore about African American television has become more and more widespread as sales opportunities abroad have opened up and international sales revenues have become central to financing domestic production. At the same time, industry lore about black and African American television has splintered into a handful of theories that serve different types of producers, distributors, and broadcasters. Today the industry lore surrounding African American television does more than just influence the circulation of African American imagery; it also determines *whether* series get made and what *kinds* of series get made. But more is at stake here than what Charles Taylor and Amy Guttmann (1992) have called the "politics of recognition," or the presence and diversity of African American representations on the world stage. Indeed, the global television industries and the lore that circulates through them ultimately set up hierarchies in which certain kinds of cultures are more valuable and more globally relevant than others, ultimately forming some of the most powerful understandings in today's world about who can and cannot communicate across national boundaries. These understandings, in turn, influence broader social beliefs about which cultures are and are not worth exploring, respecting, and preserving.

1

Roots and the Perils of African American Television Drama in a Global World

Prior to the runaway worldwide popularity of the 1977 miniseries *Roots*, few television series featuring African Americans circulated internationally, and none had sufficient success in foreign sales to catch the eyes of program merchants. *Amos 'n' Andy* (1951–1953) appeared in the United Kingdom, Australia, Guam, and Nigeria in the 1950s and 1960s, and a smattering of African American situation comedies of the 1970s sold sporadically, including *Good Times* (1974–1979) and *Sanford and Son* (1972–1977), but none of these series did much to change the dominant perception at the time that few African American television series could appeal to white American viewers, much less viewers abroad.

Roots likewise faced a good deal of resistance among industry insiders, and its global popularity not only defied conventional wisdom at the time, but also paved the way for a slew of miniseries on the world markets. In fact, the success of *Roots* abroad helped solidify a business model for funding miniseries production that relied heavily on international sales. However, prevalent industry lore at the time tended to deflect attention from the distinctly African American elements of *Roots* in explaining the miniseries' success abroad, focusing instead on historical themes and supposedly universal family themes. Consequently, the majority of miniseries that followed in *Roots*' wake told stories about white American and European history.

Roots grew out of a moment of racial ferment in the United States. The early 1970s had witnessed the growing economic, political, and cultural clout of diverse African American groups, including black nationalists, black separatists, and the Black Power movement. *Roots* picked up on and recirculated a range of African American discourses, chief among them the extreme psychological, cultural, and communal ruptures that slavery caused; the importance of reconnecting with the past and with Africa; and the historical and contemporary culpability of whites and white power structures. At the same time, the miniseries retained more conservative discourses of racial integration, the American melting pot, and the availability of the American Dream; simply the alteration in the subtitle between Alex Haley's book and David Wolper's television series—from *Roots: The Saga of an American Family* to

Roots: The Triumph of an American Family—reflected this conservatism for numerous contemporary observers.

Many progressive and radical discourses underlay the popularity of *Roots* abroad and the institutional labors that the miniseries performed, even in predominantly white European markets. At the same time, while African American discourses obviously resonated with audiences and programmers in nonwhite and non-Western markets, programmers in several Western European markets seem to have used the miniseries as a way to begin to exorcise white guilt for the treatment of domestic minorities. In nearby Eastern Europe, the details of African American history intersected with the history of imperial exploitation at the hands of Western powers, as well as the political interests of the socialist parties. In other words, in Western Europe, *Roots'* representations of racial exploitation, guilt, and overcoming fit the institutional needs of public broadcasters, while for Eastern European state broadcasters, slavery served as a metonym for capitalist exploitation in general.

The specific institutional, economic, and cultural forces that shaped the worldwide circulation of *Roots* produced African American television portrayals rooted in historical settings and storylines and roles related to slavery. The majority of miniseries that followed in *Roots'* wake only tangentially included African Americans, and those that did were set in the Civil War, in large part because the economics of production required sales to Western European broadcasters to recoup costs. The exception was the sequel to *Roots, Roots: The Next Generations,* which is notable in its own right for telling the story of African American political struggle through the civil rights movements of the 1960s, but whose popularity was explained away by the popularity of the original and consequently did not influence wider televisual portrayals.

Roots and the Struggle for International Distribution

So many myths have sprung up around the *Roots* miniseries and its journey from concept to network blockbuster that it can be difficult to separate fact from fiction. One of the most popular myths is that its success took everyone involved with the project by surprise. The ABC programmer Fred Silverman, reportedly worried that the miniseries would be a ratings bust and destroy the network's January sweeps numbers, presciently decided to schedule the episodes back-to-back in order to minimize the potential ratings damage for ABC. The result was a relentless and crescendoing buzz among viewers that culminated in the largest single audience for any fictional television program at the time, when 71 percent of the viewing public tuned in to watch the final episode, or about thirty-six million viewers (Warner Brothers, n.d., a). ABC had sold advertising slots based on an expected 35 percent audience share, so the miniseries obviously did exceed the network's expectations by a large margin (Quinlan, 1979). Still, Silverman had doubled both the length and the budget of the miniseries when he arrived at ABC in 1975, suggesting that he might have had more confidence in the series' performance than is popularly assumed (Wolper, 2003).

Regardless of the precise facts, however, it seems clear that both trepidation and high hopes circulated around the *Roots* project from the beginning. Its budget surpassed that of even the most expensive television genre of the time, the movie of the week, topping $500,000 per hour versus an average $425,000 per hour for television movies (Russell, 1975). Nevertheless, the producer David L. Wolper went more than $1 million in debt to help finance the project, a debt that surely contributed to his decision to sell his production company to Warner Brothers in early 1976 for $1.5 million (Wolper, 2003). Always the astute businessman, however, Wolper retained his domestic and international syndication rights for *Roots* in the deal, demonstrating his confidence in the profitability of the program.

The uncertainty about whether *Roots* would become the hit television program that its producer was sure it would infiltrated the international markets as well, where Wolper turned, rather unsuccessfully, to help finance his increasingly ambitious and expensive undertaking. Wolper pursued both direct sales to foreign buyers and arrangements with well-known international syndicators in his efforts to garner sales revenues up front. Channel 7 in Sydney, Australia, bid early for the project, and feverishly worked to retain its purchase rights after Wolper sold his company to Warner Brothers, which had an exclusive distribution contract with its rival Australian network, Channel 10 (Kinging, 1976). Apparently, both commercial broadcasters had high hopes for the miniseries. Meanwhile, half a world away, the British Broadcasting Corporation (BBC) had similar interests in acquiring the series, and requested the opportunity to preview the rough cuts of the first few episodes in 1976 (Somerset-Ward, 1976). Rounding out the main English-speaking markets at the time, Canadian buyers were split on acquiring *Roots*. The Canadian Broadcasting Corporation (CBC) declined to purchase the miniseries in 1976, ostensibly due to Canadian Content (CanCon) regulations, which required that 60 percent of prime-time programming come from Canadian producers. According to Merv Stone (1976), the manager of program purchasing for the CBC, a twelve-hour series would have been too difficult to schedule effectively while respecting CanCon regulations.

Regardless of such difficulties, however, the CBC managed to import many television dramas from the United States at the time that comprised far more than twelve hours of programming per season. More likely, the CBC wished to pass on the series and simply used CanCon regulations as an excuse for turning the series down. By contrast, Simcom International, a Canadian distributor, believed that the series would sell well to commercial broadcasters in Canada, fetching perhaps more than $100,000 (Simpson, 1976).

Outside English-speaking markets, Wolper turned to U.S. distributors with experience in international syndication for help selling the series, but to no avail. David Raphel, president of Twentieth Century Fox International Corporation, wrote to Wolper that although the script was "extremely interesting," he did "not believe that much [could] be done with it overseas" (Raphel, 1976). Wolper got a similar response from United Artists when he approached them about an international syndication deal. Desperate, Wolper sought to edit the first three hours of the miniseries and release it in theaters abroad as a feature film, even promising Twentieth Century Fox that he could "add things that you may want for the feature (more violence, more sex, et cetera)" (Wolper, 1976). However, international distributors passed on this project as well.

Wolper's perception that the miniseries might perform better as a theatrical film and his offer to make the story more spectacular reiterate the perceived dailiness of television in comparison with popular film, as well as the impact those perceptions can have on black representations. In 1970s Hollywood, black male bodies became synonymous with sex and violence due to the popularity of blaxploitation films, while at the networks, even realistic dramas such as *Roots* only nominally included such portrayals. Thus, some of the main ways blackness has come to be portrayed in globally distributed Hollywood action films are understood as inherently at odds with industry-wide perceptions of the television viewing experience, which tends to work against the production and circulation of African American television dramas.

Roots' unprecedented success in the United States almost guaranteed that foreign broadcasters, who typically show strong interest in the most popular U.S. television series, would pick up the miniseries. However, nothing could have prepared either Wolper or Warner Brothers for its phenomenal performance abroad. In Australia it achieved audience ratings that were nearly equivalent to those in the United States, averaging a 66 share over eight nights ("*Roots* a Hit," 1977). In West Germany it posted similar ratings, garnering a 49 share on its first night and a 55 share on its second (Seeger, 1978). One West German network spokesperson exclaimed, "We never expected it to be the biggest hit of all times" ("West Germans Tune In," 1978). In Italy, too, *Roots* brought in a record number of viewers for an imported series, attracting nearly twenty million viewers per night ("*Roots* Sets TV Records," 1978). Outside Europe, the Japanese broadcaster Asahi TV claimed to be "delighted" with the miniseries, which performed especially well with young men and reportedly sparked a nationwide fascination with rediscovering one's ancestors (Chapman, 1977). These are just a handful of examples that found their way into U.S. newspapers. By the end of the decade, Warner Brothers (n.d., a) promotional materials listed forty-nine territories that had broadcast the miniseries, and rights to the sequel *Roots: The Next Generations*, which performed less well than the original in the United States, were sold to eighty-six countries, according to internal Warner Brothers (1994) fiscal reports.

Despite these impressive statistics, awareness of the worldwide popularity of the miniseries seems to have dawned slowly on Warner Brothers executives. Of course, reconstructing historical industry perspectives on the international marketability of a particular series is a speculative undertaking, given that interviewing is impossible and most corporate archives are closed, leaving us to interpret those perceptions from extant comments in trade journals and marketing activities. Nevertheless, it seems clear that Warner Brothers did not have strong confidence in the sales potential of *Roots*. At the April 1977 Mip-TV international sales market, Warner Brothers representatives refused to report its sales figures to *Broadcasting* magazine, typically a signal that sales are poor. By contrast, MGM executives reported in the same article that their miniseries *How the West Was Won*, which had aired a month after *Roots* on ABC, had been sold to thirty territories ("U.S. as TV Programmer," 1977). Most likely, the same doubts about *Roots* that executives at United Artists and Twentieth Century Fox had expressed earlier to Wolper also fueled concerns at Warner Brothers.

A comparison of promotional advertising for *Roots* designed for domestic and international buyers reveals uncertainty about how to frame *Roots'* domestic popularity in a way that would appeal to potential foreign buyers, especially European public service broadcasters. While the ad designed for domestic trade journals emphasized the ratings performance of the miniseries in major markets, an ad in the April-May 1977 edition of *Television International* listed only the awards that the series had earned. The accompanying text reads, "Rarely has quality been so richly rewarded" (Warner Brothers, n.d., a). Apparently, Warner Brothers did not believe that the popularity of the series in the domestic market alone could guarantee sales abroad, and felt it necessary to emphasize the "quality" of the miniseries over its popularity.

Table 1.1. Nations Importing Roots *Prior to 1981*

Abu Dhabi	Finland	Qatar
Argentina	France	Saudi Arabia
Australia	Germany	Singapore
Austria	Holland	Slovakia
Bahamas	Hong Kong	Spain
Belgium	Jamaica	Switzerland
Bolivia	Jordan	Syria
Brazil	Kuwait	Taiwan
Brunei	Nigeria	Thailand
Canada	Norway	UK
Chile	Peru	Uruguay
Colombia	Philippines	Venezuela
Denmark	Poland	Yugoslavia
Dominican Republic	Portugal	Zambia
Ecuador	Puerto Rico	

Source: Data from undated Warner Brothers promotional kit for post-broadcast syndication of *Roots*. David L. Wolper Archives, 300-002, University of Southern California, Los Angeles.

The international ad is an obvious attempt to counteract the belief that *Roots* was little more than a popular story for American viewers, but also a high-quality television series for the ages.

By November 1977, Warner Brothers reported in its internal corporate magazine *Warner World* that the miniseries had been picked up "in almost every major country in the world" (McGregor, 1977, 18). A couple of words in this quotation bear closer scrutiny, specifically the words "almost" and "major." Even in internal promotional copy, the company cannot claim that *every* major country has purchased the series, or that many smaller countries had done so. One year later, Warner's promotional kit for international syndication made a much stronger case, calling *Roots* "the world's most-watched television drama" and listing forty-nine territories that had purchased the miniseries (table 1.1).

Warner Brothers' apparent lack of confidence in *Roots* suggests that its executives bought into the industry lore that African American dramas could not sell well internationally, especially when we compare their efforts with the confidence that MGM expressed toward *How the West Was Won*, a historical miniseries set in the American frontier in the nineteenth century and focused on white American rather than African American historical experiences. This industry lore was summed up succinctly by an anonymous network executive who told reporters five months after the blockbuster success of *Roots* that the same white viewers who enjoy black ethnic comedy shows just aren't about to accept a black hero in a serious dramatic program. If it's not a comedy, they just won't accept it. And the economic realities we live by tell us that we can't exist by appealing to only a black audience. (Deeb, 1977)

It is perhaps not surprising that prevalent industry lore in the late 1970s militated against exporting narratively complex, dramatic stories about African American suffering during slavery. Television merchants, after all, are not primarily cultural theorists, but businesspeople, and as such they cannot be expected to know the common experiences and bonds that non-Europeans around the world share due to the history of colonialism. They are, however, cultural interpreters who decide which projects will get production funding based on estimations of their potential international sales revenues, which programs will get heavy promotion at international trade shows like Mip-TV, and how those programs will be positioned via advertising in relation to other programs on the market. In the case of *Roots*, industry lore about the appeal of African American television complicated production funding, depressed international sales, and may have facilitated the spectacular portrayal of black male bodies.

Competition, Broadcast Economics, and the Rise and Demise of the Miniseries

Despite dominant industry perceptions that African American dramas could not appeal to white viewers at home, much less foreign viewers, a combination of forces led to efforts to develop the miniseries *Roots* in the late 1970s. These included technological, regulatory, economic, and cultural changes, specifically the deployment of communication satellites; the FCC's passage of the "open skies" plan for satellites; the move on the part of television networks toward expensive, "prestige" programming; and the black revolution of the 1970s. Production costs for the miniseries genre, however, made it particularly dependent on international sales revenues, and ultimately undermined its viability.

Into the 1970s, the television broadcast networks faced little competition from cable and satellite programmers. Although the technology of cable dates back to the beginnings of nationwide television in the United States, cable was used primarily for rebroadcasting network programs, rather than carrying original cable programming. Similarly, communications satellites began broadcasting nationally and internationally in the 1960s, but the FCC stymied development of that industry as well, in order to shore up the incumbent broadcast networks. By the mid-1970s, however, broadcast network power had begun to erode. The Nixon administration's famous disdain for broadcasters led to an opening up of competition early in the decade, in particular the open skies policy, which freed any company to operate, uplink, and downlink satellite television services. As a result, Time Inc. launched the first satellite and cable network, Home Box Office (HBO), which transmitted a combination of movies and sporting events. HBO was joined by the nation's first superstation, WTCG (soon to be renamed WTBS and later TBS), in 1976, which programmed a combination of sports and network reruns. The networks could see the handwriting on the wall, and began to focus on the kind of prestige programming events that only they could afford, in order to price any potential competitors out of the running for top prime-time audience ratings.

Miniseries had the added advantage that they ran during sweeps weeks, the monthlong periods during which the A. C. Nielsen Company tracked audience ratings at local stations in order to set advertising rates for the upcoming quarter. Sweeps weeks are notorious for the stunts that programmers pull in an effort to artificially raise viewership; miniseries became an effective tool in these efforts. Finally, throughout the 1970s, competition between the three major U.S. networks had grown increasingly fierce, as ABC continued to siphon viewers away from the traditional leaders, CBS and NBC. In 1976 ABC finally toppled their dominance and became the top-rated network for the first time in history (Quinlan, 1979).

Miniseries also offered the networks an opportunity to portray socially relevant and politically dicey programming, much like the movie-of-the-week genre, which attracted both critical acclaim and affluent urban viewers. While "relevance" had become a buzzword among network programmers since the debut of *All in the Family* in 1970, the concept had begun to disappear from regularly scheduled weekly series by the middle of the decade, replaced by what were derisively referred to as "jiggle" series aimed at youthful viewers, such as *Three's Company* (1977–1984) and *Charlie's Angels* (1976–1981) (Levine, 2007). These series were less likely to worry advertisers but performed as well among audiences as relevant programs. Additionally, changes in the cultural mood of the nation probably contributed to this shift away from relevance in weekly series. The ending of the Vietnam War and the resignation of President Nixon did much to take the wind out of the sails of the 1960s student movements. Nevertheless, social relevance continued to be the most obvious marker of quality television at the time, and socially relevant television shows continued to draw good ratings among young urban demographics, which were becoming increasingly important for the networks (Alvey, 2004). Thus, while relevance increasingly disappeared from weekly series of the 1970s, it persisted in "one-off" programs such as movies of the week and miniseries (Gitlin, 1983).

The costs of miniseries productions, however, skyrocketed immediately upon the genre's introduction. While *Roots* was originally approved a budget of $375,000 per hour in 1974 and ultimately cost more than $500,000 per hour, per-hour costs for the miniseries *Shogun* reportedly topped $2 million in 1980.[1] In large measure, these cost increases stemmed from the star-studded casts and exotic location shoots that defined the genre, as well as the historical nature of most miniseries, which called for extensive costuming and set budgets. However, domestic markets for miniseries had difficulty absorbing these additional production costs. For networks, which typically paid a license fee to broadcast a miniseries twice per season, the fact that the second broadcast tended to attract significantly smaller audiences made it difficult to justify high fees. Meanwhile, in the domestic syndication markets, where syndicators sell programs to each individual local television station for broadcast in off-prime-time hours, the miniseries genre proved equally troublesome, because most stations preferred the flexibility of half-hour series.

The high costs and poor domestic sales potential of the miniseries genre made it especially reliant on revenues from international syndication. The 1977 miniseries *Washington: Behind Closed Doors*, which told the story of the Watergate scandal, only made back its production costs through international syndication (Funt, 1979). *Roots: The Next Generations* (1978) earned more than $9 million from foreign syndication, and only $8.6 million from domestic syndication. Although the *Roots* sequel earned more than $15 million from domestic network license fees, foreign syndication obviously represents a significant portion of the miniseries' overall revenues (Warner Brothers, 1994). Moreover, the *Roots* sequel was able to fetch a high network license fee because of the popularity of its predecessor—an opportunity that few other miniseries enjoyed.

The Cultural Politics of *Roots*

Roots intervened in a long history of African American television portrayals, and its specific textual strategies both relied on and departed from those earlier representations, at the same time that it prepared the ground for future series. The miniseries opened up a variety of representational avenues for African Americans, some of which eventually became well trodden, others of which were never fully pursued. Some of these representational strategies were central to the series' ability to succeed abroad and, although the international labors of the miniseries did not directly influence domestic production practices, buyers' institutional needs and the forms of televisual blackness that helped them meet those needs did get folded back into television's representational logics at the time.

Generically, *Roots* was a miniseries—a term that refers primarily to the limited run of the series, as opposed to full-length series—as well as a melodrama, a term that refers more specifically to the content, rather than the length and scheduling of the program. At its most basic, the term "melodrama" refers to any dramatic portrayal that also includes a musical accompaniment, but in television, melodrama has taken on a variety of additional traits as well. Television melodramas typically feature one-dimensional characters that are clearly marked as good or evil. They use a variety of aesthetic techniques, including dramatic music, extensive close-ups, and lighting cues to construct highly emotionally charged stories rooted in everyday life. David Thorburn (1987) writes that most scholarly and elite observers see television melodrama as "denoting a sentimental, artificially plotted drama that sacrifices characterization to extravagant incident, makes sensational appeals to the emotions of its audience, and ends on a happy or at least a morally reassuring note" (628–29). However, rather than trivializing or papering over complex social issues, Thorburn suggests that these conventions "can be perceived as the *enabling conditions* for an encounter with forbidden or deeply disturbing materials, not an escape into blindness or easy reassurance" (630). Especially in terms of the potentially volatile political material represented in *Roots*, at a time when the nation was still reeling from the racial unrest of the 1960s and 1970s and beginning to deal with the social changes ushered in by civil rights legislation, Thorburn's description of the capacity of melodrama to allow viewers to experience volatile issues through familiar formats seems particularly apt. Evidence that *Roots* served such a function comes from the oft-told stories that, during the broadcast, multiracial groups would gather around the water cooler at work to discuss the prior evening's episode, along with contemporary race relations.

At its most obvious level, *Roots* dealt with the horrors of black chattel slavery in the United States. This historical frame could work to bracket the current forms of structural and individual forms of racism that the miniseries depicted, assigning them to a bygone era. Such was the case in the final scene of the final episode, when the now-free descendants of the enslaved African Kunta Kinte rode off to claim their own land and their own piece of the American Dream. At the same time, the very current discourses of the civil rights and Black Power movements were never far below the surface, capable of being accessed by viewers who were looking for them, and perhaps even some who were not.

The effects of slavery were figured primarily through the individual psyche and the integrity of the nuclear family, as opposed to a more public and political framing, such as the African American community in general or the African nations that provided most of the slaves. As with much of television, this framing emphasized personal and individual explanations for racism and violence, rather than the structural and institutional racism that supported slavery. Herman Gray picks up on this conservative discourse of racism and slavery when he states that "*Roots* was an indictment of bad people and of certain forms of brutality, but in terms of the entire edifice of American political, social, and economic structure, it came off pretty unscathed" (quoted in Riggs, 1991). The conservative framing of racism and slavery coexisted in the miniseries with more progressive and radical discourses. Although its happy ending brought together the individual and historical frames to produce a powerful conservative ideology that downplayed the persistence of racism and its foundational role in the intellectual, political, social, and economic worlds of contemporary *and* antebellum America, *Roots* also activated progressive and radical discourses of black separatism, militancy against white authorities, and racial pride, including the adoption of African hairstyles, clothing, names, languages, and more. Indeed, simply broadcasting a realistic portrayal of the horrors of slavery on American television was itself a racially liberal political act: because television has always been a creature of the state and corporate America, it carries the imprimatur of these powerful social institutions, making the broadcast of *Roots* tantamount to an admission by these powerful institutions of the real psychological, physical, social, and cultural damages that slavery caused.

Roots provided a kind of Rorschach test of 1970s U.S. race relations. The explosiveness of the thematic material that *Roots* covered, combined with the day-to-day rollout of the miniseries genre, made it particularly difficult for the series to contain within its formal structures the social forces it unleashed. Indeed, the formal structure of each individual episode, which exhibited a fairly open versus a closed narrative structure, encouraged discussion and speculation among viewers and worked to open up different reading positions, interpretations, and perspectives.[2]

Undoubtedly, the melodramatic elements of *Roots* contributed to the reading of the series as a socially conservative text, but these same generic traits also help account for the show's strong emotional appeal. In fact, television is probably at its most powerful as a medium when it brings large social issues down to the level of the individual and the emotional, and the overall structure of the *Roots* narrative, which ends with the descendants of the African slave Kunta Kinte settling in Tennessee on their own piece of land, cannot contain the power of these more emotional elements, even though those elements do not directly map onto identifiable political projects. As one contemporary observer noted when comparing *Roots* with a much more accurate BBC production of the time, *The Fight against Slavery* (1977), the latter "dramatized the events [it depicted, but] lacked a dramatic focus." *Roots*, on the other hand, "is a saga that is told from the black standpoint," and "gets the human cost of slavery across to whites" (Diamond, 1977, 6). Although Diamond does not mention the word "melodrama," his obvious preference for the way *Roots* told the story of slavery stems from the individualization of black suffering and white violence.

I want to concentrate on two prominent emotional themes that the series develops: the importance of ancestry and the question of white guilt. Along with global anticolonial struggles that drew on and contributed to the American Black Power movement, the themes of ancestry and white guilt were the most commonly taken up themes among viewers and broadcasters abroad. With regard to ancestry, I specifically explore the issue of naming, without which ancestry becomes impossible to trace, and the rediscovery of ancestral names among African Americans. Of the many things lost in the Middle Passage and the adjustment to slave existence in the United States, names, including both personal and ancestral names, were perhaps one of the most precious.[3]

The centrality of naming and ancestry in *Roots* becomes visible in the very first scenes, as do the related themes of rebirth and renewed hope. The opening scenes of the first episode pan across verdant images of the African savannah, lush with plants and animals, and come to rest on the village of Juffre, whose residents seem to be as much a part of the African landscape as the animals. As Omoro paces along the river, his wife, Binta, screams in labor inside their hut. After much difficulty, Binta finally gives birth to a son, and we see in ensuing scenes Omoro troubling over what to name the child. Eventually, Omoro takes him out into the night and removes his wrap, as mysterious music with a slightly African flavor of drums and voices plays in the background. Exclaiming, "Kunta Kinte, behold! The only thing greater than yourself," Omoro holds his son skyward, and we cut to an extreme long shot of father and son bathed in a single circle of light, an ocean of bright stars shining overhead. On the soundtrack, a woman's voice breaks into an ecstatic song as a single, powerful, discordant note echoes. For African American viewers, most of whom had been denied knowledge of their ancestors, such an emotional scene might have held powerful resonance. The repetition of naming scenes when new male children were born into the family suggested the continuation of rituals that linked contemporary African Americans to the African homeland.

The theme of naming surfaces again in the third episode, when the overseer gives Kunta Kinte the slave name Toby, but he refuses to respond to it. After a failed escape attempt, Toby is savagely whipped until he answers to his new name. Again, the brutal imposition of the Western name not only demonstrates the power of naming when it comes to acquiescence and resistance, but also ties into the rage felt by many African Americans at the time about the erasure of African names and, thereby, personal and collective history. Kunta Kinte does not, of course, forget his name, but passes it along with other words to his children, and each new generation does the same, until the name reaches Alex Haley, who then reconstructs his ancestry. Thus, although the slave overseer wins in the short term, Kunta Kinte prevails over the course of history. Undoubtedly, these themes of resistance, perseverance, and rediscovery tied into Black Power discourses of the time about the need to emphasize the African dimensions of African American cultural identity in order to restore black pride and mental well-being and to cultivate a healthy racial solidarity in opposition to white America.

The Black Power movement was a controversial and feared political movement in the 1970s, and the inclusion of its themes and rhetoric in prime-time television programming is noteworthy, if not exceptional (Acham, 2004). Indeed, even black militant voices appeared in the miniseries: during the Middle Passage scenes, the wrestler character whom we met in Juffre and who was captured along with Kunta Kinte tells a despondent Kunta Kinte that he must "Eat so that you may grow strong, grow strong to kill the white man. Wa' u' tay. Wa' u' tay." Later, aboveboard, an entire group of slave men begin chanting "Wa' u' tay," to the consternation of the ship captain. Of course, the historical and linguistic gloss on the popular militant call of "Kill whitey" is unmistakable here, and one could argue that they blunt the power of the wrestler's statement by placing the words in historical rather than contemporary context. However, I believe that this is one of those instances where the aesthetics of the melodrama, particularly the historical melodrama, allow otherwise unspeakable contemporary sentiments to be spoken and explored. It must have been very hard for any viewer at the time not to feel the power of a black man, in close-up on national television, encouraging the murder of white people and not to see this as an allusion to—and a sympathetic rendering of—contemporary black militancy.

A second main theme that emerges in the early scenes of the first episode and continues throughout the story is that of white guilt and white culpability for slavery. Although Gray (in Riggs, 1991) is right to critique the miniseries for lacking a strong condemnation of European expansionism, agrarian capitalism, Christianity, and Enlightenment philosophy, all of which underwrote the institution of slavery in the United States, the miniseries does offer a powerful exploration of white racist psychology. In other words, the racial cultural politics of *Roots* depend on the simultaneous construction of blackness *and* whiteness. It is this portrayal of whiteness, I believe, instead of some sort of comforting portrayal of blackness, which in part explains the popularity of the miniseries among whites both at home and abroad.

One of the main vehicles through which this exploration of contemporary white guilt and white racism occurs is casting. *Roots* not only featured virtually every African American film and television actor of note at the time, but also provided a veritable parade of popular white television and film actors. Certainly, this use of well-known actors was one of the draws of the miniseries in the United States and beyond. But it also brought on board a tangle of intertextual allusions that worked to contemporize portrayals of whiteness and encourage viewers to read those portrayals as allegorical explorations of the general state of whiteness, rather than as realistic, historical characters. Perhaps the most apparent example of these tendencies is the character of Thomas Davies, the white slave ship captain played by Edward Asner.

Edward Asner was well known by the time *Roots* premiered not only for his role of Lou Grant on *The Mary Tyler Moore Show* (1970–1977) and *Lou Grant* (1977–1982), but also for his strident, leftist political activism, which had caused frequent headaches for CBS, the network that aired his series. We first meet Asner's character, an out-of-work ship captain, after the sequence in Juffre in the first episode of *Roots*, which ends with the naming ceremony recounted above. As the screen fades from black to reveal colonial Annapolis, Maryland, we see Davies discussing the possibility of a new commission. To his horror, he discovers that the commission involves captaining a slave ship. At the same time, we see that he needs the work. This character has frequently been cited as an example of the miniseries' conservative racial politics, because it attributes feelings of sympathy, political consciousness, and guilt to a slaver, when no historical evidence for such attributions exists. However, if we read this character not as an accurate portrayal of a slave ship captain but an allegory of whiteness—which I think we must, given Asner's intertextual identity as both a leftist political activist and the socially conscious character of Lou Grant—his character becomes an exploration of the emotional, psychological, and moral toll that slavery took even on whites of supposedly good conscience. That is, Asner/Davies shows that even principled white people are/were affected by the evils of chattel slavery and the erotics of racial violence.

Throughout most of the two episodes in which he appears, Captain Davies retains an air of moral superiority toward his follow slavers. When discussing with Mr. Slater, the slave catcher, whether to load "cargo" in a "tight pack" of 200 or a "loose pack" of 170, Davies scoffs at Slater's suggestion that the decision is a matter of "philosophy." Davies immediately turns Slater's philosophical discussion to a moral matter: responding to Slater's enumeration of the benefits of a "tight pack" of 200 slaves, Davies asks condescendingly, "And how many of them will we have left alive by your reckon?" We are encouraged to understand Davies' moralism as a function of his own guilt at being involved in the slave trade. At the end of this scene, for instance, as Davies searches for a new keg of rum, Slater intones, "I was under the impression you didn't drink, sir." To which Davies replies, "There are a number of things that I have done in connection with this voyage, Mr. Slater, that I've never done before." Davies' guilt at being involved with the slave trade is obvious here, and it makes him a more sympathetic and morally superior character.

In the course of the Middle Passage, however, Captain Davies changes irrevocably. His moral decline begins when Slater brings a young African woman to his quarters as a "belly warmer" for the night. Davies is busy with a letter to his wife, in which he tries but fails to express what has been happening to him since he began the journey. Davies initially protests the woman's presence. Then, after Slater leaves her, he lectures her on his views about "fornication" and tries to make small talk. When this fails, however, he falls silent, staring at her in close-up, lit with candle and shadows, as ominous music plays in the background. "Merciful heaven," he mumbles, almost inaudibly, and begins to advance toward her as the screen fades to black.

When the ship arrives back in Annapolis, a representative of the slave trading company comes to see Davies, who is now despondent and weakened, with dark circles under his eyes. Apparently, he has contracted some sort of disease along the way, perhaps malaria. After the company representative extols the wonders of the present economic system, the "golden triangle" of prosperity—with slaves brought to the Americas, tobacco shipped to England, and trade goods shipped back to Africa—Davies observes that "It sometimes feels that we do harm to ourselves by taking part in the endeavor [slave trade]." When the representative protests that he cannot see the harm in making money, Davies again waxes philosophical: "I doubt that you'd like to know [what harm participation in the slave trade does to slavers]. I doubt that either of us would truly like to know." In this respect, Davies' physical illness becomes a visible manifestation of his moral depravity.

Davies' character provides an opportunity to explore the psychology of whiteness in a racist society if we read him as an allegory of white identity. Going beyond questions of white guilt, *Roots* addresses the culpability of whites who benefit from a racist system, even if they are not active racists. The miniseries portrays the erotics of racial domination and sexual violence as irresistible, even for a "good Christian man" such as Davies: in a position of ultimate power over other human beings, one cannot help but become morally corrupted.

Obviously, for foreign viewers who might be unaware of Asner's intertextual persona, an allegorical reading of his character might be uncommon. Even without such associations, however, the devastating effects of slaving on Captain Davies' psyche are obvious and, as the main white character in the first episode, he provides one of the primary points of identification for white viewers. In other words, despite the narrative's efforts to reimagine the history of slavery in the United States as the triumph of African American struggle, the initial episodes of *Roots* offer a multilayered portrayal of the effects of racial violence on the white psyche as well.

Roots, then, integrated radical, progressive, and conservative racial discourses, as well as themes of black ancestry and white guilt. These discourses and themes arose from the particularities of American history and race relations, at the same time that they were part of a broader global history of European colonialism and racism. While the miniseries did portray the imaginary resolution of the racial tensions that slavery produced under the rubric of the American Dream, the genre and the medium itself lacked the capacity to contain such volatile political currents once they were let loose.

The Reception of *Roots* Abroad

The discourses of white guilt, black ancestry, racial pride, integration, and black resistance enabled the worldwide circulation and popularity of *Roots*, as did the personalized, historical treatment of racial oppression. Non-Western societies in particular seem to have latched onto the progressive and radical discourses of the miniseries and placed them in dialogue with local and international struggles against colonialism, including both political and cultural anticolonial projects. In European markets, by contrast, the popular reception and programming of the miniseries suggest that themes of white guilt and integration accounted for its success. This section concentrates on the popularity of *Roots* outside Europe, while the next compares the importation of the miniseries in Western and Eastern Europe in order to demonstrate that the specificity of political-economic and communications systems shapes the importation, popularity, and cultural politics of imported television culture as much as the political and cultural resonances between local viewers and television exports.

Before we delve into the discursive currents that propelled *Roots* overseas, it is worth examining the generic features of the miniseries that aided its successful travels. As a miniseries, *Roots* fit the scheduling practices of foreign broadcasters better than most conventional U.S. series. The world's television landscape of the late 1970s and early 1980s comprised a number of nationwide, public service broadcasters with no competition, which predominantly programmed onetime television plays and short series with clear beginnings, middles, and ends. By contrast, the commercial U.S. system favored weekly series that continued from season to season as long as their ratings remained strong. As a miniseries, *Roots* was closer to the public service model of programming, as it comprised a set number of episodes; moreover, each episode could be sliced and diced into a variety of different lengths, providing a good deal of flexibility for programmers.[4] In Germany *Roots* was shown in eleven installments, two of which appeared on back-to-back nights, and the final nine of which appeared weekly (Sollors, 1979). In France it appeared sporadically over a two-month period in ninety-minute episodes, matching the duration of most French drama series at the time (Fabre, 1979).

While formal features of the miniseries may have made *Roots* appealing to foreign broadcasters, the content itself also needed to connect with the foreign viewers' tastes and the cultural worlds they inhabited. In Africa the connection between the history of black slavery and contemporary social movements for racial justice seems to have been the primary thematic connection between the miniseries and importing cultures. In Nigeria the miniseries' broadcast led to significant discussion of the era of slavery and helped prepare the ground for government demands for reparations in the 1990s (Falaiye, 1999; Owens-Ibie, 2000, 138). In South Africa, by contrast, the proapartheid broadcaster, the SABC, refused to air the miniseries, for fear of the radical potential of broadcasting a realistic portrayal of the horrors of slavery. In an interesting twist, the U.S. consulate in Johannesburg arranged for private screenings of *Roots*, demonstrating that diplomats likewise believed in the power of the miniseries to hasten political change in South Africa; at the same time, they must likely have thought that *Roots* portrayed race relations in the United States more positively than those in South Africa (Roeder, 1978).

Remarkably similar events took place in Brazil, when the military junta forbade the commercial broadcaster, Globo TV, from airing *Roots* for fear that it might stoke the nascent black civil rights movement of the time. Here, too, American diplomats arranged private screenings instead (Straubhaar, 2007). In all of these instances, what were liberal or even conservative discourses in the United States—a recognition of the historical brutalities of slavery, coupled with a narrative of overcoming—became potentially radical in different contexts: while the Nigerian government sought to leverage these discourses to its own ends by broadcasting *Roots*, the governments in South Africa and Brazil banned the program in an effort to keep racial unrest under wraps.

The global appeal of the Black Power movement and its capacity to carry *Roots* around the world extended well beyond Africa. Even in places seemingly isolated from the history and fallout of American slavery, such as Japan, *Roots* became a smash success. To this day, "roots" is a loan word in the Japanese language that refers to ancestry. In fact, the search for and reverence toward ancestry in *Roots* seems to have struck a deep chord in 1970s Japan, a time when renewed interest in history, ancestry, and nationalism had begun to sweep the nation. To a certain extent, this was a conservative and even right-wing version of nationalism that *Roots* articulated in Japan and which continues to this day. On the other hand, an executive at the company that published the Japanese translation of Alex Haley's novel in 1978 insisted that Japanese viewers also identified with the racial oppression and the struggles for justice and dignity portrayed in *Roots* (Chapman, 1977). These ideologies, connected closely with the discourses of Black Power and anticolonial struggles in general, continue to resonate in Japan today. For instance, a Japanese anarchist group, Shirouto no Ran, staged a collective viewing of the miniseries in 2009 in an effort to stoke resistance and build solidarity and mutual support, much as the Black Power movement did (Morris, 2010).

Each of these examples demonstrates the dense weave of discursive threads that we must untangle in order to account for the popularity of *Roots* abroad, including the complex and contradictory discourses of the program itself and the complicated local and transnational discourses that intersected in the importing nation. Outside Europe and the White Dominions, at least, viewers and programmers seem to have responded in varying degrees to the miniseries' representations of nationalist desire and anticolonial struggle. Within Europe, these themes also sometimes resonated, particularly in socialist Eastern Europe. In Western Europe, however, the popular reception and institutional labors of *Roots* seem to have focused on its representations of white guilt.

Roots and the Political Economy of European Broadcasting

In examining the worldwide popularity of *Roots* thus far, I have concentrated primarily on cultural and historical continuities and discontinuities between the program and importing nations, but the political-economic and communications systems are equally important forces. By comparing the importation of the miniseries in two culturally and historically similar European nations on different sides of the Iron Curtain, we can see how these systems shape the popular reception of imported programming and the institutional labors that program imports can serve. Specifically, I show how the public broadcaster in West Germany and the state broadcaster in Hungary exhibited nearly identical orientations toward the generic and commercial elements of *Roots*, but exhibited quite different orientations to the portrayals of white guilt, ancestry, and anticolonial struggles because of their very different political-economic situations and the distinct circumstances of the national broadcaster in each country.

In both countries the generic status of *Roots*, its popularity in the United States, and its thematic material made it appealing to broadcasters, who saw the miniseries as helping fulfill their remits of bringing the world's best television to their viewers, while fitting their dominant scheduling practices.[5] Likewise, the shared history of fascism and genocide during World War II in both nations required broadcasters to manage the positive portrayal of ancestry recovery and ancestor worship in *Roots*, given their connection to the delegitimated ideologies of racial purity and nationalism in the postwar era. In West Germany, the airing of *Roots* opened up a space for wider discussions about domestic minorities, as well as a chance to reflect upon the differences between public service and commercial broadcasting systems. In Hungary, meanwhile, the importation of *Roots* demonstrated the openness of the society to foreign ideas and the dangerous nature of global capitalism.

Despite the similarities between *Roots* and domestic programming in Germany and Hungary, however, significant differences remained to be managed. *Roots* is basically a melodramatic serial, not unlike a soap opera in its narrative structure and characterizations, and the genre of soap opera was, for many European programmers, the epitome of commercial television schlock. Similar attitudes about the melodramatic elements of *Roots* animated European programmers' responses to the series. German newspaper critics panned the miniseries as "historic schmalz," "serialized kitsch," and "pure melodrama" (Reid, 1978; Sollors, 1979, 42–43). One observer complained that "For ARD [German national broadcast channel Arbeitsgemeinschaft der öffentlich-rechtlichen Rundfunkanstalten der Bundesrepublik

Deutschland] to revel in such trashy stories full of sweat and tears, sex and crime, shows that the WDR [regional broadcaster Westdeutscher Rundfunk] has far fewer scruples than problems" (Umbach, 1978). In Hungary newspaper critics worried about the "layers of commercial excess" in *Roots* that threatened to obscure "the core of the series' . . . social critique" ("Gyökerek Gyökerei," 1980). Both broadcasters surrounded the first episode with paratextual features—a documentary on slavery in Germany, a panel discussion in Hungary—in an effort to counteract the program's supposed historical inaccuracies and its appeal to emotions over intellect (Sollors, 1979). While there may have been different political impetuses behind these decisions, they also share similar cultural roots, namely, a distrust of commercialized American popular culture that predates the division of Europe. The French public service broadcaster, too, introduced the miniseries with a panel discussion similar to the one in Hungary (Fabre, 1979). Unlike the discussions in France, however, commentators in Hungary did not use the opportunity to discuss domestic ethnic problems or the nation's history of anti-Semitism. Instead, the focus remained on deflecting the commercial excesses of the program and underscoring the horrors of chattel slavery.

Roots and White Guilt in West Germany

While difficult to accommodate in its programming structure and general remit, in Germany the more popular elements of *Roots* also performed important institutional labors for the public service broadcaster, which was beginning to feel the pressure of commercial television, especially commercial cable channels. A long-anticipated government report on the feasibility and desirability of commercial cable television was released in 1976. Although such channels did not begin to appear until 1984, the late 1970s and early 1980s were nevertheless periods of anxiety for ARD, as it began to confront the real possibility of direct competition for the first time (Bleicher, 2004). In this new environment the popularity of programming, as measured by audience ratings, began to take on importance, and popular imported series helped greatly in this regard.

While *Roots* obviously addressed quite different historical material, the representation of white guilt and white culpability for the genocide of racial minorities provoked discussion of the Holocaust for perhaps the first time in German broadcasting, and opened a discursive space and an institutional willingness in West German television that ultimately led to the watershed broadcast of the *Holocaust* (1978) miniseries the following year. Despite efforts to revisit and reexamine the horrors of the Holocaust, the appeal of

Nazism, and the culpability of average German citizens in German cinema beginning in the 1960s, television broadcasting came to these issues much more slowly. Although West German television had dealt with World War II in a variety of television programs and genres, most of them had concentrated on the impact of the war on regular Germans or the culpability of the war generation; those programs that did broach the subject of the Holocaust tended to do so in abstract or emotionally distant ways, as opposed to the portrait of everyday life under Nazism that *Holocaust* represented (Geissler, 1992). Again, because public service broadcasting in particular carries the imprimatur of the state in a way that film does not, a broadcast about the horrors of the Holocaust on West German television would have carried a far greater degree of government authorization. Moreover, a melodramatic treatment that relies on realistic settings with heightened emotions might have been quite disturbing to viewers. In fact, Michael Geissler (1992) argues that, while West German television did indeed carry stories about the Holocaust prior to the broadcast of *Holocaust*, the miniseries had such a powerful impact because it was the first to portray everyday Jewish life in Nazi Germany.

The importation of *Roots* caused a similar stir, allowing ARD to broach the subject of the Holocaust. The portrayal of black genocide might not have been *intended* to spark these discussions, but it is difficult to imagine that the programmers who purchased the miniseries didn't consider the parallels. Certainly, critics picked up on the similarities, noting that "If our respect for *Roots* is limited this may—subliminally—reflect the fact that in Europe, in this century, we have experienced unimaginably more horrible scenes of genocide," and that "in Germany, too, a German Jewish family chronicle could only succeed if it discreetly ended in the middle of the nineteenth century" (Sollors, 1979, 43). While these commentaries do not take up the role that *Roots'* portrayals of white guilt might have played in the miniseries' popularity in Germany, they certainly recognize the similarities between the American and German situations and envision only the potentially cathartic impact that the miniseries might have on white viewers, not nonwhites.

If popular critics ignored the potential importance of *Roots* for nonwhite German viewers, they did recognize the presence—and potential dangers —of the themes of ancestry and racial pride, which stirred up troubling connections with the Nazi era. As one observer put it, "the rhetoric of ethnicity (or the interest in family trees) always evokes memories of the National Socialist past" (Sollors, 1979, 43).

Roots, then, labored in service of ARD's remit, not only to bring the best of the world's television to German viewers, but also indirectly to broach issues of current relevance to German citizens. In addition, the popularity of

Roots gave German viewers familiarity with the historical miniseries genre that likely made the aesthetics of *Holocaust* more acceptable, at the same time that *Roots* proved the genre's potential to German broadcasters. *Roots'* portrayal of black victimization during slavery served institutional needs for popular, limited-duration series that could broach the subject of Europe's racist past and present. At the same time, the themes of ancestry and racial pride and the melodramatic elements of the miniseries required broadcasters to work hard to bend the miniseries' particular aesthetic practices to their specific needs. The decision to use documentaries about slavery helped in both of these efforts, potentially counteracting the melodramatic treatment of historical material and framing ancestry and racial pride as issuing from unprecedented racial violence, as authenticated by a more veracious genre.

Roots and African American Struggle in Socialist Hungary

While the German public broadcaster ARD deployed *Roots'* portrayals of white guilt in an effort to begin to come to terms with its nation's history of racial exploitation, the Hungarian state broadcaster MTV (Magyar Televízió) used its representations of racial exploitation and anticolonialism to help distinguish socialist societies from the supposedly corrupt capitalist nations to their west. Simultaneously, imported Western series such as *Roots* began to be used in the late 1970s and early 1980s to demonstrate the purported openness of the Hungarian regime, ostensibly one of the most open societies of the Eastern Bloc.

Socialist state broadcasters walked a tightrope in their efforts to appear independent of the state while continuing to serve as party mouthpieces. MTV at times operated as a state broadcaster, championing the policies and the wonders of socialism, and at other times as a typical public service broadcaster, attempting to educate, inform, and entertain viewers with high-quality television programming. The importation of Western programming, especially a program such as *Roots* that implicitly critiqued the racial politics of the United States, helped broadcasters immensely: the willingness to air such imports demonstrated the openness and independence of broadcasters, while the content of the programming served the interests of the party.

Roots was broadcast in Hungary from December 3, 1979, to February 24, 1980, with one-hour episodes aired every Tuesday night, except for the first night, which featured a two-hour episode, and Christmas and New Year's holidays, during which MTV interrupted its normal scheduling. Of course, given the broadcasting system of the time, it is impossible to get audience ratings figures to judge the popularity of the series. However, several contemporary newspaper articles suggested that the miniseries was a major success. One commentator discussed how watching the miniseries had replaced normal daily activity. End-of-year reviews of television programming in 1980 invariably mentioned the miniseries and its importance and popularity. The series was also actively promoted in the newspapers prior to its broadcast, especially the party mouthpiece *Népszava*.

Roots also had had a hand in constructing Hungarian prime-time schedules, which were fluid prior to 1979. MTV broadcast six days a week, Tuesday through Sunday, with no broadcasts on Monday. *Roots* appeared in Tuesday prime time at 7:30, immediately after the nightly news, and was stripped weekly. Near the end of its run, it was followed by a French documentary series, *The History of Aviation*. Together, these two series established Tuesday as the main night for prominent television series for a decade to come, stabilizing MTV's prime-time schedule for the first time ("Gyökerek és Emberek," 1980). While such stabilization may appear unnecessary for a noncommercial broadcaster, it provided ways of increasing viewership for the broadcaster's more state-oriented functions. For instance, *Roots* served as a lead-in for an interview with the country's powerful agricultural minister, as well as a live broadcast of a party congress.

As evidenced by the panel discussions that took place prior to the broadcast of *Roots*, the depictions of black suffering at the hands of white landowners, as well as the struggles against that exploitation, permitted MTV to reconcile its simultaneous function as a party mouthpiece and a public service broadcaster. The scheduling of the first installment of the miniseries, with two episodes aired back-to-back, was part of this strategy to emphasize the critical elements of the series. The first episode concentrates on preparations to capture and ship slaves and the idyllic African society where Kunta Kinte lives, ending with his capture. While it does allude to the evils of slavery, it does not depict those evils visually, and also provides us with the sympathetic white character of Captain Davies. By contrast, the second hour takes place almost exclusively on the slave ship, and rawly depicts the cruelties of slavery, including the corruption of Captain Davies. Again, a writer for *Népszava* praised this scheduling because it left the viewer with a clear impression of the evils of slavery rather than naive idealism, as would have been the case if only the first episode had been aired ("Mit Látunk," 1980).

Another example of the efforts to promote the critical elements of the series appeared in the summary of the final episode in *Népszava*. The ending of the series has generally been criticized by scholars because it depicts the achievement of African American freedom and integration in the United States, which many have seen as a whitewashing of historical and contemporary facts (Gray, 1995; Riggs, 1991). However, the summary in *Nép-szava* ("Mit Látunk," 1980) made no mention of this happy ending, concentrating instead on what it called the "deprivation of intellectual and material equality" that slavery produced, "and which African Americans continue to face." In this way, the newspaper attempted to frame the miniseries as a whole as a critique of the *contemporary* corruption of the U.S. capitalist system.

Observers at the time not only identified the evils of slavery, but also contrasted that history with the history of Hungary, Eastern Europe, and socialist nations. A writer for *Magyar Nemzet* commented how so much of the official discussion of *Roots* had focused on the fact that black chattel slavery was a Western experience that had no corollary in Eastern European history (Lócsey, 1980). Again, this provided MTV, as a state broadcaster, with an opportunity to demarcate Eastern and Western European societies and position the former as superior. In fact, the most commented-upon historical corollary mentioned was serfdom, and the serf, along with the worker, was the privileged subject of the Hungarian socialist system. *Roots*, then, allowed MTV to offer not only a critique of Western capitalism but also an implicit celebration of the idealized subjects of Hungarian socialism, the peasant and the worker.

The legal scholar Mary Dudziak (2000) and others have suggested that the treatment of African Americans and the struggle for civil rights in the 1970s was a major weapon of the socialist system in its propaganda war with the West. The plight of African Americans, it was suggested, clearly demonstrated the evils of Western capitalism. This analysis is reinforced by a comment in *Népszava* that linked the *Roots* phenomenon to the Watergate scandal. *Roots*, the party newspaper told its readers, created "almost the same amount of storm" as Watergate ("Gyökerek Gyökerei," 1980). Of course, one of these was a television event and the other a political scandal, which makes the comparison tenuous, but the obvious underlying logic was that both of these phenomena demonstrated the moral bankruptcy of the American system.

Although the depiction of black suffering in *Roots* helped Hungarian broadcasters and observers articulate the global struggle against capitalism with the global struggle against European colonialism, the recent history of racialization and genocide in Hungary, coupled with the uncomfortable history of Hungarian nationalism, made the depictions of ancestry and minority exploitation problematic as well. In contrast to Germany, where the representation of minority exploitation prompted discussions about the treatment of Jews and others during World War II, in Hungary such discussions rarely surfaced. Although some historians believe that Hungary was largely an unwilling German partner in World War II, the fact remains that Hungarian fascists, supported by ultranationalists, did in fact take over the country from 1944 to 1945, passed racial purity laws, and deported Jews and others to Nazi concentration camps. The absence of this topic during the panel discussion prior to *Roots'* broadcast demonstrates one attempt to avoid the subject of Hungarian genocide of Jews. Comments in official reviews and previews that framed the miniseries as exclusively focused on the West represent a similar attempt at circumventing such connotations. In fact, the one commentator I have found who did broach the subject wrote for the relatively independent newspaper *Magyar Nemzet* and argued that, despite all official attempts to quell the connections between *Roots* and the national-socialist Arrow Cross Party's reign in Hungary, viewers still tended to draw such inferences (Lócsey, 1980). MTV did not import the miniseries *Holocaust* during the socialist period.

In both Hungary and Germany the history of anti-Semitism and its relationship to nationalism formed inevitable historical backdrops for the themes of ancestry and racial pride explored in *Roots*. While German observers and broadcasters promoted the exploration of this racist history by emphasizing the theme of white guilt while largely ignoring African American struggles and their connection with antiracist and anticolonial struggles elsewhere, Hungarian broadcasters and critics took quite the opposite tack, emphasizing racial struggle and resistance, while largely ignoring questions of white guilt and culpability for Hungarian genocide. The differential reception of the miniseries in the two nations had less to do with cultural or historical differences than with the quite different political-economic systems in Western and Eastern Europe. In addition, the institutional labors that *Roots* performed for broadcasters and the particular themes of the miniseries that served those needs differed, due to the unique priorities of each institution. For ARD in Germany, the exploration of white guilt in *Roots* and its capacity to open up a space for the *Holocaust* miniseries permitted the broadcaster to program more popular fare in the face of potential commercial competition, while maintaining the basic tenets of public service. For MTV, by contrast, the themes of racial brutality and resistance helped resolve the potentially conflicting demands to demonstrate an openness to Western programming while fulfilling its propagandizing role.

Conclusion

Roots was a bona fide commercial success, and it led to the expectation among some observers that the days of serious African American drama had finally arrived in American television. Unfortunately, the business model that underwrote the miniseries' production funding was heavily dependent upon international syndication revenues from Western European national broadcasters—broadcasters who sought to address undifferentiated national viewers and imagined those viewers as white. As we saw in the German case, even a program as focused on the African American experience as *Roots* got deployed in a manner that emphasized the themes that white German viewers could identify with. Given these economic conditions, it is not surprising that conventional industry lore at the time discounted the importance of African American themes, and instead struck on the idea that historical miniseries about white Europeans and Americans were best suited for international markets. Miniseries such as James Michener's *Centennial, The Awakening Land,* Herman Wouk's *Winds of War,* and *North and South,* all of which concentrate on white history with minimal African American contributions, were the primary beneficiaries of the international trail that *Roots* blazed.

The fact that *Roots* failed to change the industry lore about the poor international appeal of African American themes and characters was rooted in the political economy of the television industry. However, these political-economic realities themselves were deeply shaped by historical discourses of whiteness and an industry lore built upon that foundation. While sales to Western Europe and the nations of the White Dominion accounted for 58 percent of foreign revenues for the *Roots* sequel, more than $4 million came from beyond Europe. Consequently, a production and syndication strategy targeting non-European markets would have been possible and lucrative at the time, and such a strategy would have undoubtedly led to quite different forms of industry lore. The fact that the American television industries did not pursue this possibility says more about the inability of executives to think outside the bounds of whiteness, which tends to universalize its own culture while particularizing nonwhite cultures, leading to the perception that non-European markets could not possibly have anything culturally in common with each other. In other words, the political economy of the industry, its prevalent institutional practices, the cultural content of exported television series, and both global and local social discourses determine one another in complex patterns as well as the global circulation patterns of African American television.

Ultimately, the costs of the miniseries genre, combined with its poor domestic syndication potential and the difficulties of selling programming abroad, particularly in European markets, doomed the miniseries, and with it the dominant mode of portraying African American experiences and themes in dramatic television. By the end of the decade, industry observers were proclaiming the death of the genre due to skyrocketing production costs, poor syndication potential, and growing fear on the part of the networks about the competition from cable and pay-television, including Home Box Office (HBO), which led the networks to concentrate more on fiscally conservative projects such as situation comedies, rather then lavish, risky miniseries. In 1979 the three networks scheduled no miniseries during January sweeps and, although the genre experienced a renaissance two years later after the blockbuster success of *Shogun* (1980), it was short-lived. These newer miniseries such as *Shogun* and *Winds of War* were funded through international coproductions, making them even more reliant on the perceived preferences of international viewers than their predecessors (Funt, 1979; Martin, 1980).[6] Not surprisingly, the international partners that American producers allied with preferred material that reflected their own societies and histories over African American stories like *Roots*.

2

Integrated Eighties Situation Comedies and the
Struggle against Apartheid

In the late 1970s and early 1980s, prime-time, episodic television featured African Americans almost exclusively in integrated, middle-class situation comedies. Despite the massive domestic and international popularity of *Roots* in 1977, U.S. television executives remained unconvinced that African American themes and characters could generate the kinds of audience ratings that warranted the greater expense of dramatic genres, relegating them instead to cheaper genres such as the sitcom. At the same time, international buyers generally shunned U.S. sitcoms because they considered them too culturally specific to translate to foreign markets. As a result, African American television did not circulate widely for most of the 1980s.

A notable exception, highlighted in this chapter, was the renegade black South African broadcaster Bophuthatswana Broadcasting Corporation, or Bop-TV, which programmed integrated U.S. sitcoms to construct a distinctly antigovernment, antiapartheid political stance. American race relations, as signaled through the integrated settings of these sitcoms, provided a racially progressive alternative to the strictly segregated broadcasting policies of the government-controlled South African Broadcasting Corporation's (SABC) channels. However, as the chapter demonstrates, the representations of race relations in American imports, while central to Bop-TV's institutional strategy, were no more important than the broadcaster's scheduling practices. Indeed, while the programming carried a range of political potentialities, it was only through Bop-TV's scheduling practices that particular political content became realized and articulated to specific commercial and political projects.

During the 1980s, scheduling was primarily a national or subnational practice, though, as we saw in the scheduling of roundtable discussions surrounding broadcasts of *Roots* in different parts of Europe in chapter 1, the seeds of transnational scheduling practices had already been planted. Due to the localized nature of scheduling, transnational industry lore had a difficult time forming, because every broadcaster tended to use imports differently. In subsequent chapters we will trace how, as scheduling practices standardized beginning in the late 1980s, transnational industry lore began to flourish.

Despite their inability to influence wider industry perceptions at the time, the institutional labors of integrated U.S. sitcoms in South Africa in the early 1980s do point to different cultural dynamics, trade routes, and industry practices than those that dominate the pages of the trade journals, reminding us that the history of globally traded African American television programs is more complex and diverse than dominant industry lore admits. In particular, we will see how the trend toward media liberalization that swept the world in the 1980s, combined with global discourses of human rights, antiracism, and anticolonialism, met with local discourses of race, nation, ethnicity, and economic globalization to produce the institutional conditions that led Bop-TV to program integrated American imports in politically radical ways.

The International Market for Situation Comedy

The situation comedy genre has never fared well in the estimations of global television merchants. Klaus Lehman, president of international sales for the independent U.S. distributor Metromedia Producers Corporation, which produced some of the most memorable television shows of the seventies and eighties, including *Charlie's Angels,* (1976–1981), *Hart to Hart* (1979–1984), and *Starsky and Hutch* (1975–1979), struck a common refrain in 1977 when he explained, "Most of the comedies produced in America have unique meaning to American viewers. Will foreigners really be receptive to a black American junkman, a working woman in a Minneapolis newsroom, and a blue-collar bigot?" ("U.S. as TV Programmer," 1977, 49). This attitude continued well into the mid-1980s, appearing frequently in trade journal articles. In 1985 Bert Cohen, senior vice president of international sales at Worldvision Enterprises, explained, "You can't translate comedy into another language, because much of it is too Americanized" ("U.S. Programmers Converge," 1986).

The idea that situation comedy is too culturally specific to translate across cultural and language borders was not, however, uncontested, particularly among distributors with a number of sitcoms to sell. Bruce Gordon, president of international sales at Paramount, for example, claimed, "I've sold every comedy Paramount has ever had to Japan, which is probably the most difficult market in the world for comedy" ("U.S. as TV Programmer," 1977, 49). The one exception he mentions, interestingly enough, is the TV adaptation of Neil Simon's *Barefoot in the Park* (1970–1971), which featured a predominantly African American cast. "The Japanese couldn't make head or tail" of it, according to Gordon. We see here the presence of a nascent industry lore that would become more widespread in the 1990s, in which sitcoms perform poorly abroad, and sitcoms with recurrent African American characters perform especially poorly. When trade journal articles do mention African American sitcoms, they are almost always held up as examples of programming that is too culturally specific for international syndication, as evidenced in the comment above about the limited international appeal of a "black American junkman" (i.e., *Sanford and Son* [1972–1977]).[1]

In the early to mid-1980s, even well-performing integrated sitcoms such as *Diff'rent Strokes* (1978–1986) were most commonly used as filler at emerging commercial channels in Europe. As such, their impact on prevalent industry perceptions about the universality of the genre or of African American characters and cultures was minimal. However, in the case of South Africa, integrated U.S. imports had a marked impact on politics, programming practices, and even the broadcasting environment of the nation itself, forcing the introduction of a fourth government-run channel devoted to entertainment television.

Integrated U.S. Sitcoms on Bop-TV

On New Year's Day 1984, Bop-TV began broadcasting to the black South African homeland of Bophuthatswana, a jigsaw puzzle of oblong areas carved out of Transvaal Province (see fig. 2.1). The first commercial television station in South Africa, Bop-TV was retransmitted to predominantly black South African areas outside Bophuthatswana as well, including the Johannesburg suburbs of Soweto and Kagiso. With a mixture of international news feeds, locally produced current affairs, and imported U.S. sitcoms, action-dramas, and specials, this "handful of American trash on a tinpot TV channel" (Cowell, 1984) became an overnight success in black and white households alike.

Because Bop-TV originated in one of the ten South African homelands, which had been founded in the 1970s in an effort to reassign the national identities of all blacks and strip them of South African citizenship, the South African government considered the channel a foreign broadcaster. Although no other government recognized the independence of Bophuthatswana, the South African government had ceded nominal independence to the homeland, including the right to originate radio and television broadcasts. In return for assurances that Bop-TV would not adopt an overtly antigovernment editorial stance, South Africa agreed to retransmit the channel to blacks in the Johannesburg area (Cowell, 1984). This agreement did not, however,

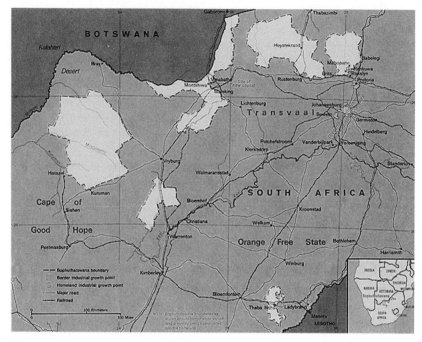

Figure 2.1. This 1977 map of the South African homeland of Bophuthatswana shows the homeland (shown as white areas) as well as some of the Johannesburg suburbs that could receive the Bop-TV broadcast signal.

prevent Bop-TV from crafting an antigovernment, antiapartheid message, which it articulated through creative counterprogramming of South Africa's three state-run channels.

Bop-TV's signal emanated from Mmabatho, the capital of Bophuthatswana, about two hundred kilometers west-northwest of Johannesburg, and was boosted and rebroadcast to black viewers in the western suburbs of Soweto and Kagiso (Lander, 1984). Of course, whites in the western Johannesburg suburbs could also receive Bop-TV. Viewers in Roodepoort, Krugersdorp, and Bekkersdaal reported watching Bop-TV, as did viewers in the eastern suburbs of Germiston and Boksburg. During the first quarter of 1984, approximately 20 percent of Bop-TV's viewers were white, according to research conducted by All Media Products and Services (Correia, 1984b).

White viewers often went to extremes to bring in the distant Bop-TV signal, spending as much as $200 on high-power aerials (Cowell, 1984; Lander, 1984; Van Slambrouck, 1984). Beginning on July 13, 1984, however, several white viewers noticed that they could no longer receive Bop-TV, or that their reception had sharply degraded. Many speculated that, in order to maintain its advertising revenues and dominance over the ideological content of television, the SABC was jamming Bop-TV's signal. For its part, the SABC claimed that any change in Bop-TV's signal quality in white areas owed to the corporation's efforts to boost the quality of the signal in black areas. Besides, SABC officials insisted, viewers had long been warned that the "spillage" of the Bop-TV signal in white areas was only temporary ("Bop-TV Blackout," 1984).

White viewers went ballistic: they accused the SABC of censorship, paternalism, and fear of competition. If the SABC wanted to eliminate the competition from Bop-TV, went a common refrain, it should concentrate on improving its own channels rather than blocking Bop-TV (Correia and Faulkner, 1984). The fallout from the conflict between the SABC and white fans of Bop-TV continued through the summer and fall of 1984, often making the front page of the *Rand Daily Mail*, an English-language, antigovernment Johannesburg newspaper (Pfister, 2005, 22). Fans collected more than sixty thousand signatures on a petition demanding that Parliament allow free access to Bop-TV ("Bop-TV Petition," 1984). Foreign Minister Roelof Frederik "Pik" Botha and members of the opposition Progressive Federal Party clashed publicly over the Bop-TV issue multiple times ("Bop-TV Issue," 1984; Cowell, 1984). Even the international press got wind of the controversy, and articles appeared in the *New York Times*, the *Christian Science Monitor*, the *Globe and Mail*, and the trade journal *TV World*, mostly praising American-style commercial television for giving black viewers what they wanted and turning the tables of racial exclusion on whites ("Bop-TV Petition," 1984; Cowell, 1984; Lander, 1984; Van Slambrouck, 1984).

Despite protests from Bop-TV's white fans, the Parliament ultimately ignored their petition and the channel remained out of reach for most white South Africans at the time ("Bop-TV Petition," 1984). Still, as newspaper accounts from the time make clear, the Bop-TV incident became a lightning rod for debates among white South Africans themselves about freedom of the airwaves, apartheid, and the paternalism of the National Party government that pointed up strong political divisions among English-speaking and Afrikaner whites. In the wake of the Bop-TV controversy, the SABC reorganized its channels and began offering a fourth channel that provided a broader range of popular imported programs aimed at a cross-racial audience. Combined with black South African resistance, the divisions among whites that surfaced in the Bop-TV debates would eventually lead to the dismantling of apartheid in South Africa ten years later.

Bop-TV ignited such strong political divisions at the time because of its reputation as anti-Nationalist and antiapartheid. It achieved this reputation primarily through program selection and scheduling practices that tapped into political and cultural similarities among white and black viewers, in which integrated U.S. sitcoms played an important role. In other words, Bop-TV's channel identity and the political debates it engendered stemmed primarily from the ways executives positioned the channel in relation to existing competitors. Bop-TV's intervention rested predominantly on three program categories: international news feeds that portrayed a wider variety of foreign news than the SABC; local news and current affairs programming that, while relatively tame, nevertheless allowed viewers to hear people and viewpoints excluded from the SABC; and integrated U.S. imports, particularly sitcoms, that showcased interracial harmony and equality. These programming strategies allowed Bop-TV to associate itself with integrated programming, cosmopolitanism, and modernity.

Reading Television Program Schedules

If television programs are imported into preexisting broadcasting environments that profoundly influence their institutional labors (Ellis, 2000), the identities of broadcasters and the ways they conceive of and target viewers are significant elements of that environment. Much of a broadcaster's image comes from how it organizes its program offerings into schedules that compete with other broadcasters. A good deal of this chapter focuses on a critical analysis of program schedules in South Africa during apartheid, reading those schedules for how they privilege particular discourses and position viewers. While not nearly as common as textual analyses of television programs or genres, analyses of television schedules are similar in that they seek to read the processes of domination and resistance that circulate through popular texts (Ellis, 2000; Havens, 2008; Scannell, 1988; Silverstone, 1994; Williams, 1974). However, while an analysis of a single program or genre tells us only how that program or genre imagines society, a reading of program schedules tells us how entire channels or entire national broadcasting systems imagine viewers' identities, sympathies, and relationships.

Programmers in competitive markets use their schedules to construct a particular brand or channel identity in comparison with other channels, most often with counterprogramming techniques, which seek to appeal to audience segments that other channels ignore, or to cobble together several segments in a manner that differs from other channels. Bop-TV, for instance, sought to bring white English speakers and black viewers together by counterprogramming the SABC's channels with internationally oriented programs.

In addition to counterprogramming, television broadcasters use scheduling to capitalize on "inheritance effects," or the tendency of well-performing programs to increase the ratings of prior and subsequent programming on the same channel. Scheduling, therefore, involves both vertical structures internal to a specific channel's programming, and horizontal structures that develop in relation to competitors' program offerings. Thus, the fact that Bop-TV's news included coverage of domestic unrest and was scheduled against the SABC news not only suggested the inadequacy of the latter's coverage, but also contributed to Bop-TV's definition of itself as antigovernment. In what follows, I read the vertical and horizontal constructions of South African television schedules in the mid-1980s in order to understand how they imagine the similarities and differences among racial and linguistic groups, with a particular eye to how integrated U.S. sitcoms fit into the overall organization of its program schedule.

Bop-TV in the South African Broadcasting Landscape

Prior to Bop-TV's launch, the SABC programmed three channels divided along racial and linguistic lines. TV1, aimed at whites, broadcast in English for half the day and Afrikaans the other half. TV2 targeted black Xhosa and Zulu speakers, the two largest black linguistic groups. TV3, meanwhile, broadcast to black viewers in Sesotho and Setswana languages. Thus, the SABC's programming structure reflected the apartheid system of the government that it served, dividing white channels from black at the same time that it envisioned a unified white audience and a black audience fragmented by language and ethnicity (Goldberg, 1993).

The segregated SABC channel lineup was the outcome of struggles among whites over the meanings and functions of television in South African society. While most national governments around the world found the integrative powers of television useful for mobilizing nationalist sentiment among the citizenry, South African nationhood was built on the idea of difference and incommensurability among the races (Barnett, 1995; Nixon, 1994, 50). Combined with concerns about the influence of secular capitalist modernity on the religious, premodern Afrikaner culture, the National Party forestalled the adoption of television until 1976, when increased terrestrial and satellite signals from abroad forced the government to develop its own channels in response (Nixon, 1994, 76). As was the case in Western Europe and elsewhere, then, the liberalization of broadcasting regulations—in this case, the legalization of television broadcasting—followed the introduction of new technologies that slowly encroached upon government broadcasting monopolies (Papathanassopoulos, 1989; Tomaselli, Tomaselli, and Muller, 1989).

The animosity of the Nationalists toward television and modernity was not shared by all whites, most notably English-speaking whites, many of whom were economic elites with little political power. Many English-speaking whites considered the Afrikaners to be impediments to economic progress and the inclusion of South Africa among First World nations (Nixon, 1994, 68). The refusal to allow television broadcasting was, for them, symbolic of the problems with South Africa, a sentiment that spilled over into apartheid politics.[2]

Although the Afrikaner-controlled National Party acquiesced in television broadcasting, the SABC generally refused to program the contemporary U.S. and U.K. imports that many English-speaking whites wanted. In part, this refusal stemmed from a ban by Equity, the U.K. actors' union, on program sales to South Africa. Thus, while English-speaking South African whites got access to Western communications technologies, they remained largely isolated from Western popular culture. The sense that the SABC perpetuated South Africa's isolation from Western modernity is nicely captured in this comment from the *Rand Daily Mail*'s television critic at the time: "When we watch SABC, its [*sic*] like climbing on to the back of an oxwagen [*sic*]. . . . In almost every aspect of our lives we are in step with the Western world. But SABC lags sullenly behind" (Michell, 1984).

Bop-TV managed to cut across the segregated South African television landscape by exploiting the lingering tensions between white English speakers and Afrikaners. While the broadcaster ostensibly targeted black Setswana speakers in Soweto and other black neighborhoods near Johannesburg, it also drew large numbers of white viewers in the surrounding areas. During the second quarter of 1984, the channel attracted an average of 81,000 white viewers per day on weekdays, as compared with 165,000 black viewers (Correia, 1984b). While it is impossible to know the total number of white viewers that Bop-TV reached, and therefore how popular the channel was compared with other channels, a survey conducted by Complete Media at the time claimed that the channel averaged 3.37 viewing hours per day in white households capable of receiving it, as opposed to 1.13 hours per day for the white channel TV1 in the same households (Correia, 1984a).

Bop-TV built its appeal to white English speakers around the programming of imports, especially American ones. Although some British distributors sold programming to Bop-TV in defiance of the ban by Equity (Leavy, 1990), the availability of British programming was meager in comparison with U.S. programming. Bop-TV programmers would have preferred to feature popular British programs as well, as the importation of the Channel 4 soap opera *Brookside* (1982–2003) attests (Leavy, 1990), but international conditions restrained them. In this manner, geopolitical realities shaped how Bop-TV chose to target South African viewers.

Domestic political considerations also set limits on Bop-TV's programming practices. As we might expect, these limitations particularly targeted news coverage, which nevertheless tended to offer a broader range of international news and slightly less censored domestic coverage than the SABC channels. Bop-TV's news included feeds from the British service UPITN, a joint venture of United Press International and the Independent Television News, while its local news included occasional footage of local unrest that went so far as to quote strikers and activists (Lander, 1984). Its current affairs programming sometimes featured discussions with people who were banned from speaking in public in South Africa, ANC leaders, and other critics of the National government. While documentaries on the SABC addressed topics such as the founding of the Afrikaans language, Bop-TV's documentaries included the story of the founder of the black nationalist movement in South Africa, Steve Biko (Cowell, 1984; Michell, 1984). Still, Bop-TV's news remained relatively tame. Reports on corruption and human rights violations in Bophuthatswana were rare, due at least in part to a news director with pro-Mangope sentiments (South African Truth and Reconciliation Committee, 1997). Bop-TV's news programs as well as its entertainment programs were allowed to critique the Nationalist policies of apartheid, but not internal Bophuthatswanan policies.

In the face of domestic and international pressures, Bop-TV nevertheless managed to connect with black South African viewers by programming U.S. imports featuring racial integration and cross-racial interaction, which were generally taboo on the SABC (Spiller, 1990). Integrated American sitcoms such as *Benson* (1979–1986), *Gimme a Break* (1981–1987), and *Diff'rent Strokes* populated Bop-TV's schedules (Spiller, 1990). A local jeans company that aired different versions of the same commercial on the SABC and Bop-TV in 1984 demonstrates well the broadcasters' different programming sensibilities. Both commercials featured a black male hand stroking the torso of a white woman in jeans. In the version run on Bop-TV, the man's hand also patted the woman's buttocks and ran up and down her thighs; in the SABC version, these latter scenes were edited out (Games, 1984).

Bop-TV's handling of controversial content, as compared with the SABC, helped define the former as modern and subversive and the latter as a backward tool of the government. While television critics certainly bemoaned the sad state of the SABC in comparison with broadcasters in other nations prior to Bop-TV's launch, Bop-TV gave critics and viewers clear evidence of the limitations of the SABC's offerings. Letters to the editor of the *Rand*

Daily Mail in the summer of 1984 frequently compared programming on TV1 and Bop-TV in order to take the SABC to task for failing to provide compelling entertainment and objective news ("Big Brother," 1984; "Bop-TV's Fare," 1984).

Its antigovernment stance made Bop-TV appealing to both white English speakers and black viewers, even though the groups' grievances against the Afrikaner-controlled National Party differed. Despite these differences, however, Bop-TV's success demonstrated unequivocally that black and white viewers had a great deal in common. As mentioned, Bop-TV could bring these viewers together in this way only because it entered a preconstituted, segregated television environment. While different program offerings were an important dimension of Bop-TV's appeal to both black and white viewers, so was its strategy of counterprogramming the SABC channels in real time, which worked to draw together white and black audience segments in specific ways.

Scheduling Racial Integration

Examining in detail the juxtaposition of programs on the three SABC channels and Bop-TV can help us interpret the institutional labors that U.S. imports performed to help identify Bop-TV as dramatically different, non-Afrikaner, antigovernment, and antiapartheid. Table 2.1 summarizes the Johannesburg-area television schedule for Sunday, August 26, 1984, including TV1, TV2, TV3, and Bop-TV, all of which broadcast from about 3:00 to 10:00 P.M. TV1 broadcast in English from 3:31 to 8:00, and in Afrikaans from 8:00 to 10:00. TV2 broadcast Xhosa programs in the afternoon, including *Ikhaya Labantwana* (Home for Children) and *Ubhazil Nopekora* (Bazil and Kora), and Zulu titles such as *Imisebenzi Yenkolo* (Works of Faith) and *Ukholo Lunje* (Such Is Faith) in the evening. Meanwhile, TV3 scheduled Setswana programs such as *Legae la Bana* (Home for Children) in the afternoon and Sesotho programs such as *Mahlasedi A Tumelo* (Waves of Faith) in the evening.[3] Bop-TV's original programming used a mixture of Setswana and English that was familiar to many black viewers, while its imports were aired in English. At first glance, Bop-TV's and the SABC's program offerings look quite similar, including imported U.S. and U.K. series, sports programs, news, current affairs, music programs, and religious fare.[4] Upon closer examination, however, we see that the broadcasters schedule these similar programs in very different ways, articulating quite distinct visions of the nation, its viewers, and their political and cultural sensibilities.

Table 2.1. Johannesburg-Area Television Program Schehdule for Sunday, 26 August 1984

	SABC TV1	TV2	TV3	Bop-TV
3:30	Baby Crockett (UK animation) (3:31) The Saga of Noggin the Nog (3:33)	Educational (5)	Educational (3:40)	Sport (3:00)
3:40	Cheesecake (UK animation) (3:43)			
3:50	Tom 'n Jerry (U.S. animation) (3:45)			
4:00	This Happy Breed (UK Film, 1944) (3:59)			
4:50				Tales of Washington Irving (U.S. special, 1970) (4:48)
5:40				Studio Service (5:38)
5:50	Flare: A Ski Trip (sport) (5:45)	Ikhaya Labantwana (Home for Children)	Legae la Bana (Home for Children)	Religious Discussion (5:53)
6:00	Country Comes Home (concert) (6:04)	From the Book Ubhazil Nopekora (6:05)	From the Book The Story of the Bible (6:05)	
6:10		Story of the Bible		AO Ultwile (talk/variety) (6:08)
6:20		Imisebenzi Yenkolo (Works of Faith) (6:25)	Le Reng? (What Do They Say?) (6:23)	
6:30	Cherokee Trail (U.S./Aus series, 1981) (6:27)	Ukholo Lunje (Such is Faith) (6:32)		Benson (U.S. series, 19791986) (6:34)
6:40			Mahlasedi A Tumelo (Waves of Faith) (6:37)	
7:00		News	News & Weather	UPITN Roving Report
7:10	Crossroads (religious) (7:13)			
7:20				Project UFO (7:25) (U.S. series, 1978)
7:30		Harvest Jazz: Stan Getz (7:32)	Sedibeng (To the Wells) (7:33)	

(continued)

Table 2.1 (continued)

	SABC TV1	TV2	TV3	Bop-TV
7:40	Thy Kingdom Come (7:38)			
8:00	News & Weather	Genesis Project	Good Times (U.S. series, 1974–1979) (7:59)	
8:10				News & Weather (8:15)
8:20			Harvest Jazz: Bobby Hutcherson (8:25)	
8:30	Kruis & Kroniek (talk) (8:33)	Maynard Fergusson (sic) (8:28)		Jesse Owens Story (U.S. movie, 1984)
8:50	Helena van Heerden (classical music) (9:00)	The Green Man	New Media Bible (8:54)	
9:10		In Concert (9:20)	Genesis Project (9:12)	
9:30	Arabesque (Ballet)			Benny Goodman Special
9:50	Lig vir de Wereld (Light of the World)			

Source: "Your Full Weekend Television Guide," *Rand Daily Mail*, 25 August 1984, 11.

Programming Apartheid on the SABC

While TV1 divided its broadcast schedule equally among English and Afrikaans programming each day, with the language groups switching between afternoon and evening time slots every day, Afrikaans language and culture retained a superior position: TV1 chose to program prime time in Afrikaans four days a week and in English three days a week. Moreover, it is significant that the channel chose to program prime time in Afrikaans on Sundays in particular, which avoided offending the strict religious sensibilities of the politically influential Calvinist Afrikaner churches (Loader, 1985, 287).

TV2 and TV3, meanwhile, took significantly different approaches to programming for black linguistic groups. TV2 broadcast in Nguni languages, mostly Xhosa and Zulu, while TV3 broadcast in Sotho languages, predominantly Setswana and Sesotho. Moreover, as table 2.1 demonstrates, TV2 and TV3 offered identical programs in different languages for portions of their broadcast schedules. While much of the work in media and cultural studies emphasizes the integrative nature of such shared viewing experiences for constructing imagined communities, TV2 and TV3 divided the black community with this programming strategy (see also Tomaselli, Tomaselli, and Muller, 1989). Thus, although language distinctions were far less clear than these strict programming divisions suggest, with many people speaking several African languages as well as English, the schedule gave the impression that black viewers were irreconcilably divided by language, a division that was reinforced every time a viewer selected whether to watch *Legae la Bana* (Home for Children) in Setswana or *Ikhaya Labantwana* (Home for Children) in Xhosa at 6:05, or whether to watch the news in Zulu or Sesotho at 7 P.M. Hence, TV1 created the appearance of an integrated if somewhat unequal white viewing public, while TV2 and TV3 articulated a linguistically divided black audience.

The SABC's construction of English-speaking and Afrikaans-speaking whites, then, was contained within the vertical structure of the programming schedule of TV1, while its construction of black South Africans was dispersed horizontally across TV2 and TV3. Examining TV1's English-language program offerings in table 2.1 more closely, we can see that the channel imagined white English identity as rooted in historical rather than contemporary differences, with cultural preferences that aligned with Great Britain rather than the United States. With the exception of *Tom 'n' Jerry* (1965–1972), the animated children's shows from 3:31 to 3:59 were imported from Great Britain, as was the film at 3:59, *This Happy Breed* (1944). This historical film, along with the imported American series Louis L'Amour's *Cherokee Trail* (1981), represented British culture in the interwar period and eighteenth-century America, respectively. Indeed, the only present-day programs targeted at white English speakers were sports at 5:45 and the imported American concert program *Country Comes Home* (1982).[5] In this way, TV1 distinguished white English speakers from white Afrikaners by way of language and ethnic roots, rather than contemporary cultural or political differences. Indeed, by airing religious programs in both languages as well as cultural programs that overcame language differences, TV1 gave the impression that white viewers of both ethnicities had a great deal of cultural similarity.

TV2 and TV3, meanwhile, constructed an image of black South Africans as ethnically divided, culturally inferior, politically disinterested, and largely disconnected from black struggles worldwide (see also Tomaselli, Tomaselli, and Muller, 1989). The programming in table 2.1 consists primarily of religious programs, educational children's programs, jazz concerts, and thirty minutes of news at 7 P.M. We have already seen how the distribution of programs across TV2 and TV3 created an image of a linguistically divided black audience. In addition, the program offerings indicate an audience in need of social uplift. Children's programs on TV2 and TV3 from 3:45 and 3:40 to 5:50, respectively, were educational, as opposed to the entertainment-oriented programs aimed at white children and families at the same time. From 5:50 to 6:20, both TV2 and TV3 programmed almost identical religious shows. For most of the rest of the evening on both channels, the programming alternated between religious programs and jazz. Very few entertainment programs appeared on the black channels. Evoking the idea of the white man's burden under apartheid, the program offerings on TV2 and TV3 aimed to enlighten and ennoble viewers rather than provide them with culturally relevant programming.[6]

Not only do TV2 and TV3 position black viewers as culturally backward, they also imagine them as apolitical. Thus, the only program about Africa, *The Genesis Project* (TV2 at 8:00, TV3 at 9:12), is a nature documentary about efforts to preserve African elephants and rhinoceroses (Botha, 2006). Magazine programs like *Le Reng?* (What Do They Say?) focused mostly on personal, middle-class black concerns rather than contemporary political issues (Botha, 2006; Tomaselli, Tomaselli, and Muller, 1989). Meanwhile, although religious services and discussions such as *Imisebenzi Yenkolo* (Works of Faith) and *Ukholo Lunje* (Such Is Faith) might have addressed political issues from a religious perspective, the largest black religious bloc at the time, the independent churches, were generally apolitical and did not actively challenge the racial status quo (Loader, 1985, 281).

Ironically, evening jazz programs may have carried the most radical political voices on TV2 and TV3. While jazz music was decidedly less political in connotation than African music or imported rock music of the day, it did possess immediate associations with the Sophiatown black renaissance of the 1950s, which had been crushed in 1955 when blacks were forcibly relocated and the city was razed and replaced with white suburban dwellings (Nixon, 1994, 11–13). Thus, the inclusion of jazz music in the program schedule does allude to cultural associations that run counter to the Nationalist ideology. The alternating jazz programs on TV2 and TV3 also allowed for cross-linguistic viewing among black audiences. Indeed, white viewers, especially English speakers who didn't care for the cultural offerings on TV1, may have turned to these channels to watch the integrated jazz bands perform.

The SABC's approach to imagining the national audience along racial and ethnic lines, then, articulated a white audience that may have been divided by its roots, but shared a common culture. The schedules of TV2 and TV3, on the other hand, portrayed black viewers as literally incapable of communicating across language differences. Program offerings identified black audiences as largely apolitical and culturally backward. However, this program structure also allowed for, and even sometimes encouraged, a degree of cross-linguistic and cross-racial viewing, suggesting that the neat boundaries of race and language that the SABC had constructed suppressed other possible categorizations of viewers and their cultural and political sympathies (Tomaselli, Tomaselli, and Muller, 1989). This was the broadcasting landscape into which integrated U.S. sitcoms were imported and from which Bop-TV's programmers imagined their institutional labors.

Constructing Integrated Audiences on Bop-TV

Bop-TV's program schedule reflected a concerted effort to imagine and assemble an integrated viewing audience, even while maintaining its primary identity as a black channel. While U.S. imports were an important component of this effort, they were only one ingredient in the overall strategy. At different times of day, Bop-TV adopted different programming strategies that identified the channel as an integrated alternative to the SABC channels' image of the South African nation.

At 4:48, for instance, Bop-TV counterprogrammed educational children's programs on TV2 and TV3 with an entertainment-oriented animated U.S. import, *Tales of Washington Irving* (1970). Not only did this choice demonstrate a more populist approach to programming for black children, it also acknowledged, though obliquely, the imagined cultural sensibilities shared by black South African and American cultures. Furthermore, the scheduling of *Tales of Washington Irving* also countered the British slant of TV1's programming with a distinctly American children's program. Thus, Bop-TV created an integrated audience among children at this time of day by tapping into a shared interest in American stories.

At other times of the day, Bop-TV programmed head-to-head against the SABC's black channels, abandoning its integrated audience for a predominantly black one. Beginning at 5:38, Bop-TV programmed a church service and a religious discussion against religious programming on TV2 and TV3. *Studio Service* and *Religious Discussion* were self-produced studio shows that featured mostly black participants who spoke a mixture of English and Setswana, which may have been difficult for some English-speaking white viewers to understand. The abandonment of white viewers helped identify Bop-TV as a distinctly black channel that appealed sometimes to white viewers because of shared tastes and sensibilities, rather than a channel that valued white and black audiences equally.[7] Although the views of Bop-TV's religious programs were likely more critical than those of TV2 and TV3, religion nevertheless played an important role in Bop-TV's construction of its black audience.

As the evening progressed, Bop-TV began to imagine an integrated black and white family audience as members of the modern, Western world, predominantly through the use of imported U.S. programs with integrated casts. Beginning at 6:34, Bop-TV counterprogrammed the SABC channels with *Benson*, which featured the African American actor Robert Guillaume as a wisecracking butler who works for a white state governor and rises in the ranks to become budget director and eventually lieutenant governor. Unlike the rival Australian-American program on TV1, Louis L'Amour's *Cherokee Trail*, *Benson* was a popular American series set in contemporary times that dealt with current political and racial issues. Bop-TV's airing of the series identified the broadcaster with integration, modernity, and America, in contrast to TV1's association with whiteness, history, and the racist frontier spirit that helped settle the American West and South Africa alike. Meanwhile, by countering TV2 and TV3's religious programming in this time slot, Bop-TV addressed black viewers as members of a taste culture that included not only English-speaking white South Africans, but also multiracial viewers in the United States. By employing both head-to-head and counterprogramming strategies in relation to TV2 and TV3, Bop-TV was able to imagine a black South African identity that was locally distinct yet interconnected with white South Africans and the international community.

Bop-TV reinforced and extended this international connectedness when it returned to a head-to-head programming strategy against TV2 and TV3 at 7:00 with the imported British news program *UPITN Roving Report*, which also counterprogrammed TV1. Due to its capacity to reach across racial divisions by airing in English, the *UPITN Roving Report* imagined both black and white viewers as part of an international political system, as opposed to the parochial news broadcast on TV2 and TV3 at the same time. Significantly, TV1 showed no news or current affairs programs in English on Sundays, which was also the only day that Bop-TV programmed the *Roving Report*.

A close comparison of U.S. imports on the SABC and Bop-TV helps clarify how the broadcasters constructed quite different images of America. At 7:59, TV3 aired the imported American sitcom *Good Times* (1974–1979), a "pluralist" (Gray, 1995) television series that featured an almost exclusively black cast living in a segregated world. Although early seasons of the series did feature numerous scathing critiques of racism in the United States, the show remained segregated. Moreover, given the intense comparisons that the Nationalist government often drew between South African and U.S. racial politics (Nixon, 1994), such a segregated image of the United States reinforced the perception that segregation was a widespread international practice.

By contrast, Bop-TV's earlier showing of *Benson* drew a very different picture of contemporary U.S. race relations.[8] Herman Gray (1986) has written that *Benson* promoted an assimilationist ideology of blackness, framing racial difference in solidly middle-class terms that required no sense of change or sacrifice on the part of whites to achieve assimilation. Although the main character, Benson, served as the ethical center of the series and retained a communicative style rooted in African American culture, particularly his cutting, mumbled, and sometimes subversive sense of humor, he had no connection with the wider African American community, encountered few difficulties because of his race, and always worked to resolve conflicts well within the bounds of polite, white, middle-class society. Still, in order for this assimilationist ideology to work effectively, the series needed to reference the historical racial unrest that the world of *Benson* had supposedly transcended, if even obliquely. Such references came across perhaps most strongly in the opening sequence of the pilot, which depicted Benson arriving at the governor's mansion, only to be sprayed with water by the lawn sprinkling system and chased by guard dogs. These tamed images of the violence that white authorities, including southern governors, had unleashed against civil rights activists in recent decades subtly suggest how far the United States as a nation had come with regard to race relations and racial violence. But the allusions to more difficult race relations than those that predominated in *Benson* were, nevertheless, present, both here and throughout the series.

In South Africa the integrated idyll of *Benson* must have seemed quite distant indeed, much more a utopian dream than a representation of contemporary race relations, as it may have been perceived in the United States. While *Benson* may have created a false sense of the true state of U.S. race relations, the series' utopianism also provided an imaginary release from the day-to-day racial exploitation that South African blacks faced, large numbers of whom were employed as domestic servants in white households, much as was Benson. Finally, it is important to note that *Benson*, along with other integrated U.S. sitcoms, portrayed the *domestic* space as integrated, as opposed to the workplace, a move that might have seemed particularly radical in the South African context due to undertones of interracial sexual and marriage relationships. A sitcom such as *Gimme a Break*, which told the story of an African American live-in maid who worked for a widowed white police officer and was widely panned as a racist throwback to 1940s film portrayals of African American women, might have been quite differently regarded among South African viewers for this reason. Many of Bop-TV's imports demonstrate a preference for integrated domestic U.S. series, substantiating claims by two Bop-TV program buyers that they specifically sought out such programming (Spiller, 1990).

If Bop-TV addressed black viewers as locally distinct, yet cosmopolitan and already integrated into South African society, it projected an image of the white audience as incompletely integrated into Western capitalist modernity. Because Bop-TV remained primarily a black channel, with white viewers forced into the position of eavesdroppers who had to invest both effort and money to bring in the signal, the channel served as a persistent reminder of the Nationalist government's censorship of Western popular culture and its refusal to fully join the Western world. Letters to the editor of the *Rand Daily Mail* made it clear that many English-speaking whites resented the isolation that Bop-TV made them aware of, at the same time that they reinforced the isolation among viewers far beyond Bop-TV's broadcast signal by informing them, often in detail, about the programs they were missing. One viewer in the white suburb of Krugersdorp wrote to the English-language *Rand Daily Mail's* television reviewer, "Please Mr. Michel, let us have reviews on Bop-TV as well. Even though many readers can not tune into Bop-TV, I am sure they would like to know what they're missing" ("Bop-TV's Fare," 1984).

Although the petition for greater access to Bop-TV failed, the broadcaster had a lasting impact on the South African television landscape. Throughout 1984, TV1 imported greater amounts of current, popular American fare, including the integrated 1980s police drama *Miami Vice* (1984–1990). In 1985 the SABC launched a new channel, TV4, which targeted an integrated audience with entertainment programming, in a move that some observers saw as a direct response to Bop-TV's popularity (Correia, 1984c; Reynolds, 1984). Bop-TV's broadcast signal continued to be limited to black areas, and the broadcaster continued to associate itself with antiapartheid politics through its importation of programming that addressed African American cultural, political, and historical themes.

Program Scheduling as Culturally Embedded Institutional Labor

In this chapter I have gone into some depth analyzing South African television schedules in the mid-1980s and the ways programmers used imported U.S. series, particularly situation comedies, to bring together certain segments of the black and white viewing public and to project an integrated, cosmopolitan channel identity. The image of the audience that Bop-TV projected developed in the way that it did only because of competing constructions of the audience on other South African channels, specifically the representation of viewers, through scheduling, as consisting of a racially coherent white audience and a black audience fragmented by language and ethnicity.

Scheduling, then, serves as a primary site where institutionalized perceptions of viewers' tastes, affiliations, and identities become available for analysis, where cultural processes and commercial imperatives interact to produce industry lore. In the case of Bop-TV during apartheid, the dominant industry lore held that racially integrated American programs, particularly those centered in the home, served the broadcaster's needs best because they identified Bop-TV as irreverent, thus drawing in a broad range of disaffected South African viewers of all races.

This industry lore, meanwhile, arose from a complex tangle of local and transnational discourses and institutional practices. The SABC promoted a "separate-but-equal" ideology through its racially and linguistically targeted channels and segregated imports, while Bop-TV's scheduling and imports advanced a vision of racial integration that drew upon long-standing transnational discourses about the universality of white values (Fiske, 1996), as well as the history of civil rights struggles in the United States and elsewhere. The appeal of Bop-TV's integrated imports also arose in part from the global circulation of the discourse of cosmopolitanism, as opposed to provincialism, as the hallmark of contemporary modernity. Bop-TV's scheduling, meanwhile, was deeply influenced by uneven economic development and the global movement to divest Western business from apartheid South Africa. That is, Bop-TV's decision to import integrated American series stemmed not from the fact that it was the best *possible* way to meet its institutional needs, but rather because such programming represented the best *available* alternative. American, British, and Australian programming was abundant on the market at the time, while programming from other African nations, other predominantly black markets—even other nonwhite markets—was virtually nonexistent due to the historical exploitation and consequent economic underdevelopment of these societies. And finally, the transnational discourses of antiapartheidism and divestiture had led the U.K. television industry to ban sales of current programs to South Africa, again shaping the ways Bop-TV could enact its particular form of antigovernment, antiapartheid cultural politics.

The realization that program trade is deeply embedded in local and transnational institutions and discursive flows recognizes that program buyers and schedulers act as cultural interpreters. Certainly they work within constraints imposed by larger economic, political, historical, and cultural forces, but they nevertheless exert personal agency in their decision making, which articulates a host of similarities and differences among domestic tastes and foreign television culture. While their perceptions of the commonalities among communities worldwide do not determine audience members' perceptions, they do determine cultural flows. Thus, while numerous textual features may resonate across national boundaries, only those features identified by the local gatekeepers of global cultural trade shape the kinds of cultural products that circulate internationally.

This idea that programmers actively articulate the cultural connections between viewers, channel identities, and imported texts stands in stark contrast to the dominant industry lore—and perhaps conventional wisdom more broadly—that black viewers abroad prefer imports with African American characters primarily because skin color similarities decrease the foreignness of the imports. Several sales executives, for instance, have explained to me that African American programming does well in South Africa and other African nations because "there's a high population of blacks" (personal communication to the author from anonymous sales executive at a Hollywood distributor, June 28, 1999). By contrast, Cawe Mahlati (1999), the last CEO of Bophuthatswana Broadcasting before its incorporation into the SABC, identifies the role that cultural and political sensibilities played in Bop-TV's preference for acquiring African American programming over the years:

> Because we are a black station, the preference for acquisitions are television programs where African Americans appeared or acted. For a number of reasons. The one being that African Americans have got a very, very great influence on South African black urban culture. And therefore, they've always been thrown up as role models. For instance, if you look at the dressing style and also if you look at the music . . . and the whole neighborhood thing, the whole dancing. . . . Consequently, it makes sense, then, for one to show programming that contains images that people in South Africa can relate to. Secondly, as well, Bop television has shown most of the movies that depict the African American experience in the U.S. There's a lot of resonance in South Africa for that kind of programming.

Mahlati's comments demonstrate the inherently cultural considerations that acquisition executives take into account in constructing linkages between black communities worldwide, while the more conventional wisdom of the Hollywood sales executive sees those acquisitions choices as natural expressions of skin color preferences.

Given the highly localized nature of program decision making traced here, it is perhaps a wonder that worldwide programming trends ever developed.

Of course, the limited amount of programming to choose from is one factor that helps create those trends, but even in the early 1980s, tens of thousands of hours of programming were available on the international markets. Today that number is likely in the hundreds of thousands of hours. The solution to the riddle of worldwide programming trends lies in the active efforts of program merchants, especially syndicators, to influence buyers' perceptions about which imported programs can best serve their institutional needs. In addition, the increasing numbers of global advertisers utilizing similar demographic categories in every market, as well as specialty channels that target those demographics, have created political-economic conditions that further facilitate similar thinking about channel identity and viewers' preferences across national markets.

3

The Cosby Show, Family Themes, and the Ascent of White Situation Comedies Abroad in the Late 1980s

Beginning in the mid-1980s, changes in both domestic and international media industries led to increased international sales revenues for U.S. programming of all genres. These increases were particularly noticeable in the formerly resistant markets of Western Europe, which had tended to view U.S. programs as overly commercial and ill-suited to their public service broadcasting environments. With the introduction of commercial television in Europe and growing demands for European public service broadcasters to demonstrate their popularity with a broad cross section of the national audience, numerous channels began programming U.S. imports in unconventional ways that led to revisions in the dominant industry lore about the kinds of programs that transfer well across national borders.

The impact of these political-economic changes on conventional industry lore and the institutional labors of U.S. exports abroad was profound, both for U.S. television in general and for African American television in particular. Rather suddenly, buyers from specialty channels, commercial channels, and reorganized public broadcasters revised their images of their potential audiences and the kinds of programming techniques that could hold their attention. Buyers were more willing to experiment with imported programs than they might have been only a few years earlier due to the comparative cheapness of program imports and uncertainty about how to attract this newly imagined audience.

Such moments of significant political, economic, and regulatory change in the world's media systems reshape prevalent industry lore because of the uncertainty they produce for both buyers and sellers. They permit—require, really—industry executives at home and abroad to search out new ways of imagining foreign and transnational audiences and their potential connections to imported programming. As part of this search, long-ignored cultural alliances, new historical developments, submerged transnational discourses, historical similarities, and informal cultural flows get activated and, potentially, filter up into conventional industry lore.

In the case of U.S. situation comedies, dominant perceptions about their exportability began to change in the late 1980s and early 1990s. While most program merchants remained skeptical about the genre's overall appeal, they began to realize that certain types of sitcoms, especially family-oriented domestic sitcoms, could appeal to both niche and general audiences abroad under some conditions.

The Cosby Show (1984–1992) was central to revising industry lore about sitcoms. A certifiable hit in its domestic market, *The Cosby Show* attracted more viewers and made more money than any series in television history, netting over $1 billion in domestic syndication sales and close to $1 billion in ad revenues for NBC during its eight years in prime time. Internationally the series was almost as popular in many markets, consistently topping the ratings in such diverse places as the Philippines, Lebanon, Indonesia, Hong Kong, Australia, the Caribbean, and South Africa. Across Europe the series became the top American import and beat out previous international favorites like *Dallas* (1978–1991), *Dynasty* (1981–1989), and *The A-Team* (1983–1987) in terms of popularity and total number of markets where the series aired.

Drawing on the insights of the previous chapter, it seems reasonable to argue that the explanations for the popularity of *The Cosby Show* abroad are probably at least as numerous as the number of territories that imported the show. Extant viewers' comments from around the world exhibit voyeurism and fascination with black bodies in Sweden; appreciation of the dignity of Bill Cosby's character—as compared with conventional, satirical portrayals of black men in popular culture—among black South Africans; identification with family size, communication patterns, and the ability to retain one's cultural identity in the face of white, Western pressures in Lebanon; and dislike for the series' portrayals of masculinity, feminism, and youth culture in Barbados (Havens, 2000).

Despite the range of viewer responses to the series, however, a coherent industry lore grew up around the series among American, European, and some non-Western executives, identifying "universal family themes" as *The Cosby Show*'s primary appeal abroad. In this chapter I examine how technological, industrial, representational, and discursive forces worked together to produce this industry lore. While the previous chapter explored how *programmers* worked with local and transnational political trends, discourses, and political-economic developments to produce radical television schedules in apartheid South Africa, this chapter zeroes in on the global television *merchants*—buyers and sellers of African American television—and how this distinct, transnational interpretive community developed a coherent lore about the audience appeal of one of the most successful global television programs of all time.

The Changing Economics of Global Television Trade in the 1980s

While the economics of television broadcasting both at home and abroad had encouraged international program trade from the late 1950s through the early 1970s, as nations around the world added television broadcasting capabilities that relied heavily on imports to round out their schedules, television syndication since that time had been largely a domestic affair. Certainly, program trade existed in the mid-1970s and early 1980s, but U.S. syndicators made far more money from domestic syndication to local broadcasters and independent stations than they did from international trade (Havens, 2006).

Since 1970, U.S. networks had been legally barred from owning or profiting from the programs that they aired during prime time. Consequently, Hollywood studios and independent producers created most of the prime-time programming in the 1980s, including *The Cosby Show*. The networks licensed the rights to broadcast prime-time programs from the producers, generally for two prime-time runs per season, after which the rights to sell programs into syndication reverted to the producer. These syndication rights included international sales, and the ratio of profits from international and domestic sales differed significantly by genre. As we saw in chapter 1, for instance, the miniseries *Roots* earned more than half of its revenues overseas, in contrast to the situation comedies we examined in the previous chapter, which earned perhaps 10 percent of their revenues abroad.

For a number of reasons, the market for global television trade and the balance between domestic and international revenues changed dramatically in the mid-1980s. Domestically, one of the most significant changes was the 1984 Cable Act, which paved the way for several competing cable channels to challenge the traditional terrestrial broadcasters—ABC, CBS, and NBC—and led to steady declines in network audience ratings. By 1985 Nielsen Media reported that prime-time viewership had fallen below 50 percent of the total potential audience, a decline of about 20 percent from ten years earlier. Along with audience ratings, network advertising revenues fell and program production costs grew, as the networks spent lavishly on signature programs in an effort to stand out from their cable competitors. Decreased advertising revenues prompted the networks to lower the license fees that they paid to program producers, while increased production costs forced producers to seek greater syndication revenues from abroad to cover the difference (Barns, 1981; Boyer, 1986; Richter, 1986).

Meanwhile, governments abroad relaxed restrictions on commercial broadcasting and cable television, thereby expanding the number of international buyers for U.S. programming. Between 1984 and 1997 the number of cable and satellite channels in Europe grew from 10 to more than 250 ("Europe's 'Other,'" 1997, 57). Most of these startup channels depended heavily on imported programming to build audiences and fill out their broadcast schedules. In Europe in 1992, for instance, 75 percent of new channels used imported programming for at least half of their schedules ("Transformation Scene," 1992, 40).

This wave of deregulation and privatization started in Western Europe but quickly spread to many parts of the globe, aided by the rise of neoconservative governments in the United States, the United Kingdom, Canada, Australia, India, and other nations, who shared a disdain for the concept of public service broadcasting and preferred to place broadcasting in commercial hands (Herman and McChesney, 1997, 156–58). Between 1984 and 1989, U.S. syndicators' foreign revenues nearly quadrupled from $500 million to $1.7 billion (Havens, 2006). In fact, one of the main reasons the U.S. networks sought to decrease their license fees at the time was the understanding that syndicators in the mid-eighties could recoup production costs from these international sources.

The Selling of *The Cosby Show*

The Cosby Show was produced by the boutique production firm Carsey-Werner and syndicated domestically and internationally by Viacom, which at the time was a small television distributor, not the global behemoth that it is today. Along with macro-level political-economic changes at home and abroad that prepared the ground for a revision of industry lore about sitcoms, micro-level business practices at Viacom also contributed to the ascension of *The Cosby Show* as the most popular U.S. export of the late 1980s. The fact that *The Cosby Show* became a prime vehicle for revising prevalent industry lore shaped that lore in specific ways. That is, the perception that universal family values facilitated the series' export would have been impossible to sustain if, for instance, the Fox sitcom *Married . . . with Children* (1987–1997), often referred to as "not *The Cosby Show*," had become the most popular U.S. export. A close examination of Viacom's international marketing strategies reflects the company's slow-but-sure recognition that, against conventional industry wisdom at the time, sitcoms could achieve popularity on the international markets.

Viacom was created in the wake of rule changes by the FCC that made it illegal for the networks to have a financial stake in the prime-time programming they aired. In response to these new rules, CBS spun off its syndication wing into a separate company, Viacom. By the mid-1980s, however, Viacom's library of 1970s CBS hits such as *The Mary Tyler Moore Show* (1970–1977) was aging, and the company was on the lookout for new programming. Before it found *The Cosby Show*, its previous efforts had netted only such forgettable shows as *Dear Detective* (1979) and *The Lazarus Syndrome* (1979), though the company also held the rights to some B movies and *Perry Mason* specials. Therefore, when Carsey-Werner ran into trouble financing *The Cosby Show*'s high budgets, Viacom agreed to pump in extra funds in return for the right to distribute the show worldwide (Richter, 1985).

Observers estimate that *The Cosby Show* never earned more than $100 million in international revenues.[1] While this figure pales in comparison with the more than $1 billion the series brought in from domestic syndication, it still represents wide international appeal, given that international buyers paid significantly less than their domestic counterparts for the rights to air the series. In addition, although *The Cosby Show* quickly soared to the number one spot in the United States, Viacom was unable to recoup most of its investment until 1987, when enough episodes had been produced for domestic syndication.[2] For three years, then, international sales offered the only revenues from the series other than NBC's license fee while the company awaited domestic syndication profits (Flanigan, 1987; Lippman, 1992; Richter, 1985).[3]

The Cosby Show far outperformed any of its domestic competitors in international sales. *Family Ties* (1982–1989), for instance, which occasionally challenged *The Cosby Show* for the top-rated position in the U.S. market and was sold internationally by Paramount Pictures, performed well only in Europe and Australia. *The Cosby Show*, by contrast, appealed to audiences in these predominantly white markets as well as in nonwhite markets in the Middle East, Latin America, Africa, and East Asia. The similarities between these two sitcoms are striking and begin to give us a glimpse into the importance of race in explaining their differential success. Paramount Pictures was just as interested as Viacom at the time in establishing a presence as a successful international distributor. The quality of the writing and acting in *Family Ties* rivaled that of *The Cosby Show*, and many remember the series as *The Cosby Show*'s "white obverse" (Taylor, 1989, 163). Each series offered a comparable vision of the American Dream, in which material comfort allowed family members to escape the drudgery of daily work and concentrate instead on personal and familial well-being. In fact, the racial difference between the Huxtables and the Keatons is perhaps the only salient difference between these two sitcoms that can account for their very different export patterns.

The details of Viacom's international distribution strategy for *The Cosby Show* are difficult to reconstruct. In all likelihood, the strategy was mostly opportunistic and haphazard, rather than carefully planned, due to low expectations for the series in international markets (see fig. 3.1).

Most of the international sales in 1984 and 1985 were to either Scandinavian or non-European general entertainment television networks. These European markets were still dominated by one or two public broadcast networks that paid low license fees for imported programs. In Denmark and the Netherlands the state broadcasters reported that *The Cosby Show* was the top-rated import in 1986. In South Africa, where the show consistently ranked number one, the SABC began airing the show in 1985 on the newly introduced TV4, which targeted a multiracial audience. The monopoly socialist television network in Poland reported that the show was popular in the fall of 1986. State-run channels in Israel and Lebanon likewise reported in 1988 that the series had been an unqualified success for more than a year (Fuller, 1992; Hall et al., 1986; Mufson, 1986; Raschka, 1988; "What's Hot," 1986). Obviously, the institutional labors to which these varied broadcasters put *The Cosby Show* differed greatly and can be reconstructed only through the kind of close analysis of the political, cultural, and broadcasting environments that we undertook in the previous chapter. Nevertheless, these details suggest that interest in *The Cosby Show* in small markets mostly came from established broadcasters who used them to attract undifferentiated audiences.

Because these early sales took place in markets that paid small license fees, it was easy for Viacom's executives to either ignore the show's popularity in these territories or write it off as little more than a curiosity. Slowly, however, the growing success of *The Cosby Show* in international markets began to sink in at Viacom, particularly as a handful of larger European territories started broadcasting the show. In these increasingly lucrative and competitive territories, the show performed best in newly commercializing markets at small television stations. The show flopped in Belgium in 1985, where it was carried on the state broadcast system prior to the introduction of commercial television. In Italy, which had had pervasive, if illegal, private television since the mid-1970s, the show performed well on the private station Canale 5 from 1985 onward. France's M6, a theme channel dedicated to popular entertainment, began programming the show in 1988, soon after private television broadcasting became legal, and continued with good ratings for at least six years. In the United Kingdom, meanwhile, the series began airing in 1985 on Channel 4, a commercial broadcaster aimed at affluent viewers. While the series achieved only a "cult following" of between two and three million viewers per episode, it was one of the top-rated shows on Channel 4 and received high Appreciation Scores, which measure viewers' levels of

Figure 3.1. We can see Viacom's low expectations of *The Cosby Show*'s international syndication potential reflected in the way it advertised its programming in *TV World*, one of the main international television trade journals at the time. In 1984 and 1985 the company's slogan, "The World Turns to Viacom for Great Drama," was repeated in several advertisements for drama programming, especially the miniseries *Peter the Great* (1986). The first mention of *The Cosby Show* came in a February 1985 advertisement promoting four series—*Me and Mom* (1985), *Star Games* (1985), *Peter the Great*, and *The Cosby Show*—in which mention of *The Cosby Show* is buried at the end of the second paragraph of copy (Viacom, 1985a). Obviously, Viacom did not view the show as a lucrative international commodity at the time.

enjoyment. Finally, in Germany, the public broadcaster ZDF began broadcasting the series in 1987, but it did not develop much of a following until it moved to the commercial broadcaster Prosieben in 1989 ("Belgian Parliament," 1986; Buxton, 1985; Fuller, 1992; Henry, 1986; "La Cinq," 1989).

In each of these examples, programmers used *The Cosby Show* as a cheap way to attract an audience that was interested in popular commercial programming, but otherwise largely undifferentiated in terms of gender, class, income, and other demographic variables. Moreover, the distribution patterns within and beyond Europe demonstrate that buyers looked to the performance of the series at similar channels in other markets in their region when purchasing the series. Thus, for instance, buyers from state-run broadcasters in the Middle East or public broadcasters in Europe could look to one another to gauge the show's potential performance when making buying decisions, demonstrating the transnationalization of industry lore and perceptions of how African American imports can help accomplish institutional goals.

Viacom's growing awareness of *The Cosby Show*'s European popularity, combined with the promise of new, private channels across the continent that would require cheap American imports to fill out their broadcast schedules, led the company to take a more aggressive approach to promoting the show (see fig. 3.2). By 1986 Viacom reported sales of *The Cosby Show* in more than sixty countries. However, international sales revenues remained tiny in comparison with domestic sales, even in the largest foreign markets, in part because many of the channels that bought the show had comparatively small audiences. The United Kingdom's Channel 4 reportedly paid between £10,000 and £15,000 per episode ($16,000–$23,000 in 1990 dollars), while France's M6 paid between 20,000 and 30,000 French francs per episode ($3,000–$4,500 in 1990 dollars). Domestic sales, meanwhile, amounted to more than $4 million per episode (Henry, 1986; "La Cinq," 1989; Viacom, 1986).

Viacom held low expectations for the international marketability of *The Cosby Show* because of its status as a situation comedy and the impression at the time among global program merchants that sitcoms sold poorly abroad, as we saw in the previous chapter. While this impression did not extend to everyone involved in program trade, it was widespread enough to shape Viacom's marketing strategies. Given the international performance of other top-rated U.S. television series in the recent past, particularly the impressive success of *Dynasty* and *Dallas*, we can only conclude that the modest expectations for *The Cosby Show* abroad stemmed from negative attitudes toward the sitcom genre in general.

Regardless of the challenges of selling sitcoms internationally, however,

Figure 3.2. In February 1986 Viacom thought it financially worthwhile to take out a full-page ad for the show in *TV World* announcing that the domestically renowned series was available for international distribution. By November 1986, we find a full-page ad announcing that *The Cosby Show* is "The World's Newest Superpower," and claiming that the show "has transcended language and culture." Although the show had overcome non-European languages and cultures before this ad was published, sales to Western European markets provided the catalyst for Viacom's revised international marketing strategy and somewhat hyperbolic claims.

the genre had become increasingly popular in domestic syndication in the mid-1980s. In the United States, sitcoms attract desirable young demographics, are easy for television stations to schedule because they last only thirty minutes, and retain more of their audience in reruns than any other genre. Furthermore, sitcoms are generally the cheapest fictional genre to produce because they have traditionally been shot in-studio, usually with a stationary, three-camera setup that requires few changes in production equipment from episode to episode. *The Cosby Show* was an exception to this rule, with per-episode production costs topping $500,000 in 1985 due to costs associated with shooting in the Bronx rather than Los Angeles—a price tag that rivaled the costs of more expensive dramatic genres (Boyer, 1986) and contributed to Viacom's efforts to recoup its costs overseas. Despite this anomaly, however, most of the sitcoms that followed in the wake of *The Cosby Show*'s popularity remained comparatively cheap to produce. Therefore, U.S. distributors found their libraries stocked with sitcoms in need of international buyers (Heuton, 1990).

By the mid-1990s negative attitudes about the international marketability of sitcoms had been revised. As one commentator wrote in 1998, "the old paradigm against the international appeal of sitcoms has changed. It's not that sitcoms don't work, it's that some kinds of sitcoms don't work" (Spring, 1998, 6). A number of similar reports appeared in several trade journals around this time, virtually all of which credited *The Cosby Show* with a pivotal role in changing the industry lore.

The Cosby Show's Worldwide Appeal

The changes in the television industries across the globe outlined above help explain why *The Cosby Show* might have appealed to the raft of upstart channels that began in the mid-1980s. In addition, Viacom's efforts to promote the series as a universal success undoubtedly shaped buyers' decisions. Ultimately, however, the explanation for the popularity of *The Cosby Show* abroad lay with viewers who, despite differences of region, nationality, race and ethnicity, class, and so forth found value in the series. These viewers exhibited a wide variety of reasons for enjoying the series, and their comments give us insights into the kinds of diasporic sensibilities that exported African American television culture can harness (Fuller, 1992). Furthermore, the diversity of these comments, as compared with the uniformity of industry explanations, which we examine below, demonstrates how program merchants operate as cultural mediators who interpret and process complex audience trends in manageable and institutionally useful ways.

Although no comprehensive research into international viewers' reasons for watching *The Cosby Show* took place at the time, several newspaper articles did report viewers' attitudes in various parts of the world. A scholarly article about the show's reception in the Caribbean and a book that includes some written comments alongside statistical reports on viewers' satisfaction levels also give us glimpses into the kinds of pleasures that viewers got from watching the show (Flanigan, 1987; Fuller, 1992; Henry, 1986; Mufson, 1986; Payne, 1994; Raschka, 1988). In addition, a review of some of the main textual features of the series can help us understand why it might have become popular abroad.

Unlike most shows before it, *The Cosby Show* presented a picture of a comfortably well off, upper-class African American family that faced few problems from the world outside its living room walls. The heads of household in the series were Heathcliff Huxtable (Cliff), an obstetrician played by Bill Cosby, and Clair, an attorney played by Phylicia (Allen) Rashad. For the majority of the series' run, four Huxtable children rounded out the cast: Denise, the eldest, played by Lisa Bonet; Theo, the only son, played by Malcolm-Jamal Warner; and younger daughters Vanessa, played by Tempestt Bledsoe, and Rudy, played by Keshia Knight Pulliam.

Based on discussions with numerous black and white American focus groups from across the socioeconomic spectrum, Sut Jhally and Justin Lewis (1992) in *Enlightened Racism* argue that the show struck a politically conservative chord by failing to portray the economic and social hardships that so often constitute part of what it means to be black in the United States. The authors criticize the show for ignoring these thorny issues and leaving white viewers with the impression that African Americans no longer faced economic barriers in American society, at the same time that it flattered African American viewers by avoiding traditional buffoon characters. Whatever the reader may think of these arguments, the fact that *The Cosby Show* avoided most overt references to American economic hardships may have made the show more accessible to international viewers, who might have found such allusions unfamiliar and confusing.

When political discourse did surface on *The Cosby Show*, it mostly involved issues with long histories and international currency, such as civil rights, antiapartheid, and education movements. In one famous episode, for instance, the family watched a rebroadcast of Martin Luther King Jr.'s illustrious "I Have a Dream" speech. Huxtable son Theo displayed an antiapartheid poster on his bedroom door in the first several seasons. And the importance of education for personal and racial uplift, especially the role of historically black colleges and universities in educating African Americans, became a recurring theme in the series. Due to the long history of these political issues and their international visibility, international viewers would have found them much easier to understand than the kinds of flash-in-the-pan political issues that dominated series such as *Murphy Brown* (1988–1998) and *West Wing* (1999–2006).

The Huxtable family's economic status was also reflected in the allusions that the show made to high-class African American culture, rather than the hip-hop references that would come to fill many later African American sitcoms. Episodes of the show often featured jazz, blues, and R&B music. Work by African American painters, many with black figures and scenes, decorated the living room walls. As Herman Gray (1995) points out, the series made accessible to viewers an African American upper-class lifestyle that had been around for centuries but had rarely gotten noticed by popular culture. In fact, the main cultural work of the show was this effort to uncouple portrayals of African Americans from their prior connections with poverty and popular youth culture. In this way, the series was able to achieve a comparatively dignified depiction of African Americans, shorn of conventional reliance on black stereotypes, inner-city settings, and youth culture. Moreover, as Gray points out, as a result of the use of African American high culture, it was impossible to treat the characters' race as "an object of derision and fascination" (81). Much like their African American counterparts, nonwhite viewers abroad appreciated and enjoyed the fact that the show portrayed nonwhites with dignity rather than derision.

Despite the show's break with conventional popular images of African Americans, it nevertheless retained a good deal of physical humor, which has been prevalent in African American culture since the days of slavery (Watkins, 1994; White and White, 1998). For instance, in one episode, all of the family members perform a lip-synch pantomime of Ray Charles and the Raylettes' "Night Time Is the Right Time," to the delight of the Huxtable grandparents. Much of the humor derives from Bill Cosby's exaggerated facial expressions and reaction shots. In international markets *The Cosby Show*'s physical forms of comedy may have retained their humor because they were not based in verbal expressions, which often lose their subtlety and effect in translation.

Finally, *The Cosby Show* tried to include something for every viewer in order to gather the entire family in front of the set at a time when cable channels were focused on fragmenting the family into demographic niches. Episodes frequently featured multiple storylines that highlighted family life, the romance between Cliff and Clair, the travails of teenage life with Denise and later Theo and Vanessa, and childhood with Rudy and later Olivia. Thus, viewers from a wide range of circumstances could find characters and story-lines that intersected with their own lives and interests. This diversity of character portrayals extended beyond the borders of the United States as well, as we frequently witnessed international characters and plots. Theo's math teacher Mrs. Westlake, for instance, was Portuguese. In the final episode we discovered that Denise has moved to Singapore. As John Downing (1988) has written, these "aspects of international culture are part of the Huxtables' taken-for-granted world" (62). As such, we might expect the show to appeal more to international viewers than a series focused solely on a single slice of American life.

Black viewers from around the world responded well to the show's unique depiction of black dignity, as expressed in the show's humor and the trope of African American high culture. Consider these comments from black viewers around the world:

I like this show because it depicts black people in a positive way. I think [Cosby] is good. It's good to see that black people can be professionals.
—United States (Jhally and Lewis, 1992, 121)

Black people in this show are not isolated, no fun is made of Blackness, and the characters are shown leading wholesome normal lives.
—Barbados (Payne, 1994, 235)

The show makes me proud of being Black.
—South Africa (Fuller, 1992, 111)

Obviously, in order to feel the racial pride that these viewers expressed, they needed to share a belief that blacks had been historically ridiculed in white popular culture and that *The Cosby Show* was breaking with those traditions. In fact, these comments offer a good reminder that the international circulation of culture has been happening for centuries and is not a new feature of the electronic media age. Furthermore, the ridicule of blacks—and nonwhites in general—has been a part of that trade since the sixteenth century (Nederveen Pieterse, 1992). Apparently, this fact did not escape the attention of black fans of *The Cosby Show* around the world. As we shall see in the final chapters of this book, current African American television flows exhibit a high degree of ridicule and satire as well, though the politics of those forms of satire are more ambivalent than earlier forms.

Black viewers also derived solace from the show's depiction of well-to-do African Americans. A black South African viewer, for instance, explained,

> *The Cosby Show* . . . is saying, "Come on you White guys [in South Africa], the Blacks are not so bad as you make them out to be. Look at us, we are having a good life and normal problems here in America. Give those guys down there a chance. Let's change for the better and live together, not apart." (Fuller, 1992, 114)

For this viewer, the show imagined a world free of racial violence, economic hardship, and political disenfranchisement. As Downing (1988) has noted regarding domestic viewership, the setting of the show "is not simply a matter of blanking out the ugly realities of continuing oppression, but also offers some sense of resolution to the grinding realities of racial tension and mistrust in the United States" (70). It would seem the show offered similar solace to black viewers abroad.

Perhaps more surprisingly, other nonwhite viewers also expressed feelings of pride and hope watching *The Cosby Show*. Some Lebanese viewers thought that the Huxtables "came across as successful and smart, without having sold out to white culture." Another Lebanese viewer commented that "American blacks are a little like us. They have big families" (Raschka, 1988). Obviously the first statement demonstrates that these viewers considered the maintenance of one's cultural identity a respectable goal, and the dignified portrayals of black high culture in the series signaled for them the family's refusal to "sell out." Furthermore, we see again the show's ability to create an idyllic world for these viewers, where cultural integrity and material plenty can go hand in hand. This representation is starkly different from the integrated situation comedies of the early 1980s, which we explored in the previous chapter, which minimized or erased racialized cultural integrity. In fact, this comment reflects the recognition among Lebanese fans that material success for nonwhites worldwide was a dangerous proposition that had the potential to destroy local cultures. Certainly we see evidence in both comments that the presence of African American actors and the ways blackness was linked with high culture and material success played an important role in these viewers' enjoyment of the show.

For some white viewers abroad, the race of the characters was also a part of *The Cosby Show*'s appeal. A Swedish journalist wrote, "the fact that [the Huxtables] are Black also plays into [her enjoyment of the show]. They are so much more attractive than White people" (Fuller, 1992, 107). While this comment is complimentary, it also reflects hundreds of years of libidinal preoccupation with black culture among whites. Black culture has long aroused fear and rebuke in white society, at the same time that whites have been intrigued by the perceived energy, sexuality, and naturalness of black culture.

Most writers agree that this perception of black culture has more to do with what is repressed in white culture than what is actually present in black culture, and the fascination typically works to exacerbate differences and stereotype blacks as primitive (Lott, 1993; Nederveen Pieterse, 1992).

In a similar vein, a white South African viewer commented, "You'd be surprised what [Cosby] has meant to the Afrikaner. The Afrikaner doesn't mix with Black men. The television brings the Black man's quality right into his living room" (Mufson, 1986). Again, while this viewer commented positively about blacks, he still demonstrated a desire to experience black "difference" vicariously in the form of a nonthreatening sitcom. At least for some white viewers, the fact that *The Cosby Show* featured black actors was integral to their enjoyment of the show because it gave them a glimpse into the lifestyle of a group that has historically been defined as fundamentally different from them.

Not all viewers abroad considered race an important feature of *The Cosby Show*. For example, two very different reactions illustrate that, for some, the national origins of the show trumped the show's racial content. First, a pro-apartheid viewer in South Africa claimed,

> The greatest divide between Black and White in this country is not the color of one's skin but the First- and Third-World values and attitudes displayed by the different race groups. . . . Therefore, we do not see *The Cosby Show* as being about Black people, but we see it as a very entertaining sitcom displaying beliefs and values we can associate with. (Fuller, 1992, 14)

For this viewer *The Cosby Show* was primarily a Western show that extolled American values, and the race of the characters was of lesser importance. Likewise, several Bahamian viewers disliked the show because of its Americanness. "The North American influence coming from the show I believe to be detrimental on the whole," said one viewer. "Especially the norms of the children's behavior and their fashions I believe have a negative effect on [Bahamian] youth" (Payne, 1994, 243). Each of these comments is perhaps somewhat surprising and becomes comprehensible only when we realize that the show was simultaneously black and American. Consequently, the potential cultural connections and disconnections between viewers and the show were multiple and complexly interwoven.

As the foregoing overview of international audience responses to *The Cosby Show* demonstrates, foreign viewers found a variety of pleasures in the series. The upper-middle-class domestic setting offered admirable values for some and idyllic goals for others, while emptying the series of controversial and parochial political issues. This setting also provided the series with a transnational cosmopolitanism that international viewers could identify with. The dignified portrayals of blackness, especially the series' allusions to African American high culture and the absence of traditional stereotypes, appealed to nonwhite viewers worldwide, who share a history of stereotyping and ridicule at the hands of white Europeans. At the same time, some white viewers around the world found the portrayal of a slice of black life different enough to be titillating, yet similar enough to be comforting.

Perhaps the most masterful thing about the series was its ability to please so many viewers in such different ways, without alienating others. Of course, not every viewer enjoyed the series, but even the comments from those who disliked it are useful in helping us understand what kinds of messages international viewers saw in the show. While we have no way to determine how widespread any of these attitudes were at the time of the series' international broadcasts, or whether other kinds of responses were more common, the similarities of some of these responses from different parts of the world is striking. To what degree, then, did international television executives recognize these dimensions of the show's popularity abroad, and how did the show's performance influence industry lore regarding the sitcom in general and African American sitcoms in particular?

Program Merchants, *The Cosby Show*, and Universal Family Themes

By 1996 Jim McNamara at MCA (Music Corporation of America) estimated that the major Hollywood studios found international buyers for about 70 percent of their sitcoms, up from only 5 percent in the early 1980s. McNamara wasn't alone in his assessment. Lisa Gregorian, former vice president of marketing and research for Warner Brothers International Television, commented, "I think, in general, comedies have a much more significant place on the international (broadcaster's) schedules than they once did ten years ago" (Huff, 1996). Tony Lynn, a former executive vice president of international television at MGM/UA, also agreed that "American comedies [became] accepted in international broadcast during the eighties" (Mahler, 1990).

The primary change in industry lore that *The Cosby Show* helped usher in was a belief that family-based sitcoms could be successful internationally. While other series, including *Full House* (1987–1995), *Fresh Prince of Bel-Air* (1990–1996), *Family Matters* (1989–1998), and *The Golden Girls* (1985–1992), also contributed to the rethinking of the genre, *The Cosby Show* was the earliest and most successful example of the trend (Curtis, 1997; Huff, 1996; Spring, 1998; Tobin, 1990).

Virtually every European and American television merchant seems to agree that *The Cosby Show*'s "universal" family themes allowed the show to overcome cultural barriers of nation, race, and language. Consider, for instance, these strikingly similar explanations for the success of the series from executives from around the world:

> The Cosby Show was a universal hit. It was conveying universal values of family and generosity. One might think that this guy was typically American, but he was not thought of as such around the world.
> —Arthur Dela, former chair of Paris-based Arathos, owner
> of satellite systems in Eastern and Central Europe (Mahler,
> 1990)

> The Cosby Show . . . is such a universal experience of a man trying to raise children. . . . These are like universal issues of family.
> —Vice president of international television at a major
> Hollywood distributor (interview with the author, 1999)

> [The] Cosby [Show] is universal. . . . It's not just purely a black comedy with black actors. It's a comedy that reaches out to all cultures and generations because the problems they face are general problems that everyone faces every single day.
> —Jeff Ford, controller of acquisitions at U.K. Channel 5
> (interview with the author, 1999)

> [The] Cosby [Show] . . . is universal, I mean, it has nothing to do with America. Things that happen in every household, it happens in Cosby as well.
> —Frank Mulder, director of program acquisitions and sales,
> NOS (Dutch Public Broadcasting) (interview with the
> author, 1999)

While these comments may be accurate, international audience research is underdeveloped in many territories, and even the most advanced ratings data do not tell us why viewers watch a particular series, but only that they watch. Furthermore, as we saw above, the investigations that have been conducted into why viewers around the world enjoyed the show almost uniformly identified racial and national identities as important.

One striking element of executives' comments about *The Cosby Show* is how similar they are to many white American viewers' observations that the Huxtable family didn't come across as black (Jhally and Lewis, 1992, 36–48). Two factors explain these observations: first, as discussed here, the show did not depict African American culture in the same way as its predecessors, but through allusions to African American high culture. Consequently, the typical association between blackness and poverty was severed, and program executives, much like middle-class white viewers, interpreted the lack of the latter as the absence of the former. Second, because the show extolled strong middle-class values in an upper-middle-class setting, many middle-class white viewers and television executives could easily identify, demonstrating again the degree to which such executives function as an interpretive community. For example, several executives referred to the show as either "white" or "not black":

> The black sitcoms we've been involved in have been the Cosbys. And that's not a black sitcom.
> —Herb Lazarus, president, Carsey-Werner International
> (interview with the author, 1999)

> The reason [for the success of] shows like . . . *Cosby* . . . is the fact that a lot of them are very white.
> —Director of international research at a major Hollywood
> distributor (interview with the author, 1999)

> The black sitcom works best if it's, let's say, as white as possible, which is surely the case with *The Cosby Show*.
> —European television buyer (interview with the author, 1999)

By calling the series "white," these executives deny the presence and importance of African American elements in the show, at the same time that they implicitly suggest that truly "black" shows lack the appropriate focus on family themes and settings that sitcoms need in order to succeed in international trade. Perhaps most importantly, this category of familial experience is implicitly associated with being white.

The logic whereby industry executives erased the racially specific dimensions of *The Cosby Show* and its worldwide appeal helped smooth the export of white American sitcoms. First, program merchants misinterpreted the show's depiction of an upper-middle-class African American lifestyle as a depiction of white American norms. Second, because most African American series that followed in the wake of *The Cosby Show* targeted teenagers and young adults, few of them were considered appropriate for international markets. By contrast, the international syndication revenues of white American sitcoms, which continued predominantly to address middle-class family settings and issues, benefited from *The Cosby Show's* international popularity and the industry lore about universal family themes that developed to explain its success.

Why did television professionals discount race when discussing the reasons behind the series' global success? While this is a complex question, the political economy of the television industries in the 1980s, which itself arose from centuries of Western capitalist expansion and exploitation (Miller et al., 2005), provides at least part of the answer. At the time, the two main industry organizations for American television and film exports—the Motion Picture Export Association and the American Film Marketing Association—reported that more than 60 percent of international TV sales revenues came from European sales. Also among the "elite eight" nations that accounted for nearly three-quarters of U.S. audiovisual exports were the predominantly white nations of Canada and Australia.

A second, related reason that television professionals ignored the importance of blackness in their interpretations of *The Cosby Show's* success had to do with the fact that they imagined the global viewer as white and middle-class. Consequently, it is not surprising that these executives would revert to a fairly conventional understanding of the appeal of culture beyond its nation of origin, the concept of universal values. Roland Barthes (1972) has suggested that this concept papers over the real, fundamental differences that historical injustices and exploitation have wrought among human societies:

> Any classic humanism postulates that in scratching the history of men a little, the relativity of their institutions or the superficial diversity of their skins . . . one very quickly reaches the solid rock of a universal human nature. Progressive humanism, on the contrary, must always remember to reverse the terms of this very old imposture, constantly to scour nature . . . and at last to establish Nature itself as historical. (100)

Undoubtedly the idea that "family values" are "the same everywhere" stems from the kind of classical humanist assumptions that Barthes writes about. In addition, the process of universalizing human experience is one of the founding discursive operations of whiteness. As Fiske (1996) explains, "whiteness contains a limited but varied set of normalizing positions from which that which is nonwhite can be made into the abnormal; by such means, whiteness constitutes itself as a universal set of norms by which to make sense of the world" (42). The industry lore about the universal themes that inhere in globally popular television programs, then, is not merely a passive observation; it is, rather, a discourse rooted in and perpetuating the history of white Western domination of the rest of the world's cultures. Of course, in the case of the industry lore surrounding *The Cosby Show*, this power was not deployed primarily for political purposes, but because the ability to universalize white worldviews served the institutional needs of American distributors and European commercial and public service broadcasters. Consequently, a consistent use of *The Cosby Show* developed in the most lucrative international markets and shaped wider industry lore about sitcoms in a way that led to increased budgets for U.S. family sitcoms, which were predominantly white.

The Cosby Show's Continuing Influence in Global Television

The Cosby Show helped establish the belief among international television executives that some American sitcoms focused on middle-class family issues can overcome worldwide cultural differences and become successful. Even more impressive is the fact that the show seemed to accomplish this feat without a great deal of promotion on the part of its distributor, Viacom, which instead considered the series' international sales prospects to be marginal due to prevalent attitudes at the time about sitcoms. Published audience comments suggest that, much as in the domestic market, *The Cosby Show*'s abilities to bring together different segments of the audience by refusing to alienate anyone were central to its appeal abroad. This capacity allowed the show to draw viewers from various national, racial, religious, and economic backgrounds as few television shows ever had.

What truly made *The Cosby Show* a global hit, however, was the combination of its capacity to speak to a broad cross section of viewers worldwide and its ability to serve the economic needs of quickly internationalizing domestic and foreign television industries during the 1980s and 1990s. The rapid expansion of channels and buyers around the world created a sudden spike in demand for programming from the global markets, which American distributors were well poised to capitalize on. Professional events, international trade journals, and executive training courses all provided new opportunities for programmers and distributors from around the world to come together and evolve similar kinds of programming solutions to similar kinds of problems. For instance, *The Cosby Show* was the solution to drawing in good-sized, general family audiences on a budget. Moreover, since many of the upstart channels were commercial ventures, they conceptualized their domestic audiences along demographic lines standardized by the global advertising industry, leading programmers everywhere to think about the similarities and differences between domestic viewing groups in similar ways. In contrast to the programming of integrated American situation comedies in South Africa earlier in the decade, where Bop-TV's articulation of disaffected white and black viewing segments drew from local political and cultural developments, most programmers of *The Cosby Show* abroad worked from a conceptualization of their audience that came from the advertising industry.

Not only was *The Cosby Show* key in revising prevailing attitudes toward the sitcom genre among international television professionals at a time when sitcoms were becoming more numerous in the domestic market, it also gave rise to the now common practice of figuring international sales revenues into domestic production budgets for sitcoms from the outset. Today television executives must consider a sitcom's international sales potential before they are willing to sink a great deal of money into a project.

Although *The Cosby Show* revolutionized the financing and thinking of international television distribution, more profound insights about the global circulation of television programming went unnoticed by executives, specifically the fact that the national and racial origins of the characters were central to international viewers' enjoyment of the series. According to one veteran international distributor at a Hollywood studio, nearly ten years after *The Cosby Show*'s worldwide success, "I think there is a general sense [in the industry] that if [a show] is too tied to the African American experience, then it won't work internationally" (interview with the author, 1999).

African American sitcoms after *The Cosby Show* often targeted cross-racial teenage and young adult audiences, typically by tapping into their shared interests in rap music and African American pop stars. Sitcoms such as *Living Single* (1993–1998), starring Queen Latifah, *The Sinbad Show* (1993–1994) and *Martin* (1992–1997), featuring African American comedians, *Moesha*, starring the pop star Brandy, and *The Fresh Prince of Bel-Air*, starring the crossover rap star Will Smith, may have shared some of the trappings of middle-class domestic sitcoms, but they were primarily seen as niche programs with little or no appeal abroad. However, much like *Roots* and *The Cosby Show*, some of these programs would also become international hits despite conventional industry wisdom to the contrary. In contrast to these earlier phenomena, however, the textual potentialities and institutional labors of this newer batch of sitcoms made it more difficult for industry insiders to ignore the importance of African American culture in explaining their international appeal.

4

The Fresh Prince of Bel-Air, Channel Fragmentation, and the
Recognition of Difference

While white American situation comedies came to dominate the U.S. prime-time landscape in the 1990s, African American series, especially situation comedies, tended to feature youth themes addressing multiracial audience segments. This trend followed the growing popularity of rap music and hip-hop culture among teenage and young adult fans of all races. The appeal of rap music quickly reached beyond the boundaries of the United States, becoming a popular form and political force in places as diverse as South Korea, China, Brazil, Nigeria, and Italy. Likewise, youth-oriented situation comedies developed worldwide followings in the 1990s as well. Unlike their predecessors in international television trade, however, these youth series engendered an industry lore among U.S. and European executives that, for the first time, viewed African American themes as an advantage in international program trade, rather than a hindrance.

The industry lore that arose from the international popularity of youth series continued to restrict African Americans to comedic roles on television and to largely safe and inoffensive themes, where the tools of resistance were employed not against the white power structure, but against parental control. Still, these programs imagined a world in which mastery of the codes of African American youth culture and the underclass, rather than the codes of whiteness, adulthood, and middle-class culture, provided personal fulfillment and success in life. Although the popularity of rap music, as well as the discovery of ethnicity as a marketing tool among advertisers at the time, paved the way for African American youth series, significant changes in television delivery technologies and the institutional labors of the series among well-heeled buyers were necessary for these program flows to develop and to register in the dominant industry lore.

While industry insiders recognized the importance of African American themes in the worldwide appeal of these programs, that recognition was by no means universal. Even among executives within the same organization, disagreements existed about why these series were popular and whether their popularity signaled a shift in the fortunes of African

American programs among European audiences and buyers. Indeed, this era represents the beginning of the end of a coherent industry lore among U.S. and European executives about many things, including African American programs. While some industry insiders continue to assert that African American programs have trouble abroad, others insist that consistent rules no longer hold true.

Domesticating Youth Resistance in *The Fresh Prince of Bel-Air*

The Fresh Prince of Bel-Air (1990–1996) was the progenitor of the African American youth sitcom. Starring the aspiring rap artist and actor Will Smith and set in a palatial mansion in the exclusive Los Angeles suburb of Bel-Air, *Fresh Prince* told the story of a teenage African American boy from the inner city of Philadelphia whose mother sends him to live with his rich cousins in California, the Banks family. Although the Banks also have two daughters as well as a mother, the majority of the stories revolved around Will, his cousin Carlton, and his Uncle Phil.

Superficially, *Fresh Prince* appeared to address themes and concerns similar to those of *The Cosby Show*. Both were set in intact and exceptionally well-off nuclear families. Both featured strong father figures who emphasized in their personal history and their interactions the importance of education for young African American men to succeed. However, while *The Cosby Show* consistently included storylines that addressed every member of the family with themes of personal growth, responsibility, and togetherness, *Fresh Prince* centered on male relationships, particularly teenage rivalry and father-son (or uncle-nephew) conflicts. While street life and black youth culture, particularly as figured through rap music, was the persistent if unnamed other that threatened to lure Theo Huxtable away from his studies and material success in *The Cosby Show*, *Fresh Prince* celebrated the hairstyles, clothing, speech, movement, and, above all, the music of black youth culture, which had become a global phenomenon by the mid-1990s.

When the series debuted in the fall of 1990, Will Smith (a.k.a. the Fresh Prince) had already established a reputation as a rapper with comparatively tame and clean lyrics at a time when rap music was under the microscope of parents' groups and Congress for its supposedly corrupting influence on children, particularly white suburban teens. Smith's Grammy Award–winning single "Parents Just Don't Understand," released in 1988, had become indicative of his inoffensive—some would say opportunistic—persona and music. The lyrics tell of the universal difficulties of teenage life. As Will explains it,

"You know parents are the same no matter time nor place. They don't under-stand that us kids are going to make some mistakes." Musically, the backbeat and spoken lyrics reference rap music, but without the themes of inner-city life and radical politics that had come to define the center of that genre in the 1980s. Visually, the video for the song alludes to the clothing styles, hair-styles, and graffiti of hip-hop culture, but not the inner-city surroundings common in most rap music videos of the time. In this way, the visuals con-tinue the universalizing rhetoric of the lyrics, attempting to create a classless and raceless teenage landscape.

The Fresh Prince of Bel-Air picked up on the themes of universal teenage experience in order to draw in youthful and young adult audiences at a time when many U.S. households had become multichannel, multiset homes. In the period between the premiere of *The Cosby Show* and the series finale of *Fresh Prince*, the percentage of homes with multiple TV sets increased 15 per-cent to more than 71 percent of U.S. households, while 75 percent of multi-channel homes could receive at least fifty-four channels by the mid-nineties (NCTA, 2011; TVB, 2010). As households added these television services, family viewing became less and less common, and more and more family members began watching individually.

Fresh Prince was not aimed exclusively at a teen audience; it sought, in fact, to include a good amount of thematic and narrative material that appealed to parents and adults as well. Although it was the top-rated television comedy among teenagers in 1992, it was also top twenty in overall audience ratings. One contemporary critic wrote that, despite the heavy presence of youth cul-ture allusions, storylines, and characters, *Fresh Prince* was "one of the few on TV that consistently acknowledge[d] a full range of African-American lives" (Tucker, 1992). However, *Fresh Prince* needed to spotlight youth culture much more directly than *The Cosby Show*, given the changed television land-scape in the home and the ability of many teenagers to abandon the set in the living room in favor of more niche-oriented programming on MTV, BET, and elsewhere in their bedrooms.

Fresh Prince is essentially a fish-out-of-water story: inner-city Will comes to live with his rich aunt, uncle, and cousins, who live in the predominantly white suburbs. The specific theme that the series stages is class conflict, which is coded in both gendered and racialized ways (Zook, 1999). In addition, the series staged a conflict between the hip-hop generation and the older civil rights generation in the person of Uncle Phil, which Todd Boyd (2001) iden-tifies as the central division in African American popular representations of African American masculinity of the 1990s.

The series, then, drew on conflicting discourses about black masculin-ity at the time, specifically clashes among African Americans over class and racial authenticity, homosexuality, and generational differences. These central conflicts manifested as a clash between African American youth culture and assimilationist or white adult culture. In a related manner, the displacement of racial inauthenticity onto excessively rich characters worked to paper over anxieties at the time about the appropriation of hip-hop cul-ture among middle-class suburbanites, especially whites, and the role that Will Smith and the series in general might have been playing in that process (Zook, 1999). In this regard, the series took the styles, discourses, and ener-gies of the hip-hop movement and channeled them into the spaces and con-cerns of a largely deracinated suburban domestic setting.

Will and his cousin Carlton embody the clash between black youth cul-tures and white adult cultures most clearly. While Will wears bright colors, oversized clothes, and baseball caps, all commonly associated with hip-hop culture, Carlton wears prep-school styles: sweaters, dress shirts, khaki pants, and loafers. While Will speaks in street slang, Carlton uses grammati-cally proper diction and precise pronunciation. While Will's style of walk-ing, moving his head, and hand gestures allude to African American street culture, Carlton's stuffiness extends even to his bodily movements, which are reserved and uptight. The stylistic differences between these two char-acters are figured not only through class difference, but through racial dif-ferences as well, with Will alluding to black popular culture and Carlton alluding to white adult culture. This difference comes across most readily in the soundtrack. Will frequently raps in his everyday conversation and even performs rap numbers. Carlton, meanwhile, adores the white lounge singer Tom Jones and occasionally lip-synchs his songs. Through the character of Carlton, then, white adult culture gets ridiculed as misguided and boring.

In a similar vein, adult African American culture gets dismissed as overly assimilationist through the character of Uncle Phil. Philip Banks is a judge with exceptional wealth who lives in a mansion in Bel-Air, California. A for-mer civil rights activist, Banks now puts his reformist energies into raising his children well. Ultimately, though, the character represents capitulation to conventional social norms and goals of acquisitiveness. Uncle Phil shows little regard for his manservant, Geoffrey, the only recurring working-class character in the series. Furthermore, he has managed to raise two children who are utterly unaware of their own privilege, much less the history of their father's struggle. While Uncle Phil insists on the importance of education, tradition, and respect for authority, rarely does the narrative privilege these ideals. More typically, they are gently mocked, much the same way that Will repeatedly makes fun of his uncle's weight. In fact, Philip Banks's fatness serves as a metonym for the political lethargy of affluent members of the civil rights generation.

Fresh Prince participated in debates at the time about whether gayness and class differences posed threats to conventional definitions of black masculinity, and the degree to which coherent definitions of black masculinity could withstand different claimant groups. However, the series tended to privilege Will's performance as the only legitimate one, endorsing the articulation of black masculinity as youthful, working-class (or, at minimum, not upper-class), straight, playful, focused on pleasure and enjoyment, and steeped in hip-hop culture. Carlton's and Uncle Phil's performances of black masculinity are sometimes treated with sympathy and dignity, but the ridicule they endure from Will and his friends prevents them from being characters whom viewers are likely to admire.

Importantly, tensions about the racial legitimacy of upper-class African Americans are limited to male characters in *Fresh Prince*. Though the series does raise concerns about the impact of upper-class life on African American women and girls, those concerns are not *racially* coded. Instead, these concerns surface most frequently as fears about spoiling young women. Will's cousin Hillary, a self-obsessed shopaholic, is the epitome of such concerns. His younger cousin, Ashley, is more conflicted, and it is the tension between becoming spoiled and remaining true to herself that animates her character development throughout the series. Finally, his aunt Vivian is rarely a significant narrative presence. Thus, while upper-class living may present pitfalls for African American women, loss of one's racial identity is not one of them.

Of course, many of the themes and debates that *Fresh Prince* engaged would have been unfamiliar to foreign viewers. Instead, European broadcasters emphasized the conflict between youth and adulthood in their scheduling of the series, even as they recognized the importance of hip-hop culture in representing that conflict. What a series like *Fresh Prince* does is take the resistance and rebelliousness of rap music, place it in conflict with white adult culture, and privilege the former. In other words, while rap music provided a lingua franca for youthful rebellion in many places in the 1990s, African American youth television provided a vehicle for channeling that resistance into one's personal life, as well as a utopian vision of a world where mastery of the codes of youth culture, rather than adult culture, could lead to personal success and a more playful, less success-oriented world. These two themes—the importance of youthful rebelliousness and the popularity of rap music—were the primary elements of the program that found their way back into dominant industry lore at the time.

The Prince of a Place Called Bel-Air. And Spain. And Brazil. And Lebanon. And Kenya . . .

Just how successful was *Fresh Prince* in international markets? According to Warner Brothers, by 1997 the series had sold in more than seventy territories, rivaling sales of *The Cosby Show* at a time when American series faced significantly more competition in international markets. *Fresh Prince* often topped the ratings charts in importing markets. In Spain, where the series enjoyed perhaps its greatest popularity, it was the top-rated import in 1996, attracting nearly four million viewers weekly (Huff, 1996). It was still the top-ranked import in 1999, with an average 8.2 rating per episode in the first quarter, or more than one million viewers ("Top Series by Country," 1999). The upstart U.K. channel Trouble TV, a small cable channel targeting ten- to eighteen-year-olds, initially built its afternoon schedule—the channel's highest-rated time of day—around *Fresh Prince*, which aired at 4 P.M. and in 1998 attracted 160,000 viewers per episode, making it the channel's highest-rated program ("Top Import Moves Mover," 1998). In markets as far afield as Kenya, Hong Kong, and Lebanon, the series was one of the top imported television series.

While NBC's scheduling of *Fresh Prince* emphasized its familial and parental themes because of its prime-time placement, European broadcasters tended to use the series specifically to attract the youth audience, a scheduling innovation that only later appeared at U.S. syndicators, such as TeenNick, ABC Family, and Disney XD in the early twenty-first century. The United Kingdom's Trouble TV was, in many ways, the quintessential European *Fresh Prince* buyer, and the technological developments, industrial organization, and scheduling practices that led to Trouble's success with *Fresh Prince* are indicative of the series' institutional labors at channels across Europe. Trouble began broadcasting in 1998, sharing a channel with the U.K. version of Bravo, which programmed the evening time slots. Trouble identified an underserved niche of teens and tweens, an example of how the presence of global advertising helped create globally standardized conceptualizations of viewers everywhere. By the time Trouble came on air in 1998, other channels had already captured many of the more lucrative niches. In fact, Trouble's immediate predecessor, the Children's Channel, had failed to carve out a niche for young children in an overcrowded market. As the Children's Channel's fate demonstrates, launching new television channels was a risky proposition at the time, and Trouble relied almost exclusively on cheap imports to help defray programming costs. Trouble avoided placing its most expensive programs in the highly competitive prime-time hours, constructing instead a schedule focused on after-school hours, when their target audience controlled the remote.

Trouble TV's replacement of *Fresh Prince* with a self-produced magazine series only months after launching also demonstrates the precariousness of a series like *Fresh Prince* on foreign broadcasters' schedules. Working with the adage that locally produced programs outperform imported series, Trouble developed a daily series focused on "celebrity interviews, teenage talent spots, music and competitions." The executive producer for the channel, Emilia Jonson, explained that Trouble had made the scheduling change "because this is produced in-house [and therefore] you get to reflect what's going on for teenagers in this country much more than if you buy up American shows" ("Top Import Moves Mover," 1998).

Fresh Prince, then, was appealing to European buyers from small channels targeting teenagers, but was quickly replaced with cheap local programs as soon as a channel could afford it. Similarly, among larger broadcasters, *Fresh Prince* served first and foremost as an inexpensive way to bring in a consistent, if not especially lucrative, audience demographic. BBC2, which began airing *Fresh Prince* in 1991, scheduled it at 18:25, prior to its prime-time lineup. In these instances, the series was likely to stay on the air for a significant amount of time only under two conditions: first, that it perform exceptionally well; second, that the channel's production efforts were focused on other time slots and demographics.

Among international television executives, *Fresh Prince* inaugurated a new global trend that helped create new markets for African American programs. Lisa Gregorian, then vice president of marketing and research for *Fresh Prince*'s distributor, Warner Brothers, told the trade journal *TV World* that "People say Cosby started this [trend], and he undoubtedly had a major role, but *Fresh Prince of Bel-Air* broke the barriers of many territories that previously wouldn't have touched comedy like this" (Curtis, 1997, 36). Of course, Gregorian's observation was biased by the fact that she was selling the series. However, its popularity with buyers and audiences is undeniable, as is the fact that the series helped move other African American youth series and changed the way that sitcoms could be sold abroad (see fig. 4.1).

Bert Cohen, president of Worldvision, which sold the African American youth sitcom *Moesha* abroad, for instance, identified the popularity of *Fresh Prince* as crucial for driving sales of *Moesha*.[1] Similarly, Gary Schnedecker, a former acquisitions executive at Disney Channel España, commented, "I was

Figure 4.1. This advertisement for *Moesha* from Antena 3
demonstrates how the series was marketed as a tie-in with the
pop singer Brandy, rather than a family-oriented series.

working at Disney Channel in Spain. And, in Spain, the [*Fresh*] *Prince of Bel-Air* was working like crazy. That's why at Disney Channel we bought *Moesha*. We bought *Moesha* because we knew that black comedies are [a] great success and so we thought the *Moesha* . . . would work also very well" (1999). This comment shows how competitive programming environments produce national and transnational trends, as programmers constantly scan competitors and the global markets for new developments. In addition, the comment offers a good example of how programming executives work as *interpreters* of tastes, rather than diviners. That is, the recognition that *Fresh Prince* was a hit in his market could have led this programmer to buy pop-star-driven white series, family shows featuring African Americans, or any number of other combinations. The fact that he likened *Fresh Prince* to *Moesha*, which is both more family-oriented and geared toward young women's concerns, exhibits an active attempt to interpret what the appealing features of the former series were and apply them to available programming options.

Despite its eventual successes, however, *Fresh Prince* encountered the same kind of resistance among buyers when it first turned up on the world markets as many other hit African American series. Paloma Garcia-Cuesta (1999), acquisitions director at the Spanish channel Antena 3, which broadcast *Fresh Prince* in Spain, explained, "Apparently, there was no relation between those characters and Spanish people." Similarly, Torsten Dewi (1999), commissioning director of international coproduction at the German broadcaster Prosieben, expected the series to perform poorly because "Blacks are such a minority in Germany." An unnamed buyer even complained to a *New York Times* reporter after seeing *Fresh Prince* for sale at the L.A. Screenings in 1990, "How are we ever going to subtitle rap?" (Huff, 1996).

Buyers obviously thought that the language and culture of hip-hop spotlighted in *Fresh Prince* would be unfamiliar and off-putting for viewers. Nevertheless, several of them wound up with the series. For some, it was a matter of having few other purchase options. As we have seen, many came from small channels or were buying series for cheaper parts of the broadcast schedule. Others were from new, upstart channels trying to build up their audience numbers on the cheap. Both types of buyers sought to take advantage of the fact that buying imported television programming is almost always significantly cheaper than self-producing. While *Fresh Prince* might have been "idiosyncratically American," it was also comparatively cheap. Finally, a number of larger buyers wound up with *Fresh Prince* as a result of package deals, which had become commonplace in the international marketplace by the 1990s, and require buyers who are interested in broadcast rights to blockbuster films to also take a "package" of less appealing programming, including situation comedies. Several of the buyers I interviewed indicated that they had first acquired *Fresh Prince* through such arrangements.

Almost uniformly, buyers expressed surprise at how well *Fresh Prince* performed in their markets. Dewi from Prosieben, for instance, admitted that he "was surprised that [*Fresh Prince*] worked so well, because I thought . . . that it would have been much harder to establish" among German viewers. Executives at the Spanish broadcaster Antena 3 similarly claimed to be surprised by the series' performance, especially with teenage viewers, as did executives at the Mexican broadcaster TV Azteca (Durán, 1999).

Of course, the popularity of *Fresh Prince* among teenagers around the world did not take place in a vacuum, but rather built on particular historical precursors, most specifically the worldwide popularity of rap music among young people and the success of earlier youth-oriented American imports, especially *Saved by the Bell* (1989–1993). In addition, widespread efforts by global advertisers to use ethnic difference, especially blackness, as a trope for modernity and cosmopolitanism likely influenced the popularity of the series as well.

Arising from the South Bronx in the 1970s, rap music was quickly adapted to a wide range of different national contexts, in places as diverse as South Korea, China, Brazil, Nigeria, and Italy. Tony Mitchell (2001) argues that rap music became a vehicle for political agitation, minority ethnic pride, and musical self-expression in foreign lands. "In its recombination into local linguistic, musical, and political contexts around the world, rap music and hip-hop culture have in many cases become a vehicle for various forms of youth protest" (10). Mitchell also demonstrates that a good deal of exchange and collaboration occurred among rap musicians from various nations throughout the late 1990s. Among listeners, meanwhile, American rap music had become popular in the late 1980s and early 1990s. In addition, due to the growth of cable music channels, teenagers in many parts of the world at the time were inundated with the sounds and imagery of African American youth culture. *Fresh Prince* both popularized and capitalized on these broader trends by introducing hip-hop culture to mainstream television genres and audiences. Of course, as discussed above, *Fresh Prince* channeled the rebelliousness of much rap music into domestic settings and interpersonal relationships, but this move by no means precluded viewers from seeking out other, more publicly political forms of rap, whether domestic or foreign.

If the worldwide spread of rap music in the 1980s and 1990s laid the groundwork for the popularity of *Fresh Prince* among audiences, as well as recognition of rap as a global cultural trend among industry insiders, the series' precursor, *Saved by the Bell*, demonstrated the viability of a transnational teenage television audience that would all watch the same programs. *Saved by the Bell*'s success allowed industry insiders to imagine that a television series based on a popular rap artist and targeting teen viewers could potentially be a success.

Saved by the Bell was a network show produced by NBC that initially aired during the Saturday morning children's programming block, which otherwise consisted exclusively of animated programs. Network executives viewed the series as risky because no live-action series had previously performed well in the time slot, but *Saved by the Bell* quickly attracted a devoted following, and is credited with almost single-handedly identifying and capturing the tween audience demographic, or those children who no longer watch cartoons, but also don't flock to adult shows, typically identified as the nine-to-fourteen age group in the United States. Prior to the success of *Saved by the Bell*, this was not a demographic that was recognized by either advertisers or broadcasters. However, the audience fragmentation associated with increased channel capacity at the time made it possible for the demographic to emerge (Sherwood, 1992).

Despite NBC's willingness to take a risk on the series, however, its production costs required creative funding practices, including heavy reliance on international syndication revenues. The series was syndicated in eighty-five countries and reportedly sold for as much as $200,000 per episode in some markets. Foreign broadcasters such as the BBC and the German commercial broadcaster RTL II seem to have followed NBC's approach when scheduling the series, airing it on weekend mornings and during after-school hours. In addition, NBC relied on merchandising revenues to cover a percentage of production costs, though mostly in the domestic market. In these ways, NBC had largely covered its production costs for the series prior to domestic syndication, where it made the majority of its profits (Sherwood 1992; Kover, 1998).

Saved by the Bell focused on the antics of a group of friends at a California high school. Although its producers claimed the series was about the "universal" experiences of school, it addressed decidedly middle-class teenage concerns, especially personal relationships, as opposed to such working-class teen themes as balancing work and school, the impact of financial hardship on teenagers' personal relationships, or the difficulties of dealing with divorce. Despite its popularity both at home and abroad, however, *Saved by the Bell* produced few copycats beyond its own production house. The reasons behind the series' lack of followers are difficult to divine: perhaps the exceedingly low production costs were difficult for other producers to duplicate. Regardless of the reasons, however, the need for youth program imports continued and grew after the series' cancellation, as demonstrated by the inauguration of a Youth Program Screening event immediately before the global sales fair MIPCOM in 1994, which later came to be known as Mipcom, Junior. *Fresh Prince* capitalized on the same tween audience that *Saved by the Bell* had identified, although it developed a different model for attracting viewers and funding production.

Saved by the Bell targeted a tween audience at home and abroad; in contrast, *Fresh Prince* targeted a much wider domestic audience in prime-time and domestic syndication, while at upstart European satellite and cable channels it was used to draw in tweens. Of course, this was an evolving strategy, as opposed to the quite conscious demographic strategy of *Saved by the Bell's* producers. First offered for domestic syndication in 1994, *Fresh Prince* was the top-rated new series along with *The Simpsons*. *Fresh Prince* proved particularly strong among women eighteen to thirty-four and teens, and performed respectably among men eighteen to thirty-four (Tyrer, 1994). In international syndication, meanwhile, European buyers typically deployed *Fresh Prince* to attract teen and tween audiences exclusively.

Increasingly, domestic television networks abandoned the general audience for African American situation comedies in favor of more demographically focused audiences and programs. As Herman Gray (2005) has observed, African American programs have moved to the margins of the television schedule since the mid-1990s, appearing on cable networks or on the upstart broadcast networks WB and UPN. While a few general entertainment series, such as *My Wife and Kids* and *The Hughleys*, which tried to recapture the broader appeal of *The Cosby Show* and *Fresh Prince*, remained on network prime-time schedules, they slowly disappeared. Since the turn of the century, the primary outlets for African American youth series have been children's cable channels such as the Disney Channel and Nickelodeon, where they are used to attract both white and black tweens.

Industry Lore Recognizes African American Elements

Unlike the industry lore that came to surround *Roots* and *The Cosby Show*, the industry lore among European buyers and U.S. distributors about *Fresh Prince* and its descendants occasionally activated African American cultural themes when explaining the series' popularity. Specifically, industry insiders recognized that blackness signaled youthful rebellion, pleasure, and an incipient utopian vision of transnational youth culture and solidarity. Among non-European buyers, however, the industry lore surrounding the popularity of African American youth series in their territories was more continuous with prior perceptions, emphasizing the similarity of these series with prior African American imports and the cultural sensibilities of their viewers. Moreover, we begin to see disagreement in the dominant industry lore about African American programs among European and U.S. industry executives at this time that reflect the rapidly changing industrial and cultural environments of television distributors and networks.

Despite the initial hesitancy of some buyers toward a television series rooted in African American youth culture, several of them began to view such themes as central to their institutional priorities of attracting teen and tween viewers. Because of the groundwork done by rap music and, perhaps, the history of associations between black culture and such notions as pleasure, resistance, and toughness in the West, many European show buyers believed that African American youth series were better at drawing those viewers than their white counterparts. "I think because [black sitcoms] are a little more hip and the culture of music is obviously a very important part of those comedies, and therefore it does touch with the youth far more than . . . white sitcoms," says Jeff Ford, controller of acquisitions for British Channel 5. Paloma Garcia-Cuesta of Spanish Antena 3, Schnedecker of Disney Channel España, and Dewi of German Prosieben expressed similar sentiments in favor of acquiring African American youth series.

What distinguished these series from white series, in addition to the use of established pop stars as central characters, were allusions to hip-hop culture through dress, rap music, graffiti, dance, and language. Among U.S. television executives, such programs came to be called "urban" or "ethnic" television series, and nearly every executive I interviewed chose to define such series based on their use of language, rather than any of the other features just mentioned. An executive at one of the major Hollywood studios who has distributed many ethnic African American sitcoms explained, "most African American sitcoms produced today . . . definitely have a very urban skew to them, meaning there's no Russian word for 'whassup homeboy.' There's no translation for it, and most of our sitcoms really skew toward our urban African American viewers" (personal communication with the author, 1999). Bob Clark (1999), a white American and president of the commercial Russian network Story First Communications, agreed: "A lot of ethnic comedies in America don't travel particularly well to foreign audiences, because there's almost a different language in them." Given the need to translate U.S. programming in most markets, this focus on language, as opposed to other textual features, works to exclude the possibility that television programs that allude to African American youth subcultures are capable of international sales, whereas defining them by reference to other textual features would not be as damning. In the 1990s the perception that sitcoms could not travel well abroad still persisted, specifically because most humor in situation comedies of the day was based in word-play, pun, innuendo, and other linguistic forms. Most industry insiders agree that translating linguistic humor to another language is challenging, and often fails because so much of it is culturally and linguistically specific. Consequently, the suggestion that African American shows are steeped in slang makes them appear doubly difficult to translate successfully.

It is important to recognize that these impressions of the textual features that facilitate or block successful international syndication are not properties of the texts themselves, but are instead produced by television executives. In other words, they could have chosen to focus on textual features of ethnic series that help facilitate international sales when discussing these shows.

Furthermore, we cannot look to successes and failures in international sales to solve the riddle of what kinds of black cultural elements might travel well abroad, because program merchants will tend to interpret successes in a way that is consistent with their perceptions of the markets. Look, for example, at the tortured logic of one Warner Brothers executive, who is convinced that ethnic series don't sell abroad, trying to explain the success of *Fresh Prince*. "[Fresh Prince] does have a lot of vernacular in the way he talks, but not in the way the rest of the family talks," he explains. "The rest of the family talks very white. . . . So with everyone talking normally and him with the occasional whassup, I think it has more of an international appeal."

Of course, the question remains why television executives would work so hard to explain why their programming is unsalable. The answers to this are difficult to fully divine, and probably numerous: they include unexamined assumptions about race that color their perceptions, institutional priorities that favor other genres and discourage much thought about situation comedies, and an active effort to distance their companies from heavy involvement in African American programming, as a hedge against being seen as only a niche-oriented company.

It is significant to note that none of the European buyers I interviewed shared the perception that the heavy use of slang in African American youth series limited the series' potential appeal abroad. In fact, as with most of the other elements of youth culture, they tended to see the language of the program as an advantage. Dewi from Germany's Prosieben, for instance, explained that, when translating African American youth series, "They keep most of the terms like 'homeboy' and 'yo' and 'whassup' and they just translate the rest . . . —the stuff that kids also know from rap records. They listen to rap records, they know some of the stuff rappers are saying, so you can basically keep that." Garcia-Cuesta from Spanish Antena 3 sounded a similar note when asked whether the language of *Fresh Prince* and other African American youth sitcoms was difficult for viewers or translators, saying, "the black people [are] related to the teenage and American culture that they know through the cinema, music, etc." In fact, another executive for Warner Brothers, a European primarily familiar with European markets and buyers, insisted that she had "never heard" that the use of slang in *Fresh Prince* and other African American programs posed difficulties for buyers. The disagreement within Warner Brothers about the transferability of African American slang demonstrates the beginning of the dissolution of a coherent dominant industry lore regarding African American youth programs.

Despite negative perceptions of African American programs that utilize a substantial amount of nonstandard English, the tendency of such series to liberally employ visual comedy helps offset their linguistic limitations in the eyes of some television executives. Trade journal articles generally report agreement among industry insiders about the transferability of visual comedy, or slapstick, because such comedy does not require the kinds of cultural knowledge that linguistic humor does. According to a 1996 *Television Business International* article on the improved fortunes of American situation comedies on world markets in the 1990s, "what does work, say executives, are those shows with strong visual comedy or those with a strong family theme such as *Family Matters* or *The Fresh Prince of Bel-Air*" (Huff, 1996). One executive I interviewed, a president of international television at one of the Hollywood studios, concurred: "If there's physical humor or slapstick, that would translate a little better than if it's in-the-hood type vernacular." Dewi from the German station Prosieben agreed as well. "The first season of *Family Matters* did not work well for us," he explained, "but [in] the second season, when [Steve] Urkel showed up, which is a very broad, slapstick character, the show really took off."

Of course, black slapstick is controversial due to the long history in the West of stereotyping blacks through such comedy to achieve racist political ends. Since their inception in nineteenth-century minstrel shows, mainstream depictions of African Americans in white popular culture have exhibited "an overriding investment in the [black] body" (Lott, 1993, 10). While minstrelsy cannibalized and mocked slave culture with specific political consequences, the stereotypes formulated during the era of minstrelsy continue to inform representations of African American characters in popular culture, especially in comedy genres like the black sitcom. Much of the humor in these shows comes from visual comedy, such as Steve Urkel's high-water jeans, suspenders, and nerd-like gait in *Family Matters* or Will Smith's overly broad parodies of male sexuality in *Fresh Prince*, which retains its comic integrity across cultures and takes less time, and hence less money, to translate. As U.S. television programs face more and better-polished competition in the world market, especially in Europe, the practice of hiring local writers and comedians to translate sitcoms is becoming more and more common, a process that is estimated to increase the costs of translation by as much as 50 percent (Huff, 1996).

While slapstick travels well, then, it is also potentially offensive to one of the main target audiences in the domestic markets, African Americans. In fact, it would be possible to write the history of African American television comedy as a persistent effort to find ways to include slapstick without risking offense. As we will see in the next chapter, contemporary television comedies try to resolve this dilemma by ridiculing both black and nonblack cultures and by channeling criticism at media portrayals of African Americans, rather than particular communities of African Americans.

Both *Fresh Prince* and *Family Matters* solved the riddle of how to retain slapstick comedy while trying not to alienate crucial African American viewers by endowing their primary satirical characters with white cultural allusions. Both Carlton in *Fresh Prince* and Steve Urkel in *Family Matters* are made ridiculous through their association with white culture. In the case of Carlton, as we have already seen, his uptight physical movements, his frenetic dance style, his diction, and his dreams are all coded as white. Steve Urkel is made ridiculous by his love of polka music, perhaps the whitest music in America. This inclusion of African American characters endowed with white cultural values, often paired with other characters steeped in African American youth culture, became one of the primary representational strategies of African American youth series during this time. These portrayals appealed to many youthful white viewers as well, for whom white adult culture signaled stagnation, boredom, and cultural vacuousness (hooks, 1992). While European youth might not have been the primary audience, the perception that they responded to the celebration of African American youth culture and satire of white adult culture in similar ways certainly helped fuel this particular representational strategy.

A variety of industrial practices, economic demands, industry discourses, and representational strategies led to the impression among some European and U.S. distributors that situation comedies featuring young people, especially established pop stars, with allusions to African American youth culture in characters' clothing and speech, as well as through setting, music, comedy, and dance, could travel well internationally. As we have seen, this emerging industry lore was unique in its recognition of the potential transnational appeal of African American televisual portrayals. Outside the West, however, industry executives tended to understand the popularity of *Fresh Prince* and other youth sitcoms in a way that was more continuous with their perceptions of prior series, rather than as a significant break.

Buyers in Mexico, the Middle East, and South Africa who target family audiences that are less affluent than Europeans identified a connection between blackness and economic struggle that their audiences prefer, and which they identify with most African American television series. Ignacio Durán, vice president of international affairs at the Mexican broadcaster TV Azteca, claimed that "In Mexico, we don't have any Black population at all, but what we have found is that the racial conflicts have to be translated into class conflicts. . . . Black comedies will do better [than white comedies] in Mexico or in Latin America because the element of the underdog is there . . . and this will probably cause an identification with the audience" (interview with the author, 1999).[2] Perhaps somewhat incongruously, Durán included both *Fresh Prince* and the 1970s series *The Jeffersons*, a spin-off of *All in the Family* featuring a nouveau riche African American family living on the Upper East Side of Manhattan, as examples of class underdogs. The reason, according to Durán, is that both of these series focus on characters who come from poor backgrounds and are struggling to adjust to rich, white American culture.

In a similar vein Bassam Hajjawi (1999), president and CEO of International Distribution Agency, which brokers programming for major U.S. distributors to general entertainment channels throughout the Middle East, explained, "Most of the black situation comedies are about middle-class or lower-middle-class people. For many people in the Middle East, they associate and sympathize with that kind of life . . . and if they see these [white] situation comedies always with the high-brow politicians or the millionaires, they don't sympathize as much." These examples point to a clear understanding on the part of non-Western programmers targeting predominantly nonwhite viewers that important historical, cultural, and economic connections exist among nonwhites around the world.

For Khalid Abdilaziz Al-Mugaiseeb (1998), CEO of Kuwait Television Channel 2, the similarities between African American and Arab cultures also include personal style and gender relations and help target his primary family audiences much better than white sitcoms. "In white comedy," he says, "it's like the aliens talking from another planet. They're talking about rednecks and hot dogs. Black people, they talk about things in the house." In fact, Al-Mugaiseeb notes a good deal of cultural resonance between African American and Kuwaiti communication styles and comedy. "Most of what we accept from all the comedy is black," he explains. "Culturally, it's more similar. . . . Black comedy, especially the women, the way they act it's like Arabic women—the shaking of heads and such, some of it's Arab. . . . And the way [men] hit [on women] is like Arabs."

As one of the first African American series distributed abroad in the wake of worldwide privatization, deregulation, and channel fragmentation, *The Fresh Prince of Bel-Air* was capable of performing a wide range of institutional labors, from drawing in prime-time family viewers in the Middle East to helping fill newly launched niche and sub-niche channels in Europe and Latin America. Unlike the institutional labors of integrated sitcoms in South Africa in the 1980s, which we examined in chapter 2, the uses of *Fresh Prince* were widespread enough to capture the attention of some distributors, particularly those working the closest with buyers and those from independent distribution firms. Put slightly differently, the institutional labors of *Fresh Prince* among certain niche broadcasters led to revised industry lore about the suitability of certain elements of African American culture for global exchange. These elements included the satire of middle-class culture, especially white culture; the rebelliousness, sexuality, and vulgarity of hip-hop culture and rap music; and debates about authentic forms of ethnic and gender identity. This nascent industry lore was widespread but certainly not all-pervasive, leading even to disagreement among executives working for the same media conglomerate.

Arriving as it did on the cusp of the transition from the network to the "post-network" or "matrix" era of television (Curtin and Shattuc, 2009; Lotz, 2007), *The Fresh Prince of Bel-Air* was the first globally traded African American series to benefit from this new corporate logic. While its immediate successors were cut from similar cloth in terms of genre, demographic slant, and cultural allusions, the continuing fragmentation and uncertainty of the present era has led to a handful of distinctive international institutional labors and industry discourses related to contemporary African American series. In addition, one of the main consequences of the current industrial changes has been the dissolution of a single, dominant form of industry lore, which became ascendant during the era of *The Cosby Show,* and has since splintered into different pockets of industry lore centered on buyers and sellers that specialize in similar program types and demographics.

5

The Worldwide Circulation of Contemporary African American Television

Since the mid-1990s, television channels, audience configurations, and program offerings have continued to fragment both at home and abroad. The economics of this splintering landscape have proved challenging for program producers and networks nearly everywhere, and a growing number of them have turned to international markets in order to defray costs and externalize risk. The impact of these developments on television portrayals of all kinds has been a matter of much debate among media scholars. For some, these changes have introduced a degree of diversity heretofore unknown in television around the world (Curtin, 1996, 1999). Others see this diversity as superficial, and worry about the homogenization, on a worldwide scale, of viewpoints and cultural experiences due to the dominance of transnational conglomerates that place the ownership of media outlets in a small number of hands (Bagdikian, 2000; Herman and McChesney, 1997). Still others, who believe that media offerings have become more diverse, point to the growing isolation and purification of audience segments and the demise of shared values (Turow, 1997, 2005). Finally, some have argued that these developments have rendered obsolete many of the conventional ways we analyze and think about diversity in television programming (Lotz, 2006).

The evidence of increased African American television trade today is undeniable. A greater variety of genres, featuring a greater diversity of African American characters and ideological content, now travel to a wider global audience than at any time in television's history. This is not to say, however, that commercial television trade is marked by diverse, complex, high-quality stories of African American life. Quite the contrary. In fact, portrayals of African Americans continue to be enabled by specific economic considerations, business practices, organizational forms, institutional labors, and industry lore that render certain kinds of portrayals common and others unlikely. What is more, some of today's more diverse portrayals may, for some, be reactionary rather than progressive. In addition, some of the more interesting and unique portrayals are also the most vulnerable.

All of the television shows that travel successfully in today's television universe do so because they perform similar institutional labors for similar kinds of networks in different territories. That is, general entertainment broadcasters in various markets prefer programming that portrays African Americans in particular ways, while women-oriented cable channels exhibit quite different preferences. In general, these portrayals are little more than extensions of prior programming trends, but some of the newer forms do, in fact, create spaces for expressions of African American life and identity that are distinctly new. Again, I want to emphasize that the industrial conditions that I outline here and the ways they create conduits for certain kinds of portrayals to circulate among certain audiences and locations do not simplistically determine the representational practices of individual producers or programs. Instead, they encourage certain themes, genres, and forms of identity that creative workers in the television industry can—and often do —bend to their own needs. Indeed, in some instances, we see evidence of African American television producers drawing on industry trends that are potentially reactionary to create politically progressive texts.

Integration at Work: General Entertainment Channels and the Limited Diversity of *Grey's Anatomy*

In one of the quirkier moments in television history, CBS spun off the medical drama *Trapper John, M.D.* (1979–1986) from the war sitcom *M*A*S*H*, not only changing the genre of the spin-off in the process, but also bringing the spin-off forward thirty years to the present. Ostensibly the main character of the new series was based on a surgeon in *M*A*S*H* who had left the series in 1974, but the two characters had little in common except their names. In this same vein, *Grey's Anatomy* (2005–present) could be a spin-off of *The Cosby Show* (1984–1992), with Cliff Huxtable, the obstetrician, becoming a surgeon and moving to Seattle. Both shows feature similar forms of African American masculinity and both portray racial differences as minor differences of cultural style in an egalitarian American economic system that is diverse and equally open to all.

Grey's Anatomy features not just one African American in its initial cast of nine surgeons, but three, including the brilliant heart surgeon Preston Burke, the chief of surgery, Richard Webber, and the intern director, Miranda Bailey, an African American woman. In addition, three of the five featured interns are women, one of whom is Chinese American. The main storyline revolves around Meredith Grey and her cohort of interns at Seattle Grace Hospital as they strive to navigate the personal and professional relationships of the hospital and endure the difficult and grueling realities of surgical internships.

One of the framing storylines involves Grey's relationship with Derek Shepherd, with whom she had a one-night stand before starting her internship, and who turns out to be a surgeon at the hospital. This storyline continues to animate many subsequent episodes, as do relationships among interns and "attendings," as well as interns and interns, and interns and patients. Generically, then, *Grey's Anatomy* is a medical melodrama, with stories about patients and disease that generally conclude in a single episode, along with ongoing storylines about personal relationships that continue from episode to episode and season to season. In addition, each episode is structured around a recurring leitmotif that Grey addresses in voice-over at the beginning and end of each episode, as well as throughout the episode as a transition between scenes.

Grey's Anatomy is one of a slew of current network television series that feature conspicuously integrated workplace settings, typically in a dramatic genre. Robert Entman and Andrew Rojecki (2000) in their study of prime-time network television programs found that the majority of African Americans in such programs inhabited either integrated workplaces or segregated households. More recently, Herman Gray (2005) has noted the same tendency.

The trend toward portraying African Americans in workplace series that hew closely to what Gray (1995) calls "assimilationist" discourses of race is, in my opinion, a response to complaints from activist groups in the wake of the 1999 network television season. In the fall of 1999 a number of political groups, including the NAACP and La Raza, threatened to boycott network advertisers because no new series featured a nonwhite character in a lead role. Subsequently the drama series *Now and Again* (1999–2000) elevated the role of the African American actor Dennis Haysbert (Dr. Theodore Morris) and *The West Wing* (1999–2006) added an important recurring character, Charlie Young, played by the African American actor Dulé Hill. All of these characters are reminiscent of the "super-Negroes" that populated television series in the late 1960s: they are all highly competent, brilliant even, and are exceptionally well-dressed and well-spoken individuals. Beyond window dressing, the only significant difference they bring to the series is rooted in personal and communicative stylistic differences from white characters. Otherwise the medical profession, the federal government, and the ranks of law enforcement are portrayed as racially neutral work spaces that are equally open to and welcoming of people of all races, genders, classes, creeds, and so forth.

In addition to placating activist groups, the strategy of including diverse casts in contemporary workplace dramas serves the needs of the networks to reach out to the widest possible professional, middle-class viewers of all races, especially at a time when white viewers increasingly abandon the networks for cable and satellite channels, and the demographics of the United States are becoming increasingly nonwhite. I depart here somewhat from Gray's (2005) argument that the networks view African Americans only as political subjects who can cause problems for the networks if they aren't placated, rather than economic subjects whom the networks have a greater incentive to serve because they are central to the networks' commercial logics. Gray argues that the recurring appearance and disappearance of African Americans from prime-time network schedules stems from this understanding of African Americans as political rather than economic subjects: that is, because they are not economically important, the networks do not make an effort to include African Americans in television programs. However, because they are a political force, the networks do respond when threatened with boycotts, oversight, and so forth. When the political pressure disappears, the networks return to their original economic logic.

While this logic has certainly been prevalent among broadcasters for the past couple of decades, I believe that it is beginning to change as networks continue to try to hold on to lucrative audience segments. Diversity of the type we see in *Grey's Anatomy* not only works to hold a diverse audience (as African Americans become stand-ins for all forms of racial and ethnic diversity), but also marks a series as progressive for a segment of the white audiences that Ron Becker (2006) has called SLUMPies, or socially liberal, urban-minded professionals, who have become the darlings of the networks due to the rise of the digital economy. These SLUMPies are typically well educated, white, and well off, but their senses of self are deeply interwoven with progressive social policies, and they value diversity in their workplaces and cultural preferences.

Grey's Anatomy appeals not only to domestic viewers but also to a diverse array of buyers abroad. While the main markets for major U.S. distributors continue to be the European nations of France, Italy, Germany, Spain, and the United Kingdom, such upcoming markets as Brazil, Russia, India, and China are increasingly important for them (Marenzi, 2008). In addition, smaller markets such as South Africa and Indonesia are becoming more important for adding additional revenues for expensive network TV series. These series continue to follow the deficit-financing model, making them heavily reliant on international sales in the years prior to domestic syndication. Given the economic downturn since the first decade of the twenty-first century, made worse since 2007 by the collapse of credit markets, making sales to as many buyers as quickly as possible has become increasingly important for all distributors. Diversity of cast helps broaden the appeal of a series such as *Grey's Anatomy* beyond predominantly white European markets. At the same time, the specific ways racial difference is figured through the *Grey's Anatomy* text guarantee its appeal among white viewers worldwide. In other words, geo-economic differences are literally inscribed on the text of *Grey's Anatomy*.

In addition to portraying forms of difference that are nonthreatening to middle-class professional values and workplace settings, *Grey's Anatomy* and most prime-time network dramas featuring African American professionals stage the encounter with difference through white main characters. In *Grey's Anatomy*, for instance, we enter the narrative through the character of Meredith Grey, a white woman, who frames the narratives and characters in her voice-overs and operates as the main point of emotional identification. African American characters, such as Dr. Bailey, never serve as the main character identification in such stories, and the stories themselves would be quite different ideological texts if they were built around the black characters. *The Unit*, for instance, starred Dennis Haysbert (Jonas "Snake Doctor" Blane) as the leader of an elite group of U.S. Special Forces fighting terrorism, but our main point of entry into the series was the character of Bob Brown (Scott Foley), a white man who joins the Unit in the first episode, as well as his wife, who learns to adjust to the stresses of her husband's job from Blane's wife.

Miranda Bailey offers one of the more intriguing examples of how blackness is figured in a text such as *Grey's Anatomy* as a matter of personal and communicative style, rather than political and social difference. Dr. Bailey, known in initial episodes of the series as "the Nazi" because of how hard she drives interns, speaks in a direct, confident, often colorful manner that the African American interpersonal communication scholar Marsha Houston (2000) has called "fortitude" (14). In the episode "Winning the Battle, Losing the War" from the first season, for instance, she lectures a group of ne'er-do-wells whose friend, Viper, has been injured in an extreme bike race.

Is he okay? No, no. He is not okay at all. He hurled his body down a concrete mountain at full speed for no good reason. Yeah, I know you all pierce yourselves and smoke up and generally treat your bodies like your grungy asses can't break down. Hey, that's fine. You wanna kill yourselves flyin' down a concrete mountain, go to it, but there are other people walking, people driving, people trying to live their lives on that concrete mountain and one of 'em got his brains scrambled today because one of you sniveling little no-good snot rags—so no, your friend Viper as far as I'm concerned is not okay.

This tirade is obviously quite outside the bounds of conventional white American communication in a professional setting, where a doctor is speaking with the friends of a seriously injured patient. It is not at all out of character for Dr. Bailey, however, nor for African American women more generally (Houston, 2000, 14).

Dr. Bailey does not employ her distinct communication style for any social or professional purposes related to racial difference and discrimination. In fact, the distinct challenges to achieving her stature and maintaining her authority among interns, patients, colleagues, and superiors are almost completely absent from the text. When such differences do surface, they nevertheless remain so far submerged as to be nearly invisible. In an episode from season 4, "Lay Your Hands on Me," Dr. Bailey has a protracted argument with her unemployed husband, Tucker, who is a stay-at-home father for their young son. It is obvious from the argument that Tucker has trouble with the fact that Bailey is a successful professional and he is unemployed. At this point, the episode is ripe with possibilities to explore such issues as African American gender relations, the challenges that professional African American women face finding partners who are also professionals, and the distinct pressures that gender politics and economic hardship place on African American women. However, the episode addresses none of these possibilities, leaving them instead at the level of mere allusion rather than narrative exploration.

The strategy of creating diverse workplace dramas where personal problems are foregrounded over social problems has proved successful abroad as well as at home. Domestically, it solves the riddle of appealing to white viewers with nonwhite characters by foregrounding white characters, at the same time that it appeals to certain middle- and upper-class segments of the minority audience because it portrays characters who are stylistically marked as black but who are nevertheless thoroughly integrated and accepted. These images trace their history to the super-Negroes of the 1960s, but they possess a distinct twist that makes them more acceptable to African American viewers: they speak and act differently than whites. In some senses, then, these kinds of shows walk the same aesthetic tightrope as *The Cosby Show* did earlier, by offering both diversity *and* integration in the same text, depending on who the audience is.

Integrating African American Women on Television

Two additional series featuring African American women bear mentioning here, because they have been globally successful in their own right while treading similar ideological ground as *Grey's Anatomy*: *The Oprah Winfrey Show* and *That's So Raven*. Much like Dr. Miranda Bailey, the lead African American women in each of these shows are portrayed as middle-class women whose racial identities come across mainly through their linguistic styles. I do not mean to diminish the political significance of such stylistic difference. In fact, Shane and Graham White (1998) show convincingly how stylistic resistance was for centuries one of the few avenues available for African Americans. Rather, my interests lie in tracing how the institutional labors of these programs abroad help sustain portrayals of middle-class African American women who differ only in terms of their use of language.

The Oprah Winfrey Show has been a bona fide global success, airing in 145 countries around the world in 2010, predominantly on women-oriented cable and satellite channels or as daytime programming at general entertainment broadcasters. While these foreign markets certainly garner significant revenues, the show's main revenues come from the more than two hundred syndication markets in the United States that air the program and pay significantly higher license fees than their foreign counterparts.

Communicative style, rather than any particular political or ideological content, is *Oprah*'s primary marker of race and gender. A good deal has been written about the capacity of *Oprah* and other daytime talk shows to create a feminine space for the exploration of personal and political issues, to articulate a populist form of feminism, and to bring distinctly African American perspectives to issues of personal and political import (Cloud, 1996; Haag, 1993; Peck, 1994; Shattuc, 1997; Squire, 1994). However, the scholarly literature agrees, as does my own viewing of the show, that *The Oprah Winfrey Show* largely downplays issues of racial difference in the interest of shared feminine interests and female viewership.

Certainly *Oprah*, more than any other talk show, has featured African American guests and issues specifically oriented toward African Americans in general and African American women in particular. In fact, it is in these instances when Oprah Winfrey's speech becomes most clearly inflected with African American Vernacular English, and when her middle-class values of personal responsibility and self-determination come most strongly to the fore. Kathleen Dixon (2001) argues convincingly that in one such episode, "Crying Shame," which focused especially on violent crimes among African American youth, the ideological stance is all but impossible to pin down because of conflicting televisual and speech genres that crisscross the episode. Such ambiguity, however, relies on the viewer's capacity to "read" the conflicting genres and rhetorical styles, which is likely to be absent among both foreign viewers and programmers, particularly in markets where the series is dubbed or subtitled. Absent such capacity, *Oprah* winds up reinforcing the ideology that, save for minor differences of style, women's lives and issues are similar everywhere.

Abroad, programmers generally use *Oprah* to draw undifferentiated female viewers during daytime hours, when ad revenues are so low that it makes little fiscal sense to produce even cheap, domestic talk shows. The Belgian cable network VijfTV offers a typical example. Launched in 2004 into a heavily cabled market that already featured a channel targeted at women, Vijf programs *The Oprah Winfrey Show* weekdays at about 15:30 between a locally produced lifestyle program and the aging Australian serial police drama *Blue Heelers* (1994–2006). In addition to imported light entertainment and lifestyle programs, the channel features American soap operas and teleshopping.

Oprah serves as one of the anchors of Vijf's program schedule, designed to bring in at-home mothers, students, and part-time wage earners in the late afternoon. In other words, the scheduling is virtually identical to the show's scheduling throughout much of the United States. Thus, the institutional labors that *Oprah* performs for Vijf seem to exhibit shared perceptions among U.S. and Vijf programmers about who the show's audience is, how to reach them, and what they find valuable in the program. Nothing in Vijf's programming practices suggests that their programming in any way departs from domestic industry lore about the program. Here, middle-class values serve as the overriding similarity between domestic viewers, foreign viewers, and Oprah herself. While Oprah's distinct communicative style may appeal to certain audience segments, those elements and viewers are clearly secondary for programmers at home and abroad.

That's So Raven (2003–2007), a teenage sitcom vehicle for the pop star Raven-Symoné, offers a portrayal of African American womanhood that also closely tallies those of *The Oprah Winfrey Show* and *Grey's Anatomy*, despite the different generic features and demographic slant of the series. Appearing on Disney Channels around the world, *That's So Raven* provides a good example of the kind of media globalization that many critics fear, where a multinational entertainment conglomerate such as Disney exploits its cross-media holdings in television, movies, popular music, and theme parks to create a set of synergistic texts that cross-promote one another worldwide.

The multimedia model that *That's So Raven* helped launch continues to be a blueprint for Disney's teenage pop star factory, which has also launched such stars as Miley Cyrus (Hannah Montana) and the Jonas Brothers through an integrated combination of television sitcoms, pop songs, movie appearances, and live performances (Luscombe, 2009). Television series are the centerpiece of the Disney factory, introducing new stars, offering a spotlight for their songs, and allowing cross-promotion of new stars on established series (Luscombe, 2009). In other words, *That's So Raven* is only the most recent iteration of the phenomenon whereby African American television series lead to expanded international opportunities for white series and performers.

While *Raven*'s immediate predecessor, *Lizzie McGuire* (2001–2004), was perhaps the progenitor of the teen pop star sitcom genre—or "zitcom"—Disney substantially increased its international cable network holdings and revenues during *Raven*'s run, meaning that many more international channels likely carried the series. At the end of 2003, a month before *Lizzie McGuire* ended its run, Disney Channels International boasted twenty million subscribers worldwide, broadcast in fourteen different countries. At the end of *Raven*'s run in 2007, Disney had nearly doubled its number of international channels, broadcasting in twenty-six countries to fifty-four million subscribers (Walt Disney Company, 2003, 2007). Of course, *Raven* was not the engine that drove that success, but it was undoubtedly a benefactor, bringing the series and its eponymous pop star to millions of teen and preteen viewers worldwide. In fact, as Disney Channel's hottest property at the time, *Raven* was almost certainly featured prominently on most Disney Channels abroad.

That's So Raven tells the story of Raven, her brother, and her friends as they navigate teenage problems related to dating, peer pressure, and parental authority. Raven has psychic visions that foretell the future, but they typically lead not to insight, but rather to comical misunderstandings. Several episodes also include music by Raven and other performers, which Disney used to cross-promote CDs and live tours. *Raven*'s successors adopted a similar format, in which middle-class teenage life and its attendant problems were the unspoken norm. This norm fits Disney's overall teenage and children's brands, which seek to identify themselves with wholesome middle-class entertainment rather than countercultural or edgy programs. The importance and rigidity of the brand have come across most clearly in a series of recent scandals in which teenage pop stars have wound up pregnant, causing delays in production schedules and threats of cancellation, in addition to threatening Disney's wholesome brand and, potentially, young women's entire careers (Luscombe, 2009).

Although *Raven* hews closely to the established Disney format, *Raven*'s expressive style nevertheless draws on African American ones, particularly her language, her clothing, and her songs. At the same time, by including white characters who share similar styles, the series marks these expressions as the province of a general, deracinated teenage culture rather than African American culture. In this manner *Raven* is a descendant of *Fresh Prince*, but lacks the clear connection to African American cultural and political concerns that drove much of *Fresh Prince*'s narratives and characterizations. Instead, much like *Grey's Anatomy* and *Oprah*, *Raven* marks blackness predominantly as a stylistic difference in American life—a difference primarily associated with teenagers.

Along with *Lizzie McGuire* and *Even Stevens*, *That's So Raven* helped establish Disney's current teenage pop star factory, which is currently the most lucrative and growing sector of its media empire. Television series are the centerpiece of this empire, because they allow Disney to introduce potential stars through its channels, to guest-star them on established series, and to promote their music during episodes (Luscombe, 2009). While domestic markets are still the most lucrative segment of this business, Disney's financial reports make clear that global markets are increasingly important, particularly those in Latin America, Europe, and Asia. Black consumers are obviously a small part of this imagined global audience, and black televisual representations in Disney sitcoms reflect these financial priorities, making blackness a source and marker of global teenage communion and resistance. By contrast, Disney launched its first Latina teen star, Selena Gomez, in 2007 in an effort to appeal to a pan-Latino audience.

Multicultural Struggles at Home: Youth Channels and the Global Appeal of *Everybody Hates Chris*

If *Grey's Anatomy* is the progeny of *The Cosby Show* in the international markets, then the most prominent descendant of *The Fresh Prince of Bel-Air* is the CW situation comedy *Everybody Hates Chris* (2005–2009), based on the comedy of the African American comedian Chris Rock. Unlike *Fresh Prince*, *Everybody Hates Chris* got favorable reviews from buyers across the world when it was first offered in syndication (Brennan, 2005). Before the end of its first season, the sitcom had sold in the Middle East, Belgium, Ireland, Australia, Germany, Canada, the Netherlands, South Korea, Israel, South Africa, New Zealand, Finland, and a digital channel operator that broadcasts in both Spain and Latin America (Brennan, 2005).

Everybody Hates Chris shares a good deal with *Fresh Prince*. Most obviously, it is built around an established star, in this case Chris Rock, with demonstrated crossover appeal and a significant box office presence that help cross-promote the series and drive sales through inclusion in program packages abroad. *Everybody Hates Chris* is a fish-out-of-water story like *Fresh Prince*, except that Chris Rock's character, played by Tyler James Williams, is a teenager whose family has moved from the projects in Brooklyn to the

Bedford-Stuyvesant neighborhood. In addition to facing a new neighborhood, Chris must also navigate his new middle school as one of the only African American students. Finally, both *Everybody Hates Chris* and *Fresh Prince* are domestic situation comedies. However, the similarities between the series are eclipsed by their differences.

One of the clearest examples of the differences between the two series is the backstory of the characters: Will in *Fresh Prince* moves from the inner city to a posh Beverly Hills neighborhood; Chris, by contrast, moves from the projects to a neighborhood where poverty, crime, and racial tensions are prevalent. Consequently, while *Fresh Prince* handled class differences in terms of character conflict between Will and his rich cousin Carlton, *Everybody Hates Chris* embeds working-class identities in its characters, settings, clothing, and cultural allusions. Moreover, much like the initial seasons of *Good Times*, *Everybody Hates Chris* spends considerable screen time on the ways working-class African American families deal with financial hardship, as well as the impact of those hardships on families and children.

The series manages its crossover appeal by creating a second primary setting in the classroom, where the majority of the storylines revolve around teenage problems of dating and fitting in, though even here, those problems are inflected by the fact that Chris is one of the only black students in the school. The series' immediate generic predecessors, then, are *Good Times* and the nostalgic situation comedy *The Wonder Years* (1988–1993), which followed the life of a white suburban teenager growing up in the 1960s. The similarities between *The Wonder Years* and *Everybody Hates Chris* are striking: both series feature teenage leads whose lives are "narrated" by their offscreen, adult counterparts. *The Wonder Years* pioneered the use of single-camera shooting for a situation comedy, the use of a narrator, and the elimination of the laugh track, all of which *Everybody Hates Chris* incorporates. One of the main distinctions between the two is in terms of the relationship between the adult narrator and his family members, friends, life experiences and, especially, the era in which he grew up. Whereas Kevin Arnold in *The Wonder Years* struck a generally nostalgic tone toward his recollections, Chris in *Everybody Hates Chris* is far more ironic, especially with respect to the popular culture of the 1980s, which gets represented through music, hairstyles, dance, language, and dress. During the pilot episode, for instance, as we see Chris in a slow-motion fight with a racist bully, the audio track plays Paul McCartney and Michael Jackson's song of racial harmony, "Ebony and Ivory."

Everybody Hates Chris offered the only portrait of African American working-class life on broadcast television in recent years, and it did so from a frame of reference that was distinctly and unapologetically black. That is, the experiences, cultural allusions, and characterizations in the series drew from and reflected on African American perspectives, without working particularly hard to generalize those experiences to others. In the pilot episode, for instance, when he gets accosted by a bully, Chris responds in a distinctly black manner. After the bully steps on Chris's new shoes and calls him "bojangles," Chris responds, "That's not what your mother called me when I was dancing in her drawers last night." As the narrator Chris explains, "I know you think I'm crazy, but if I let him get away with that, he'd be doing it all year. I couldn't beat him, but I thought maybe I could out-black him." This scene offers a textbook example of playing the "dozens," a subcategory of what Thomas Kochman (1983) calls "woofing," or the attempt to "gain, without actually having to become violent, the respect and fear of others that is often won through physical combat" (49). Chris's response, though it does little to prevent the bully from pushing him, is a logical response that draws on African American communicative and cultural styles. Chris's mistake is not realizing that the white bully interprets his tirade as the beginning of a physical confrontation rather than an effort to avoid one. The racial politics at play in this small scene are quite complex, and require an insider's understanding of both white and black communication styles. Unlike the deployment of communicative differences without social commentary in *Grey's Anatomy*, here Chris's woofing does offer a commentary on the racism and violence that African American students often face in predominantly white educational settings.

Part of the reason that the series could inhabit a distinctly African American working-class space owed to industry economics. As a single-camera situation comedy, *Everybody Hates Chris* was particularly expensive, with per-episode costs running as high as $1.5 million, as compared with $500,000 for a conventional, three-camera series (Waller, 2006). Because it appeared on a small network, the CW, which has much weaker audience ratings and advertising revenues, rather than one of the Big Four, license fees for the program are similarly lower. Consequently, *Everybody Hates Chris* was especially dependent on syndication revenues, especially syndication in the top ten markets in the United States, all of which have a heavy concentration of working-class and poor African American viewers. These are viewers who are less likely to have access to cable and more likely to watch local CW affiliates, especially those that counterprogram local news with off-network series such as *Everybody Hates Chris*. Luring such viewers to both original and rerun broadcasts of the series with stories that match their experience and cultural sensibilities only makes sense for the network and its affiliates.

As always, international syndication revenues help fill the funding void until a television series reaches domestic syndication, which for *Everybody Hates Chris* was the fall of 2009. *Everybody Hates Chris* has aired in at least forty-eight countries, and its cocreator Ali LeRoi believes that the working-class elements of the series are largely responsible for its international popularity. "Across the U.S. and the world . . . most families are working class. And here's one awkward working class teenager trying to get a girl and not get beat up. Every young kid in Spain, France, Belgium is going through the same thing" (Waller, 2006). Despite this assertion, however, it is unclear that most of the youth audiences watching *Everybody Hates Chris* in such European countries are, in fact, working-class. Instead, European broadcasters are programming *Everybody Hates Chris* in ways quite similar to *The Fresh Prince of Bel-Air*, on channels and in day parts targeted toward a general youth audience. The Spanish terrestrial broadcaster Cuatro originally programmed the series on Saturday afternoons at 2:30 during a time slot aimed at teenagers, and the Belgian general entertainment cable channel VT4 currently strips the series at 18:20 on weekdays during a youth-oriented block of programming, between *8 Simple Rules for Dating My Teenage Daughter* and *The Simpsons* (VT4, 2008). Thus, despite LeRoi's assertion that viewers abroad respond to the class dimension of the series—and I want to emphasize that I find his assertion quite plausible—*programmers* continue to treat the series as simply another African American youth comedy, no different from *Fresh Prince*.

Foreign programmers, at least in Europe, see *Everybody Hates Chris* as part of a general youth culture that is brash, edgy, and irreverent. As a buyer from the U.K. satellite broadcaster Sky1 explained about his purchasing preferences in 2006, "I enjoyed *Everybody Hates Chris* last year, and I'm hoping we can find something [else] that's going to be quirky and noisy and a good complement" (Jenkinson, 2006). For these programming executives, then, the teenaged main character, the satirical treatment of teenage life, the creative editing of the series, and, undoubtedly, the popularity and irreverence of the cocreator Chris Rock are what make *Everybody Hates Chris* appealing, not necessarily portrayals of African American working-class life. In other words, *Everybody Hates Chris* has probably done very little to alter dominant perceptions and industry lore about the kinds of African American television programs that are suitable for worldwide trade; instead, the series and its creators make effective and creative use of dominant television codes, blending and juxtaposing them in order to tell stories that are unique, poignant, and culturally relevant. Still, though LeRoi's comments about the series' international appeal probably did little to alter dominant industry lore, the fact that he got those ideas into circulation in one of the top trade journals covering international television is no small feat, and it demonstrates the potential openness of industry lore during times of significant change and uncertainty.

Quality Television, Black Crime: Pay Television and Urban Decay on HBO's *The Wire*

HBO's *The Wire* (2002–2008) marks a distinct innovation in television series featuring African American characters. The series portrays a wide diversity of African American characters—men, women, straight, gay, sympathetic, deplorable, upstanding, and corrupt—in roles and stories that often highlight distinct social and cultural differences between blacks and whites in the United States. Over its five-season run, *The Wire* has taken multiple perspectives and highlighted a wide range of characters living in the inner city of Baltimore, including both police officers and criminals, as well as politicians, dock workers, journalists, real estate developers, and more. Taken as a whole, the series offers a biting critique of deindustrialization, urban neglect and decay, institutional and governmental corruption and malaise, and the disproportionate impact of these forces on the inner-city poor and working classes, especially African Americans.

The unique economics of HBO, which is funded mainly by cable subscriptions rather than advertiser support, along with the unique regulatory status of cable television in the United States, have enabled the discursive space that *The Wire* inhabits. However, these same forces have encouraged particular portrayals of blackness that can be not only limiting, but even anachronistic. Specifically, HBO encourages an aesthetic of gritty realism that encourages television series that focus on drugs, crime, male violence, female sexuality, and coarse language, all of which have been conventional ways of representing African Americans for centuries. While *The Wire* makes creative and effective use of these discursive trends to engage in insightful social critique, as does *Everybody Hates Chris*, this owes more to the vision and creativity of the producers than the cultural tendencies that the economics of HBO's business model nurture. International channels that program *The Wire* tend to exhibit similar economic models and similar preferences in gritty programming, which can be a double-edged sword for portrayals of African Americans: while some forms of "progressive realism" permit television creators to tell stories about African Americans that can challenge centuries of negative distortion, realism itself is a limited aesthetic, prone to promoting liberal individualism, as well as an aesthetic rooted in white European history and cultures (Shohat and Stam, 1994).

HBO, Quality TV, and Blackness

Advertising sales provide little or no revenue for HBO's original television series, and the network's definition of program success is consequently not directly tied to its ratings performance. Instead, the measure of success at HBO is more intangible and difficult to quantify: HBO wants to lure new customers to subscribe to the channel and, perhaps more importantly, to keep viewers who currently have HBO from dropping the service. Original television series have become a central strategy in their subscriber retention efforts, although their effectiveness is difficult to measure. In addition, DVD sales of original programs have become an important revenue stream, contributing an average of about 20 percent of revenues (Flint, 2005; Levin, 2004). For these reasons, HBO measures its programming via a combination of DVD sales records, critical awards, and ratings. Consequently, the network looks for programming that fits prevalent definitions of "quality" to drive awards and DVD sales.

The term "quality" has an ambivalent history in television and television studies. Most contemporary scholars agree that rather than being an identifiable set of textual features, "quality" is a relative term, which changes in response to what is considered low-brow. For instance, quality 1970s series such as *The Mary Tyler Moore Show* or *Hill Street Blues* (Feuer, Kerr, and Vahimagi, 1983) seem like run-of-the-mill programs today because the standards for low-brow and quality television have changed. Moreover, most quality television series derive that distinction because they work with the cultural preferences and expectations of better-off audience segments more effectively than their popular counterparts. For instance, writers for *The Sopranos* can integrate Shakespeare quotations into their scripts and expect many of their viewers to recognize them, whereas writers for *Everybody Loves Raymond*, for instance, cannot. The aesthetics of narratological and characterological complexity, cinematographic camerawork and lighting, and gritty realism have come not only to symbolize quality television dramas today (Caldwell, 1995), but also to help middle- and upper-middle-class viewers, especially men, distinguish their tastes from the tastes of the general public. In addition, original HBO series distinguish themselves by their ability to showcase content that broadcast networks cannot legally carry, especially graphic violence, sexuality, drug use, and profanity, all of which lead to the use of the term "adult" as another way of identifying HBO's programming.

When it comes to portraying African Americans, contemporary standards of quality are often ambivalent. To some extent, the shows represent a response to calls for more "realistic" images among some sectors of the

African American community as a way to combat the perceived distortions of television's conventional stereotyping of blacks. Moreover, the episodic nature of television series, which encourages deep exploration of characters and situations, adds complexity to the African American criminals, drug dealers, prostitutes, politicians, and police officers who populate the world of gritty, quality dramas. For example, the drug kingpin Avon Barksdale (Wood Harris), in an episode of *The Wire* from season 4, is trying to encourage D'Angelo (Lawrence Gilliard Jr.), who is at the beginning of a twenty-year prison term, to give up drugs for a few days. "I'm asking out of love," he says quite sincerely. "It's always love, D." Bringing depth and humanity to characters such as Avon is one thing that episodic television series can do far more effectively than a two-hour feature film. Therefore, although quality series like *The Wire* do trade in the same kinds of spectacular black images that dominate Hollywood films today, the cultural politics of those images are mediated and brought back down to the level of the everyday through the use of episodic narrative. Nevertheless, in terms of portraying a diversity of the life experiences and perspectives of African Americans, quality series like *The Wire* do little to widen the scope. Moreover, these series may be setting a standard for quality television that, in less thoughtful hands, winds up replicating the imagery of black, drug-infested inner cities without also adopting their humane tone.

HBO, DVD Sales, and the New Economics of African American Television

While a handful of exceptionally successful HBO series like *The Sopranos* and *Sex in the City* find their way onto broadcast and basic cable channels abroad, *The Wire* typically shows up on pay channels similar to HBO, especially movie channels, or channels identified with male action-drama, such as Sony's global channel brand AXN. These buyers program the series as a quality series much as HBO does, reinforcing the idea that a realistic portrayal of black criminal life is a primary marker of quality drama and an important tool in skimming off the cream of the television viewing audience through differential program access and pricing. Throughout German-speaking Europe, for instance, the series is carried on the digital, pay-TV platform Digital's Fox International Channel along with series such as *Lost* and *Entourage*. The British digital satellite broadcaster Sky1 carried *The Wire* on FX286, along with a collection of quality U.S. dramas, in an effort to target an upscale, twenty-five-to-forty-four male demographic (Harrison, 2004). It is important to note that the economics of the viewing arrangement, which requires subscribers to pay for the channels, encourages the same kind of devoted, appointment viewing that HBO does in the United States, a practice that is reinforced by the sales of original series DVDs abroad. Practically speaking, this means that the institutional labors that quality dramas perform are similar in many territories. Moreover, the premium networks that carry these quality series are often owned by global media conglomerates that operate similar channels worldwide, thereby further facilitating their standardized uses.

Nevertheless, we see in the circulation of *The Wire* a new development that promises to alter the ways institutions mediate the worldwide circulation of African American television programs, namely, DVD sales. Such sales are far less dependent on cultural translators who must decide which programs to purchase and how to schedule them. Of course, institutional actors must decide where and when to release DVDs and whether to promote them, but the business model of DVD sales operates more along the lines of a "pull" technology like the Internet, rather than a "push" technology like broadcasting. That is, DVD consumers have a much wider range of possible choices and make more direct selections of which domestic and foreign programming to watch, whereas television viewers face more restricted choices, even in a digital world, that are filtered through the machinations of the broadcaster, the distributor, and so forth. Therefore, although DVD viewing does not eliminate middlemen, it does decrease their influence as cultural mediators.

The conventions of contemporary, quality U.S. programming encourage portrayals of African American inner-city life, specifically of young men and women involved in the drug trade and law enforcement officers assigned to drug cases. In part, this tendency owes to restrictions on broadcast television content and the efforts of HBO and similar pay channels to use those limitations to brand themselves as distinctively adult. Given the episodic nature of television, these generic tendencies open up the possibility to explore the lives of cops and criminals in ways that are more complex, ambivalent, and sympathetic than earlier portrayals. At the same time, the articulation of inner-city black life with quality television carries with it the risk of a greater number of portrayals of black criminal behavior that serve as little more than a backdrop to other stories and vary little from conventional television stereotypes.

Television with Edge and the N-Word: *The Boondocks* and *Chappelle's Show* Abroad

In addition to pay television channels, cable outlets such as Comedy Central and the Cartoon Network have become a breeding ground for series featuring, and often controlled by, African Americans that break with conventional televisual forms and ideologies in interesting ways. Abroad, these programs typically appear on cable and satellite channels with the same or similar brands as in the domestic market (Gray, 2005). For instance, foreign versions of Comedy Central were the primary carriers of *Chappelle's Show* abroad, which was broadcast on Comedy Central in the United States as well. While these series offer unique—sometimes progressive—portrayals of African American identities, experiences, and social sensibilities, programmers typically treat them as "edgy," which means a program that hews closely to a particular viewer demographic while alienating other viewers (Curtin, 1996).

In the case of *The Boondocks* and *Chappelle's Show*, the main markers of edge are juvenile, gross-out humor; satirical references to popular culture, especially gangsta or "playa" lifestyles; and liberal use of the word "nigger." Because of the particular demographic that these programs address, they are also decidedly masculinist, though not typically overtly misogynist. Finally, such programs not only translate well to DVD, but also fit well with the demands of online and mobile TV viewing, which are becoming important revenue streams for transnational television distributors, especially those targeting young, affluent, urban male viewers.

The Boondocks (2005–present) was adapted from a long-running newspaper comic of the same title, penned by Aaron McGruder, featuring a pair of young African American children who move from the inner city to the suburbs to live with their grandfather. The main character, Huey, named after the civil rights activist Huey Newton, serves as the voice of reason in a world otherwise characterized by greed, overt and covert racism, and ignorance. His younger brother, Riley's, outlook on life has been thoroughly warped by popular culture, especially gangsta culture. Riley is fascinated with guns, thinks all women are "ho's," and idolizes gangsta rappers and thug life. Robert "Granddad" Freeman is a strict disciplinarian primarily interested in his own pleasures, and only marginally interested in raising his grandchildren. In addition to the family, the program features Uncle Ruckus, a friend of Granddad who worships white people and white culture, and the Dubois family, the interracial next-door neighbors.

The Boondocks is part of the Adult Swim lineup on Cartoon Network in the United States, which is a branded block of programming created by the production house Williams Street, a division of Cartoon Network. Adult Swim mainly targets young men eighteen to thirty-four between the hours of 10:00 P.M. and 6:00 A.M. nightly. Similar branded blocks of Adult Swim appear or have appeared on Cartoon Networks and other channels around the world, including television channels in Australia, New Zealand, the United Kingdom, Ireland, Chile, Argentina, Bolivia, Brazil, Peru, Canada, the Philippines, South Africa, Spain, Germany, and Russia.

The Boondocks is one of the most expensive and successful series to appear on Adult Swim, with production costs running $400,000 per episode, or nearly four times what many other productions cost. The debut episode of *The Boondocks* attracted 2.3 million viewers, the largest debut audience ever for an Adult Swim program, and the series maintained an average of about 2.2 million viewers per episode for the remainder of the season (Deeken, 2006; Ogunnaike, 2005; Sofley, 2005). While such ratings undoubtedly help justify the series' large production budget, they also make it necessary to derive sales revenues from international syndication if at all possible. In fact, *The Boondocks* is one of the only Adult Swim series that get sold independently abroad by Sony Pictures International Television, unlike most other Adult Swim series, which are sold as a package by Warner Brothers International Television.

Much as his comic strip did, McGruder's television series has generated a good deal of controversy among African Americans. One way to get at how this series marks itself as edgy is to examine the controversies it has raised, for it is in stoking controversy that a series creates buzz and identifies who is and is not in its target market. Two controversies in particular have caused the greatest amount of publicity for the series: an episode from the second season mocking Black Entertainment Television, which was not broadcast in the United States but is included in DVD compilations; and an episode from season 1 entitled "Return of the King," in which a resurrected Martin Luther King Jr. calls a rowdy group of African American revelers "ignorant niggers." While the issues explored in each of these episodes are important and progressive, it is ultimately language, violence, and sexual imagery that mark the series as edgy, not the political commentary.

The episode entitled "Hunger Strike" opens in BET headquarters with Debra Lee-vil, a takeoff on BET CEO Debra Lee, insisting that the purpose of the network is to "accomplish what hundreds of years of slavery, Jim Crow, and malt liquor couldn't: the destruction of black people!" When one of her junior executives suggests that BET's track record in destroying African Americans has been good, she hurls a Prada shoe at him, striking him in the jugular and causing fountains of blood to erupt. Later, the programming executive introduces the network's new fall lineup by explaining that "My Harvard education tells me that our goal should be to take all the shitty reality TV shows MTV did five years ago and make them black. Anyone who wants to see a shitty black version of an MTV reality show, well, they'll have to come to us!" At the end of this scene we discover that Huey has begun a hunger strike against BET to get it taken off the air. After it comes to the attention of Rollo Goodlove, a political activist, reverend, and former pop star, Huey's campaign begins to attract attention. However, when BET offers Goodlove his own talk show, he abandons the cause, and a resigned Huey begins to eat again.

The controversy surrounding this episode stemmed largely from the unflattering portrayal of corporate greed and exploitation at BET, facts that have been well documented by the media scholar Beretta Smith-Shomade (2007). By airing a popular portrayal of BET's poor working conditions and wages, as well as its questionable programming choices, *Boondocks* engages with thorny issues in contemporary African American cultural politics. Moreover, through the character of Rollo Goodlove, the episode offers a general critique of the political effectiveness of celebrities and the culture of self-promotion that ranges across the African American—and indeed, the American—political spectrum. However, it was not the critique that raised the ire of BET and its supporters, so much as the over-the-top caricatures of its executives, especially their use of the word "nigger." When the show is scheduled alongside other Adult Swim cartoons or as part of a Comedy Central lineup featuring *South Park*, *Chappelle's Show*, and *Reno 911!*, as it is in the United States and in some markets abroad, which use similar textual strategies to distinguish themselves from children's animation and general entertainment programming, the definition of edgy "adult" programming that emerges is one that emphasizes adult language, over-the-top violence, and gross-out jokes. While the cultural politics of *Boondocks* are far more complex than these elements alone allow, they seem to be the primary markers of adult cartooning that register with cable and satellite programmers in much of the world.

McGruder's frequent use of the word "nigger" carries both cultural and political resonances, bringing out elements of African American culture that are otherwise absent from popular television. However, these subtleties tend to be lost on programmers, who instead treat the word's frequent use as simply another expletive that identifies the program as adult- and male-oriented. In other words, much as Ali LeRoi is able to tell a unique and compelling story of African American working-class life in *Everybody Hates Chris*, McGruder manipulates the limitations and biases of the contemporary television industries to create television programs that engage elements of African American lives and experiences that otherwise are absent from television. This effort to hold up for public scrutiny those elements of African American politics that are submerged frequently causes controversy, as it did in the episode of *The Boondocks* entitled "Return of the King." The episode, framed as Huey's fantasy, imagines that Martin Luther King Jr. was shot but did not die, and wakes up from a coma to try and lead a modern-day civil rights movement. Unfortunately, his efforts meet resistance—not from the white power structure, but from "ignorant" African Americans who attend the rallies to drink and party, rather than engage in political action. At one point King loses his temper and screams at a crowd, "Would you ignorant niggers please shut the hell up!" Of course, the idea that the father of the modern civil rights movement would use such language with members of his own community was offensive to a large number of African Americans. Nevertheless, the internal dynamics that the episode points out are prevalent in African American society today, as is the popular distinction between blacks or African Americans, who are seen as contributing members of society, and niggers, who are seen as freeloaders who hobble the race as a whole.[1] *The Boondocks* did not originate this distinction, though this episode does validate it by placing these words in Dr. King's mouth, at the same time that it popularizes the distinction.

Violence, sexuality, and profanity, then, have become the markers of edge worldwide, and *The Boondocks* is able to mount the social critiques that it does because it fits these demands. We can see these particular elements of edge highlighted in the promotional video for *The Boondocks* that Sony Pictures International Television uses to promote the series to foreign buyers. The video opens with Huey and Riley meeting Kristal, a young white prostitute who will eventually date their grandfather, as she leans over for the camera, exposing her large breasts. In subsequent scenes we hear Huey telling a priest that the portrayal of Jesus as a white man in *The Passion* was "bullshit," Granddad calling Huey a "nigger," and two white women discussing when the use of the "N-word" is appropriate. We also see multiple scenes of violence, as Granddad accidentally shoots Riley in the leg and slaps him repeatedly for calling Kristal a "ho." Finally, we see the gross-out element in several scenes from "The Trial of R. Kelly" that make fun of the incident in which the rap star allegedly urinated on a young woman. And all of this takes place in just over two minutes.

The elements of edginess that we find in *The Boondocks* clearly mark the program as masculinist and male-skewing. That is, the show complicates black male identity at the same time that it relies on adult language, sexual and violent content, and gross-out gags to appeal to a cross-racial young male audience. Women, by contrast, serve mainly as sex objects or evil or corrupt characters. The only recurring female characters are the neighbors, Sarah and Jazmine Dubois, a white woman and her biracial daughter. In the comic strip, Jazmine functioned sometimes as a foil to Huey's more grandiose plans and paranoid theories about the racist adult world. In the television series, by contrast, Jazmine operates almost exclusively as a spoiled child and a sell-out, who merely validates Huey's skepticism and authenticity. Sarah similarly is portrayed as an out-of-touch, white suburban homemaker who has little comprehension of her own whiteness or privilege. Other female onetime characters are usually sex objects, such as Granddad's girlfriend Kristal and the public relations director for BET. These portrayals work to titillate and flatter male viewers, while issues related to African American men draw in those viewers and the edgy elements attract white male viewers.

In addition to incorporating these definitions of edginess, *The Boondocks* also integrates aesthetics from Japanese anime and what Deborah E. Whaley (forthcoming) calls "graphic blackness," which work to give the series an international flavor and also provide a space for exploring connections between African American and Japanese animation styles and cultures. Due to the global popularity of Japanese animation since the 1970s, anime has become one of the signature features of a global animation aesthetic that the contemporary arrangements of the television industries and the industry lore about "edge" encourage.[2]

Though a very different television show, *Chappelle's Show* (2003–2006) is remarkably similar to *The Boondocks* in the elements of edginess it incorporates, its concentration on black male identity, and its distribution and scheduling abroad. *Chappelle's Show* appeared on Comedy Central and targeted the same demographic as Adult Swim, specifically the eighteen-to-thirty-four—or more precisely, eighteen-to-twenty-four—male demographic, especially college-educated men, who are considered heavy consumers and trendsetters, and whom Nielsen Media began including in its audience ratings beginning in January 2007 (Nielsen Media, 2007; Story, 2007). Like *The Boondocks*, *Chappelle's Show* is carried on Comedy Central branded channels abroad, as well as local comedy channels, all of which target demographics similar to those of Comedy Central in the United States.

Christine Acham (2007) argues that *Chappelle's Show* effectively raises political and cultural issues important to African Americans, which are generally unavailable in other television programs, such as the arbitrariness and absurdity of racial definitions, the continuing plight of racism in America, the media's role in maintaining black stereotypes, and the rampant consumerism in some sectors of African American society. At the same time, Chappelle's preference for satirizing racial stereotypes and his reliance on "bathroom humor" (332), Acham worries, tend to blunt the show's political bite and make it appealing to otherwise racially insensitive, even racist, white male viewers. In addition, I would add, the vast majority of Chappelle's politically oriented skits address issues of concern to African American men. Unlike *The Boondocks*, however, Chappelle doesn't generally use women as foils or counterexamples; instead, they are typically absent from his skits. Basically, then, *Chappelle's Show* is able to appeal to a multiracial young male demographic by accentuating its appeal to masculinity through juvenile and prurient humor. Moreover, this model of multiracial male address fits the demands of cable programmers not only in the United States but abroad as well by expanding the audience beyond the typical white middle-class viewership that characterizes much general entertainment American fare.

The definitions of edginess that characterize *The Boondocks* and *Chappelle's Show*, along with their generic qualities, also make them particularly appealing to new television distribution platforms like mobile and online television networks. Even more than cable, the revenue models for these networks depend on reaching highly differentiated, multinational niche audiences. The problem with the adoption of mobile television—and of making money off Internet television—has long been one of content. In both settings, but particularly on mobile phones, viewers seem to watch in bursts no longer than three to five minutes. Consequently, the longer-form sixty- and thirty-minute traditional television series do not transfer well to the new technologies. In addition, bandwidth scarcity continues to dog mobile and online content, resulting in slow download speeds, high delivery costs, and poor image quality even in nations with the most highly developed Internet and mobile communications infrastructures. Given that the majority of heavy mobile and Internet video users are young people from relatively affluent backgrounds, these audiences are also the primary target of current mobile and Internet television networks, and the types of television programming that have worked best with this demographic are "extreme" sports shorts (e.g., cliff diving), fashion programs, pornography, music videos, and animation and comedy shorts. *The Boondocks*, though it is a conventional half-hour program, benefits from the fact that it is animated, and consequently uses less bandwidth than live-action series, especially given recent developments in flash-animation technology. Moreover, the series' use of short, encapsulated scenes, such as the clip of BET headquarters in "Hunger Strike" (two minutes and forty-one seconds) or Martin Luther King Jr.'s two-minute speech in "Return of the King," fits well with both the technological demands of mobile television and the ways viewers watch programming on their phones.

Online video consumption bears a good deal of similarity to mobile viewing at the moment: because of greater access to broadband at work rather than in the home, most viewing takes place on weekdays during business hours, and the average length of viewing time was 2.6 minutes in 2007 (comScore, 2007). *Chappelle's Show*, while not animated, is organized around short comedy skits that work well as online or mobile downloads. Thus, the edginess of sexual and juvenile humor and the frequent use of the word "nigger" mark these series as edgy enough to warrant downloading, while their generic organization into short "scene bites" fits the technological limitations of these new media and the ways they are customarily watched.

In 2008 the *Boondocks'* creator, Aaron McGruder, developed an online television channel on YouTube called *The Super Rumble Mixshow*, featuring live-action comedy skits reminiscent of *Chappelle's Show*, which again fit the technological and cultural demands of the online medium. As with *The Boondocks* and *Chappelle's Show*, *The Super Rumble Mixshow* is both ideologically and generically innovative. Adopting an ironic attitude toward issues of media stereotypes, American race relations, and African American culture itself, the clips include a send-up of a current-day "Black Jesus"; a segment entitled "Dear John Witherspoon," where the comedian sounds off on popular culture, the younger generation, white people, black people, and women; and fake current-affairs programming. The "Black Jesus" sketches are particularly interesting because they draw on a popular issue of debate and point of pride among African Americans, namely, the idea that Jesus of Nazareth might have been black. These satirical clips feature a present-day Jesus who hangs out with criminals, smokes marijuana, drinks malt liquor, and peppers his speech with words like "bitch" and "nigger." Still, the clips contain a good deal of humanity and social critique as well. In "Thugs for the Lord," for instance, after warning his pals against being "bitch-ass niggers" and complaining about only recently getting out of "county" jail, Black Jesus explains, "We go out and bust the devil's ass, my nigger, we need to quit killin each other, my nigger." This satirical treatment of media stereotypes of African Americans, extended even to the portrayal of what Jesus would be like if he were black and alive today, works simultaneously to critique such stereotypes and certain segments of the African American community that buy into them. At the same time, of course, a number of people worry about the degree to which satire works as an effective tool for combating stereotypes, arguing that such treatments simply reinforce stereotypical attitudes and images, rather than providing alternatives.

The question of the cultural politics of stereotyping and satire is a thorny one and, I believe, one that is highly context-dependent. Mel Watkins (1994), Henry Louis Gates Jr. (1989), Christine Acham (2004), and others, for instance, have argued that the satirical treatment of white stereotypes of African Americans has a long and progressive history in African American popular culture. Satire not only helps African Americans circulate the knowledge that such stereotypes are false, but also operates as a form of doublespeak that has helped keep alive African American resistance to white racism in the face of extreme oppression and violent threat. Moreover, as the race theorist David Theo Goldberg (1993) writes, one strategy for combating stereotypes is "to press and stress them so they collapse under their own connotative weight" (229). Certainly, this is at least part of the strategy of the Black Jesus clips here: to demonstrate how even Jesus must be made into a thug in order to fit the representational demands of the television medium. Nevertheless, as Stuart Hall (1996) reminds us, television comedy is always "two-dimensional and typecast. . . . a double-edged game in which it is impossible to ensure that the audience is laughing with, not at, the stereotype." Analyzing the cultural work of television comedy is, in other words, highly dependent on the intentions of the creator and the ways viewers receive programs.

Ultimately, I am convinced that the Black Jesus skits do demonstrate a degree of diversity in televisual representations of African American culture due to the combination of satire and straightforward social critique. Which of these gets privileged and ignored by viewers and whether the skits finally challenge racist ideas are, I believe, impossible to predict. Instead, I am interested in the ways technological and industrial forces, particularly globalization, have created the conditions where this form of representation becomes possible. Therefore, what intrigues me more than anything about *The Super Rumble Mixshow* is the degree to which it is similar to cable television featuring African American comedy, like *Chappelle's Show* and the short-lived *Chocolate News* (2008), starring David Alan Grier. All of these series take a satirical approach to stereotyped African American portrayals—what we might call black urban street culture—and include the edgy elements of drug use, sexual and excretory jokes, and adult language, especially the frequent use of the word "nigger."

Of course, the fact that current cable comedies are designed for online download helps explain why *The Super Rumble Mixshow* features skits of similar length. But the content itself owes to similar demographic targets and similar ideas about what will appeal to that demographic, regardless of whether viewers are watching online or on cable. That is, the main users of online television content are men aged eighteen to twenty-four and twenty-five to thirty-four (comScore, 2007), or the same demographic that television services such as Comedy Central and Adult Swim target both at home and abroad. Of course, it is impossible to tell the extent to which worldwide audiences are tuning in to watch clips such as Black Jesus; although the medium of the Internet is globally accessible, access, especially broadband access, is highly concentrated in North America, Europe, and the Far East. Moreover, unlike globally traded television programs, *The Super Rumble Mixshow* is only available in English, further restricting its likely foreign audience. Still the larger point that I want to make is that, as yet at least, Internet distribution has not led to representational innovations in the field of African American televisual portrayals, despite the medium's being inherently global and capable of circumventing the traditional gatekeepers of internationally traded African American television programs, including distributors, buyers, and programmers.

I want to conclude this section by briefly mentioning another online television series, *Orlando's Joint*, which sticks to cultural practices similar to *Super Rumble Mixshow*, but for reasons that I think are quite different. Syndicated through blip.tv, *Orlando's Joint* is an animated series that follows the antics of Orlando and his friends as they try to run a coffee shop after their boss dies. The boss, meanwhile, returns as a cockroach that only Orlando can hear, who offers encouragement and hurls insults. A flash-animation series using visual techniques similar to cutout animation, *Orlando's Joint* also incorporates a lesbian phone-sex worker, coarse language, and copious amounts of marijuana smoking. In other words, the demographic skew of the program and the way it targets those viewers—including rude jokes, satirical stereotypes, and adult language, especially frequent use of the word "nigger"

Figure 5.1. *Orlando's Joint* is a web series that hews closely to the aesthetics of "edge" for African American animation, as defined by the cable television industry.

—are remarkably similar to all of the current, edgy African American pro-gramming we have discussed so far. In fact the creator, Terence Anthony, draws direct parallels with edgy animated television when describing his inspiration for the series. "I wanted to do an edgy animated show—some-thing politically incorrect like *South Park* was—that spoke to the hip-hop generation," he explains.

In part, Anthony's desire to follow the conventional aesthetics of edginess may owe to his inability to think significantly differently about what might appeal to "the hip-hop generation" (Christian, 2009). More practically, how-ever, Anthony may be looking to get the series picked up by a cable network or to use the popularity of the web series to advance a more conventional television career. In explaining why he chose to syndicate the series online, Anthony says, "You're lucky if you get maybe two or three people who will read your screenplay and then they are usually people who are paid to say no unless you are truly established" (Alemoru, 2010). Knowing that network program developers are always on the lookout for popular programming, Anthony may be using *Orlando's Joint* as an attempt to establish himself as a credible television producer.[3]

Conclusion

Obviously globalization, channel fragmentation, and new delivery tech-nologies have increased the number and type of African American roles that appear on television sets and computer screens at home and abroad. Whether such increases lead to a broader diversity of ideological positions and effects than was the case with national broadcasting remains a difficult question to answer. In large part, this is the case because we have no good or agreed-upon standard among scholars as to what constitutes diversity. Is it diversity of types of roles, or is it diversity of genres, or is it something else? Certainly, television today features a wider range of African American char-acters, appearing in a wider range of genres, than at any time in the history of American television. Moreover, these images derive in part from the glob-alization of the television production industries and, as such, fit well with current trends toward globalization and fragmentation. In the final analy-sis, I consider it undeniable that these new developments have increased the diversity of African American voices in contemporary television. However, these voices are structured in dominance: they are all made possible by par-ticular economic and technological configurations, and some have wider dis-persion than others. In addition, while the scope of African American voices on television has widened, it remains highly limited, and some of the main limits on those expressions, as in earlier historical periods, are the institutional uses of those programs abroad and the industry lore that has developed to warrant those uses. In particular, the ways programmers at home and abroad imagine the appeal of African American women and their stories remain severely restricted.

6

Black Television from Elsewhere

The Globalization of Non-U.S. Black Television

In recent years the globalization of television production, the spread of comparatively cheap audiovisual production equipment, channel fragmentation, and various forms of digital video production and distribution have combined to increase the amount of television programming produced and distributed by black communities around the world. In this chapter I examine some of the ways the institutional labors and industry lore surrounding these non-American programs influence production practice elsewhere. What I aim for here is far from a comprehensive portrait of the diversity of black televisual practices worldwide, but rather an index of some of the primary ways that black television created—and often circulated—beyond the United States navigates the circuits of global commercial television, as well as the significance of those navigations for the cultural politics of the programs. I will argue that the proliferation of channels and digital distribution technologies has expanded the markets for non-American black television, sometimes accompanied by quite different industry-wide perceptions of programming and foreign viewers, which shape programming practice in quite different ways. At the same time, some elements of conventional industry lore persist even among non-American, nonwhite programmers, limiting the aesthetic and political range of these programs. While black television culture that does not fit sanctioned institutional uses and industry lore does continue to circulate, the business models of such productions are precarious.

Three case studies comprise this chapter: the first involves the animated New Zealand series *bro'Town*, which has enjoyed significant international circulation through both commercial and noncommercial programming circuits. The second case addresses the Nigerian videofilm industry known as Nollywood, which I include here because of its status as a cultural object that is both/neither film and television. Nollywood has grown to become the third-largest "film" industry in the world, and its products are distributed widely around the world, mostly through piracy and video stalls. Finally, we examine *Noh Matta Wat*, the first prime-time Belizean television series, which attracted devout viewers within and beyond Belize but faced significant funding challenges due to piracy, particularly in California. Together, these three cases demonstrate how contemporary black television programs travel, the types of funding arrangements and representational strategies that are and are not viable, the institutional labors that such programs perform, and the different forms of industry lore they produce.

"Kia Ora, World": Black New Zealanders, Specialty Channels, and Cultural Tourism

One of the most distinct elements of bro'Town, an animated New Zealand series, is its extensive use of highly local dialogue and cultural references. The first-season episode "A Māori at My Table," for instance, begins as all episodes do, in heaven, where we see Jesus trying to stop the Māori leader Hone Heke from chopping down heaven's flagpoles, a historical reference to the leader's rebellious act that helped lead to the Flagstaff War with Great Britain in 1845. When God, an Islander wearing a lava-lava skirt, appears, he chastises Jesus for his ignorance of Māori culture and tells him to watch the upcoming episode "and learn a few things about tangata whenua, or People of the Land." Produced by Firehorse Films, starring the Polynesian comedy troupe Naked Samoans, and funded through both commercial and noncommercial sources, bro'Town has been distributed to Australia, Fiji, the Cook Islands, Canada, the United States, Latin America, Africa, and Portugal. It provides a textbook example of the apparent contradiction inherent in a globalized, culturally specific text. However, an examination of the institutional labors of the program around the world and the industry lore that sustains them helps resolve this contradiction.

Classifying bro'Town as "black" might be seen as inaccurate or controversial, since the program features Polynesian teenagers living in the Morningside suburb of Auckland, New Zealand, who have no ancestral connection with Africa, and are generally not seen as members of the diaspora. Nevertheless, at least some of the Polynesian population of New Zealand, in particular members of the indigenous Māori people, have long found significant resonance with African American cultural and political movements. In addition, the master racial narratives and racist legal and cultural strategies that white New Zealand settlers deployed against the Māori borrowed heavily from American models, a fact that seems not to have been lost on the Māori, who used the rhetoric and politics of the African American civil rights and Black Power movements to counter legal exploitation. In other words, the Māori and other Polynesians have a long history of being racialized as an ethnic minority and excluded from New Zealand society; their experiences are similar to those of African Americans. Māori, in addition, tend to self-identify as "black," both politically and culturally. Consequently, a study of how a television series focused on an oppressed—and culturally specific—minority manages to navigate the commercial and cultural circuits of globalization touches upon the same theoretical questions engaged in throughout this book.

bro'Town is also decidedly not a Māori television series; it features a core group of five teenage boys, all of whom are of Polynesian decent. Only one character, Jeff da Māori, is Māori, while the others boys and their families have emigrated more recently. Still, all of the boys share similar skin colors, living conditions, and challenges in the largely white world of New Zealand. Written and acted by the all-male Polynesian comedy troupe Naked Samoans, bro'Town offers satirical portraits of both white and nonwhite New Zealanders from a nonwhite perspective; that is, white satirical portrayals of nonwhites have little place in the series. Thus, although the producer of the series claims that it "explores the New Zealand identity just as much (if not more) than the Pacific Island/Māori stuff" (Mitchell, 2009), I would argue that the exploration occurs from a decidedly nonwhite subject position.

The episode "A Māori at My Table" offers clear examples of the ethnic minority perspective of the series, as well as the ways the series remains anchored to local cultures. In addition, it demonstrates how the series appropriates elements of the globally successful adult animation genre in an effort to appeal to a global audience, as did the animated African American adult series The Boondocks, which we explored in the previous chapter.

The episode focuses on Jeff da Māori's trip with his classmates back to his ancestral "homeland," where he discovers that his favorite aunt, and leader of the community, has just died. Jeff is named the new leader and quickly becomes embroiled in a debate about whether to sell the land to Japanese businessmen who want to develop it into a mall. Uncomfortable with selling the land but unable to win over the other inhabitants, Jeff is visited by a spirit who reminds him of the ancient story that the whales will again return to Kia Ora Bay when the sacred noseflute is played in the proper location. Jeff finds he cannot play the noseflute to summon the whales, but his guitar does the job, and tourists immediately begin to show up to watch the whales, thus saving the land from development. The conclusion of the episode returns us to heaven, where Jesus and Hone Heke have reconciled, even as new disagreement breaks out between Jeff's dead aunt and the spirit who visited Jeff over which of her nephews she intended to leave in charge.

Both direct and ironic critiques of white New Zealanders, the New Zealand government, global capitalism, and white popular culture in general feature prominently in this episode, and mark it as coming from a decidedly nonwhite perspective. Lynn Grey, the boys' teacher and chaperone on their trip, is the main white character in the episode, and she is persistently mocked as a Māori-phile, especially through her efforts to incorporate Māori words into her speech and sleep with as many young Māori men as possible. The other white character, a South African immigrant boy named Joost, protests that he needs to carry a handgun on the trip in case "one of Jeff da Māori's relatives tries to rob me." In both cases, stereotypical views of whites about the Māori are mocked in a way that Māori culture is not, even as the Māori do not escape critique, as we will see below.

Meanwhile, the policies of the New Zealand government and their oppression of the Māori people are confronted more directly. This comes across most clearly in the two scenes featuring Jeff's aunt: in the first scene, a flashback to when Jeff left to move to Morningside, she explains that he has to leave because they have no more land for him to play on and tries to teach him to say "bloody thieving colonialists." When young Jeff can't say the phrase, she simply tells him to call them "Pākehās," which might translate into American English as something close to "whitey" or "honky." At the end of the episode, when we discover that Jeff was wrongly made the new leader of the people, the spirit protests that he has bad hearing because of "the poor standard of health care available to Māori."

The Japanese businessmen who want to buy and develop the Māori land represent the dangers of global capitalism for contemporary Māori, which they are able to thwart because of Jeff's faith in ancient Māori myths. However, another form of global capitalism, namely, tourism, is what ultimately saves the day. It is noteworthy, though certainly not surprising, that the creators of the series have a difficult time creating narrative closure without appealing to already existing political and economic options, rather than trying to imagine any radically new options for Māori cultural survival.

Finally, the episode's critique of white popular culture, specifically Hollywood, lampoons the conventional practice of using brown-skinned actors to play characters of a variety of ethnic backgrounds. One of Jeff's cousins, Cliff Curtis, is a Māori actor in Hollywood "who gets to act as Latin American drug dealers, terrorists, and Iraqi refugees." At the end of the episode, he proposes using the land to "build a drama school to teach Māori actors how to play other ethnic minorities in Hollywood movies." These comments serve as incisive, if somewhat commonplace, critiques of Hollywood's racial politics, at the same time that they require knowledge primarily possessed by the world's ethnic minorities, again positioning the series as a minority text.

Moreover, the critique also builds on shared, global minority experiences and knowledge.

While the episode reserves its most scathing critiques for white culture, Polynesian and Māori culture are also satirized, but the satire is balanced by more complex portraits of minority people and cultures. That complexity comes across most obviously in the boys' characters, as well as the generally respectful treatment of Māori culture that we perceive in the episode. However, Māori culture is portrayed as anything but idyllic. Perhaps most scandalously, Jeff and his buddies make frequent reference to the fact that he has "six dads," all of whom live with him and his mother. The series never makes clear whether Jeff's mother is involved in a polyandrous marriage, whether his "fathers" are mere lovers, or whether they are simply friends or family members. Still, the fact that Jeff's six dads are a satirical departure from expected social norms is quite clear, and is intended to poke fun at Māori sexual relationships.

The satirizing of both Polynesian and white New Zealander cultures can be read as an attempt to travesty all cultures and social norms, especially political correctness, and journalists and television professionals often take this position on the series. But bro'Town does not lampoon all groups equally, instead reserving its harshest criticism for white colonialist practices and mindsets, Christian religious elitism, and stereotypical portrayals of nonwhite people in Western cultural products, such as Hollywood films. In this way, bro'Town draws on a longer tradition of satirizing European colonialism, Christianity, and cultural stereotyping in Polynesian literature and storytelling (Keown, 2005). Moreover, satirical cultural practices such as these, which parody both dominant and minority groups, are common in minority comedy everywhere.

The pervasive use of satire combined with scatological humor also identifies bro'Town generically with the kinds of adult animation we discussed in the previous chapter. In the episode under analysis, for instance, in addition to the images of and references to Jeff's perpetually runny nose, we also witness a scene in which Pepelo Pepelo, the father of Vale and Valea and perpetual drunk, defecates in front of Mack's family, and we follow the excrement through the sewers until it reappears at the sewage treatment plant near Jeff's homeland. Scenes such as these have earned bro'Town comparisons to the ribald Comedy Central series South Park. Meanwhile, the series' mockery of adulthood, family, parenting, religion, school, and polite culture more generally have engendered comparisons to both South Park and The Simpsons. bro'Town is self-consciously aware of its lineage in the long history of

Figure 6.1. bro'Town, which focuses on the lives of five young
Polynesian men living in the Auckland, New Zealand, suburb
of Morningside, came to be known as "The Simpsons of the
South Pacific."

globally popular animated television series, though such allusions tend to
be far less common than in series such as *South Park* and *Family Guy*. Still,
in the present episode, one such allusion does appear when Jeff's cousin is
finally unmasked as a Japanese businessman, who complains, à la villains in
Scooby Doo, Where Are You! (1969–1972), "I'd have gotten away with it, too, if
it weren't for you meddling kids!" More than mere intertextual tributes, these
allusions to globally popular animated series also work to mark *bro'Town* as
a global television text.

bro'Town has been sold into eight foreign territories, including Australia, Canada, the Cook Islands, Fiji, Latin America, Portugal, South Africa/
Africa, and the United Sates. International syndication did not come immediately, but it did quickly become an important revenue stream. Adult animation in general is a pricey affair, and given the size of the New Zealand
market, *bro'Town*'s production costs were tough to cover, with the initial six
episodes running more than $300,000 NZD per half hour. Production fund-
ing came from a combination of public and private broadcasting funds and
extensive product placement, with New Zealand On Air kicking in $800,000
for the first season of the series and the commercial broadcaster TV3, with
assistance from the Canadian media conglomerate CanWest, providing the
remainder. Significant amounts of production work were outsourced to
animation houses in India, China, and the Philippines to help defray costs.
Despite its primarily domestic funding, however, *bro'Town* was a product of

media globalization from the beginning. The initial idea came from a meeting between a Nickelodeon executive from the United States, who had come to New Zealand looking for programming from the region, and the producer Elizabeth Mitchell, which led Mitchell to begin thinking about internationally marketable television program ideas. Indeed, Mitchell claims to have been thinking of international distribution from the beginning of the development process, even though international sales didn't begin until the series' second season (Lustyik and Smith, 2010; Mitchell, 2009).

bro'Town's buyers have ranged from general entertainment broadcasters to transnational cable channels to indigenous people's satellite networks. Consequently, the series performs a wide range of institutional labors, each of which exploits different textual potentialities. General entertainment buyers have been limited to the immediate geo-linguistic region, where cultural proximity seems to be the primary programming consideration. As initially proposed by Joseph Straubhaar (1991), the theory of cultural proximity holds that viewers will prefer domestic programming over imports, but that smaller nations that cannot afford to produce all of their own programming will tend to import from culturally and linguistically similar countries. Such was the case with bro'Town in Fiji and the Cook Islands, where the series aired on the main national broadcaster in the late evenings. As nations with a shared language, histories, and cultures, Fiji and the Cook Islands are natural cultural trading partners for the Polynesian population in New Zealand, and the fact that the series focused on five Polynesian teenagers certainly helped smooth the series' importation.

Australia, too, might seem like a natural trading partner for television programs like bro'Town, especially given the shared history of ethnic tension between indigenous people and white European settlers and a shared language culture. However, because Australia has a highly active television production industry with extensive exports of its own (Cunningham and Jacka, 1996), the major commercial broadcasters do not program many exports beyond Hollywood films and series. Consequently, bro'Town did not appear on general entertainment channels, but was imported by Foxtel's Comedy Channel and National Indigenous Television. On the Comedy Channel, bro'Town was surrounded by other indelicate and satirical adult cartoons such as South Park. In contrast to the institutional uses of the series by general broadcasters in Polynesia, the Comedy Channel exploited the satirical and scatological elements of bro'Town to position it as adult humor aimed at men in their late teens and early twenties. While such institutional uses do not erase the Polynesian and ethnic minority elements of the program, they do work to highlight the program's more juvenile aspects and address viewers as young men regardless of ethnicity, as opposed to members or onlookers of Polynesian culture in New Zealand. Buyers in other parts of the world positioned the series in similar ways, including SIC Radical in Portugal, an entertainment channel aimed at teenagers, and Cartoon Network Latin America, which reaches viewers in Argentina, Brazil, Chile, Colombia, Mexico, and Venezuela. In both of these cases, the series was programmed with other material that helped articulate it as the kind of "edgy" programming we discussed in the previous chapter.

However, the persistent use of local cultural allusions and linguistic terms in *bro'Town* distinguished it from efforts to downplay or erase those features in other kinds of programming. Together with the fact that *bro'Town* airs primarily on niche television channels, the highlighting of cultural difference in the text has led to an industry lore that favors the language of cultural translation over the language of cultural universalism. Rather than eliminating or downplaying the linguistic specificity of Polynesian youth in New Zealand, Firehorse Films has produced a *"bro'Town* Glossary" that it distributes to fans and importers to help them translate the series' dialogue into their own cultural frameworks. Moreover, scripts provided for translation are littered with definitions of specific phrases, cultural explanations, and character notes. For instance, a script from the episode "Go Home, Stay Home" contains the following footnotes for translators: "Tineke Bouchier = NZ game show hostess (1970s)—replace with anyone your audience will recognise"; "Taumaranui = name of a NZ town"; "This paragraph is Jeff's well-intentioned bastardization of a well-known Maori haka [or war chant/dance of challenge or defiance] because of his lack of Maoritanga [knowledge of things Maori]"; "Constable Bababiba desperately wants to be an actor and often misquotes lines from movies" (Firehorse Films, 2003).

Not surprisingly, questions about how to deal with the cultural specificity of *bro'Town* and how much confusion television audiences can tolerate became a prime topic of discussion when the series was translated into Spanish and Portuguese for Cartoon Network Latin America. Firehorse Films contracted with Miami-based Hola Entertainment to translate the series, with oversight from a script supervisor from Cartoon Network and frequent input from the producers. Email discussions between Firehorse Films, Hola, and Cartoon Network about the word *fa'afafine* offer an interesting glimpse into how these organizations negotiated cultural difference in order to translate the series into Latin American markets. In Samoan cultures, *fa'afafine* are boys who choose to be raised as girls and tend to live their lives as women, essentially representing a third gender category in those societies. In *bro'Town* the boys attend a community college whose principal is a *faʻafafine*, and Hola Entertainment contacted Firehorse Films about translating the word, initially suggesting "gay or transsexual." The producer at Firehorse Films, however, objected to this characterization, explaining that "*faʻafafine* has nothing to do with sex really" and insisting that the character in question was "definitely not gay." The representative from Cartoon Network conducted Internet research and suggested that *faʻafafine* are perhaps more like transsexuals, but the producer disagreed with this translation as well, because *faʻafafine* do not transition from one sex to another, but rather see themselves having always been female. Finally, the translators decided to leave the word as is, explaining, "After all, the series is a cultural journey." In an interview the producer Elizabeth Mitchell further explained that "we made the decision to leave Maori words 'un-translated' as they were embracing 'the cultural journey' we were embarking on" (Mitchell, 2009).

The idea that television trade and the viewing of imported programming are "cultural journeys" in which we learn about what is distinct not only in other cultures, but in our own as well, is a far cry from industry lore about universal values that transcend local cultures. What we see in this exchange and in Mitchell's comment is a different kind of industry lore that recognizes that cultural differences will always frustrate both the translation and viewing processes, and that both industry professionals and at-home viewers have to be willing to put up with such difficulties when it comes to importing television programs.

I would suggest that the discourse of cultural journeys is an emerging form of industry lore that originates, in part, from efforts to sell programming originated for a particular audience segment, especially audiences outside the conventional mainstream of Hollywood television, and to distribute and program such series for audiences in other parts of the world, particularly nonmainstream audiences. Broadcasters and DVD sellers have begun to refer to musical series, documentaries, and some culturally specific films about unfamiliar locales as "cultural journeys" (Birchall, 2007; Mayne, 2007).

Of course the discourse of cultural journeys is not a significant departure from the recognition among industry insiders of the appeal of African American youth culture in the 1990s, which helped stoke international sales of sitcoms like *The Fresh Prince of Bel-Air* and *Moesha*. In both instances, program merchants identify cultural difference as a positive textual feature for some viewers. What is different in the industry lore about cultural journeys is that it is a flexible metaphor that can apply to a range of programs as well as a more generalized acquisition strategy than earlier observations about African American youth series. The metaphor of the cultural journey permits both buyers and sellers to imagine television viewing as an encounter with difference, regardless of whether that difference is commodified, filtered, and packaged, and this reimaging of television viewers encourages programmers to value cultural difference.

While industry lore built around the cultural journey metaphor is arguably more tolerant, even encouraging, of the global circulation of minority programming, the cultural politics of the lore is more ambiguous, encouraging either a cultural tourism or a multicultural orientation depending on channel type and brand, programming practices, and the geopolitical power relations that exist among importing, exporting, and represented cultures. At Foxtel's Comedy Channel and Cartoon Network Latin America, *bro'Town* is surrounded by programming from Western nations, especially the United States, which features predominantly white cultural values. Such programming choices encourage comparison with Hollywood and the West in a way that tends not to challenge the supposed universality of Western values and aesthetics. One poster on an Australian discussion forum dedicated to the program complained, for instance, that *bro'Town is* "not even in the same league as *South Park*" (http://forums.whirlpool.net.au/forum-replies -archive.cfm/531328.html).

A similar form of cultural tourism got encouraged by the programming of the series in the United States, where it was available on the nonprofit satellite broadcaster Link TV. Link TV operates under the auspices of FCC regulations that require DBS providers to reserve 4 percent of their channel space for public service, noncommercial programming. *bro'Town* aired on Link TV at 8 P.M. Pacific Time (11 P.M. Eastern Time), sandwiched between world news and a documentary slot. It was one of the few non-news, non-cultural programs aired on Link TV. Consequently, Link TV's identity and programming do not invite the kinds of comparisons to Western programming that we saw above. Instead, the airing of *bro'Town* fits well the channel's slogan: "Television Without Borders." The mission of the channel is to "provide a unique perspective on international news, current events, and diverse cultures," and the importation of programming like *bro'Town* obviously fits this mission well. While such a goal is certainly laudable, Link TV comes only with a subscription to satellite television, which reaches less than 30 percent of the U.S. market, and which charges significantly more for basic service than cable television does. As a result, Link TV's viewers tend to be economically and culturally privileged, and the channel can encourage the kind of Eurocentric cultural tourism that bell hooks (1992) has called "eating the other," or a desire to consume difference in an effort to "spice up" the "dull dish that is mainstream white culture" without really challenging the assumptions of white supremacy (21). In other words, it is very easy for privileged white viewers to watch shows like bro'Town on Link TV and feel connected with the rest of the world, superior to their compatriots, but still never question their own privilege or cultural values.

By contrast, indigenous people's broadcasting networks that aired bro'Town program it in a way that encourages more comparative, multicultural orientations among viewers. These networks include NITV in Australia and the Aboriginal People's Television Network (APTN) in Canada. In both cases, bro'Town appears alongside television programs of various genres that feature indigenous cultures and people in both domestic and foreign lands. Although the majority of both channels' program schedules are made up of domestic indigenous programming, they also rely on imports, specifically imports that "have Aboriginal content, deal with Aboriginal issues and feature actors, directors or producers who are of Aboriginal descent," including "Indigenous Peoples from around the globe" (http://www.aptn.ca/corporate/producers/acquisitions.php). The presence onscreen of television programs from both domestic and international indigenous peoples provides what I would argue is a significant multicultural experience, articulating quite different notions of global cultural trade than mainstream television exchanges. Not only do such exchanges force programmers to actively think through the kinds of cultural resonances that imported programming might have, in a far more deliberate manner than simple assumptions about universal themes, they also allow programmers and viewers to consider global indigenous cultures side by side, including not only their differences but also the kinds of cultural-adaptive strategies that might be common to a range of indigenous minorities from around the world.

Collectively, the different institutional uses of bro'Town abroad fit with an emerging industry lore that views television exchange as a form of cultural journey. Both the cultural-tourist and multicultural uses of the programming fit well into this broad discourse of the cultural journey. While such industry lore in no way guarantees free, respectful, or equal exchanges of cultural programming among diverse populations of the world, it does facilitate a more complex way of thinking through cultural exchange among television insiders than does the mainstream industry lore about universal themes. Still, the producers of bro'Town have packaged Polynesian New Zealander culture into a globally recognizable format in order to increase the variety of institutional uses it can perform abroad, even as they champion an industry lore that is more accommodating of the kinds of cultural specificity that also mark the program.

Nollywood Videofilms and Illicit Global Flows

Since the 1990s, Nigerian videofilms have taken the global film industry and academia by storm. Shot on cheap videotape, often in a week or less, these "Nollywood" videofilms occupy an ontological space somewhere between films and television: like films, they are usually one-off stories, not episodic, and they are often watched in public theatres; like television, they are also frequently consumed in the home, and the history of the industry owes a good deal to the collapse of domestic television production, where many of the earliest directors, producers, and actors had cut their teeth. Nollywood, then, is relevant to our inquiry because it is the most prominent example of a transnational exchange in audiovisual culture that takes place almost exclusively through parallel economic markets. In contrast to legitimate markets, the distinction between television and film in parallel markets is almost meaningless, because both types of commodities get distributed and consumed in similar ways. In many respects, the Nollywood example suggests radically different kinds of diasporic and minority cultural exchanges than what we have encountered thus far, amounting to a highly disorganized market where the concepts of institutional labor and industry lore have little applicability. Practically speaking, this means that foreign media industry professionals and viewers have very little impact on the domestic production of Nollywood videofilms, although the videofilm trade also shows signs of becoming more organized and legitimized. As this and the following section detail, parallel economies do permit quite different kinds of programming to circumnavigate the globe, but those exchanges are predicated on a domestic market that is large enough to sustain production independently.

Unlike the other television programs we have explored in this volume, Nollywood is an entire industry that accounts for a wide variety of titles and genres of videofilm. Thus, it is impossible to tackle the entirety of the texts that Nollywood produces or the variety of foreign cultural and institutional contexts within which those texts get consumed. Instead, I have chosen to focus on a single instance of transnational exchange of Nollywood videofilms with the Caribbean islands, specifically St. Lucia. This example highlights how Nollywood exchanges work to articulate cultural resonances that fall well outside the legitimate television exchanges we have analyzed so far, at the same time that they lack transnational feedback among viewers, importers, and producers of Nollywood films.

Legend has it that Nollywood was born when a film producer and businessman found himself with an abundance of blank videotapes, and began taping Yoruba theatre performances and selling them at local markets. Since that time, Nigerian film production has blossomed into a global economic and cultural force, producing more than a thousand films bringing in revenues of more than $50 million, making Nollywood either the first or third film production center in the world, depending on which yardstick one uses (Okome, 2007). Nollywood films are popular not only in the domestic market, but throughout the Global South and, increasingly, the North, as they compete alongside Hollywood and Bollywood films on the tables of pirate street vendors in cities around the world. For some observers, Nollywood is the epitome of "vernacular globalization" (Appadurai, 1996, 10), or globalization from below, as opposed to the universalizing globalization from above that is associated with the kinds of transnational corporations we have examined thus far (Adejunmobi, 2007; Okome, 2007).

Despite the fact that Nollywood films find their way into markets as diverse as the Ivory Coast, Lebanon, and New York City, the industry remains highly localized in terms of both content and production funding. For this reason, despite Nollywood's wide global distribution, very little trade in ideas and discourse takes place among participants in the transnational value-chain. Instead, industry lore remains highly local and disorganized. Thus, while Nollywood films undoubtedly serve as a prominent example of diasporic audiovisual trade, they are nevertheless transnational cultural products primarily in terms of their *distribution* rather than their *production*. That is, consideration of foreign viewers and industries in Nollywood's production practices are minimal, given their disorganized transnational markets and their predominantly local sources of revenue. In essence, while Nollywood films do serve a variety of institutional uses abroad, the absence of a global business culture prevents the formation of industry lore about those uses, and those transnational institutional processes consequently fail to influence representational practices in Nollywood films. For this reason I would characterize Nollywood videofilms as national cultural products with transnational appeal, rather than products of transnational media exchange.

Certainly Nollywood videofilms pick up and rework a wide range of global cultural material, ranging from local stories to Hollywood genres, into a postcolonial, postmodern bricolage of narrative and filmmaking practices that resonate deeply with abject city dwellers in Lagos and beyond. In many ways, Nollywood videofilms are the products of a long history of trade and exploitation that ranges across centuries (Larkin, 2008). Shot mostly in Yoruba, English, and Hausa, videofilms have a natural linguistic market that extends well beyond the borders of Nigeria, and its English-language variants have potential markets across the world, thanks to the legacy of both

British and American colonialism (Adejunmobi, 2007). Thematically, videofilms also exhibit the twin histories of colonialization and globalization:
Christianity is a common theme, especially tensions between Christian and
indigenous religious practices, as is the vulnerability of abject urban poverty
at the fringes of capitalist modernity. In addition, the industry itself has more
direct origins in global cultural trade. According to Fidelis Duker, president of the Director's Guild of Nigeria, Nollywood developed because of the
cancellation of domestic television production in Nigeria in favor of cheap
Hollywood imports. Writers, directors, producers, and technical staff who
were laid off after this change turned to videofilm as an alternative (Sacchi
and Caputo, 2009).

Onookome Okome (2007) has identified the main genres of Nollywood
film as "the city video film, which also has as a subgenre, the occult video;
the epic video with its narrative locus on historical subjects rather than on
the dimension of the history engaged in; the hallelujah video and the comic
video" (7). All of these genres seem to transfer equally well abroad, although
the occult video and the hallelujah video are perhaps the best-known genres.
These genres share relatively modest technical standards, by Hollywood's
standards; melodramatic narrative and generic features; a reliance on the
Nollywood star system; highly current political references, made possible by
their short production schedules; and a focus on the lives and predicaments
of the world's abjectly poor urban inhabitants (Adejunmobi, 2007; Okome,
2007). Industrial considerations, in particular the threat that piracy poses
to profits and more conventional efforts to reduce risk, encourage some of
the textual practices. Specifically, the use of current political references gives
these films a short shelf life, which creates urgency among viewers to see the
newest films, and helps blunt the appeal of cheaper, downstream, pirated
copies. Moreover, the star system is a conventional commercial adaptation
that seeks to use a small number of highly recognizable actors to reduce the
uncertainties and risks involved with trying to create popular cultural commodities (Hesmondhalgh, 2000).

Piracy accounts for a good deal of the Nollywood film industry within
Nigeria, and is almost exclusively responsible for the global circulation of
Nollywood films. Consequently, Nigerian film directors and producers

> create their film narratives with the aim of making an immediate impres-
> sion on a local and national audience upon release of the film. In other
> words, and despite the fact that many Nigerian video films achieve cir-
> culation on a transnational scale, film directors and producers impelled
> both by professional and commercial considerations, work with national

audiences in mind and create narratives crafted to respond first and fore-most to the perceived interests and shifts in orientation of national publics. (Adejunmobi, 2007, 11)

Importantly, the national elements of the videofilms do not substantially block their potential cultural resonances within the West African region, due to the fact that linguistic, cultural, and trading communities do not neatly fit the national borders of postcolonial Africa (Adejunmobi, 2007). Further-more, these tales of abjection, alienation, and survival speak to millions of the world's poor as well. Only rarely do considerations of viewers outside the immediate local and national context figure into videofilm production decisions, and these seem to be more about trying to develop reputations abroad that might one day lead to sales or production opportunities, rather than immediate revenues (Adejunmobi, 2007). Of course, such drives to develop the reputation of Nollywood abroad can certainly have long-term financial consequences, as Nollywood becomes a lingua franca for the video culture of the dispossessed. However, the immediacy of parallel economies such as those that animate Nollywood do not favor such long-term industrial strategies, making efforts to incorporate the tastes of foreign viewers and needs of foreign industries into domestic production decisions disorganized and infrequent.

Once completed, Nollywood films are duplicated on DVD, VCD, and VHS, screened at viewing parlors, and sold by video stores and street ven-dors. Piracy begins almost immediately, and the producers and directors of the films have no way to track pirated sales or receive compensation from illicit sales. Pirated duplicate copies of Nollywood films, particularly those with wide popular appeal in Nigeria, follow the trade routes of the parallel economy, transported abroad by trucks, boats, human beings, and beasts of burden. Videofilms are duplicated two, three, or more times on their way to their final destination abroad. All of this travel and reduplication takes time and money, which is what prevents Nollywood from getting directly involved and trying to make money from international sales: while the time lag associated with piracy gives Nollywood a small window in which to make money off new releases, in international markets the time difference between legitimate and pirated copies disappears. Moreover, the immediacy of the political references of Nollywood films, which are likely to elude foreign viewers, eliminates the market advantage that the newest releases enjoy over slightly less new releases.

None of these observations blunt the cultural significance of Nollywood as a transnational phenomenon, but they do demonstrate that efforts to think race beyond the confines of the nation-state are not a significant part of what goes on in Nollywood. Nollywood may force cultural theorists to confront transnational aspects of race and culture, but it does not force businesspeople to do so. Similarly, the uses of Nollywood videos among street vendors demonstrate little need to consider such issues in order to turn a profit. While it still makes sense to think in terms of the institutional labors of Nollywood videofilms abroad, those labors tend to occur without much reference to the content of the programming or reflection on whether and why imported Nollywood videofilms resonate with buyers.

The example of Nollywood films in the Caribbean offers an example of the kinds of cultural resonance that videofilms activate, and the relationship between those resonances and the institutional practices of street vendors and duplicators. One observer estimated than 80 percent of pirated music and videodiscs on the market in St. Lucia came from Nigeria. Videodiscs are typically shipped first to Europe, then via Guyana to the Caribbean, with duplicators making and selling additional copies at each stop (Cartell, 2007). For instance, one of the Nollywood videodiscs that Philip Cartell (2007) examined in St. Lucia had been stamped with the names of duplication houses in both Guyana and St. Lucia. Little is known about these duplication houses, but they seem to trade primarily in the most popular Nollywood videofilms. Street vendors, meanwhile, have limited table space to devote to video- and audiodiscs, especially considering that they carry not only Nollywood films, but films from Bollywood and Hollywood as well. All of these discs are pirated and of similar quality, which tends to take away the technological edge that Hollywood—and even Bollywood—enjoys over Nollywood, and places Nollywood videofilms on a more level playing field with other national competitors than they would have if consumers were viewing pristine copies in multiplexes (Adejunmobi, 2007).

For good reason, street vendors keep their ears close to the ground when finding out about both the most popular new releases and their customers' preferences. Informal conversation with distributors and customers gives these street vendors a good sense of some of the cultural resonances that customers find in Nollywood films. For instance, street vendors in St. Lucia explain that while hallelujah videos, which often feature traditional religions as evil, are popular among their customers, occult videos that treat magic and the occult more sympathetically are not. The reasons for the difference, street vendors explain, is that local audiences tend to be far more Christian and religious than their Nigerian counterparts (Cartell, 2007).

Cartell (2007) notes a range of other resonances that Nollywood films have with Caribbean culture, including the common heritage of British imperialism that gave them a shared language, the tension between urban and rural values, the experience of abjectness, and the coexistence of Christian and traditional religions. As with other instances of commercial trade in black television, the Nollywood example demonstrates how only certain kinds of resonances filter back to domestic program providers. Certainly a good deal of informal conversation occurs among customers, street vendors, duplicators, and, ultimately, producers and directors. To some extent, these street vendors and duplicators fulfill a cultural-interpretive role, as they select from available options which videofilms to reproduce or feature on their tables. However, the absence of financial incentives to produce for Caribbean markets and the absence of more formal channels of communication among vendors, duplicators, and producers prevent the formation of transnational business networks that need to think through the questions of West African and Caribbean cultural resonance in any active manner. Consequently, while religious similarities seem to be an important site of cultural convergence among Christians in Nigeria and the Caribbean, the kinds of connections that might exist among traditional religions in both locations, and the role that Nollywood occult videofilms might play in activating those resonances, remain unexplored.

Of course, the kinds of diasporic cultural trade that we see in Nollywood videofilms do not escape the attention of legitimate economic actors for very long, nor is the line between parallel and legitimate economies clearly drawn. In fact, television seems to be a prime site of intersection between these two economies, at least in part because of Hollywood's domination of movie screens everywhere. In St. Lucia, for instance, the popularity of Nollywood films began when a local television station broadcast the occasional videofilm (Cartell, 2007). More recently, the U.S. direct-to-home satellite service Dish Network began carrying Afrotainment, a digital channel that features Nigerian and Ghanaian films. We see here both a recognition by legitimate television providers of the pirate trade in Nollywood films and the beginnings of business practices that promise to reshape transnational industry lore surrounding black and African television and film programming. Afrotainment's stated mission, to "[redefine] how African entertainment is consumed on Live Television in North America," might also apply to perceptions of African audiovisual culture among industry insiders in the United States and beyond.

Nollywood remains, nevertheless, a nationally self-sufficient videofilm market, and cannot work as a more general model for transnational trade in black audiovisual culture. In fact, as we shall see in the following section, the very technical realities and parallel economies that permit Nollywood to achieve transnational circulation can undermine the development of other kinds of diasporic television flows that do not originate from a self-sustaining domestic market.

Noh Matta Wat and the Fate of Television Culture in Small Nations

Premiering in 2005, *Noh Matta Wat* was the first and, thus far, the only dramatic television series ever produced in Belize. Focusing on the lives of the largely matriarchal Diego family, including grandmother Miss Tomasa, her daughter, Margaret, and her grandchildren, Lisani and Randy, *Noh Matta Wat* is a multistory melodrama that is generically similar to the daytime soap opera in the United States, except that the series was broadcast weekly for most of its run. Over the course of its three seasons, the series underwent a good deal of change behind and in front of the camera, and always struggled to secure production funding. Much like the actors in Nollywood videofilms, the actors in *Noh Matta Wat* worked for minimal wages and held down regular full-time jobs, as did many of the creative and technical staff. Unlike Nollywood videofilms, however, business models for making *Noh Matta Wat* profitable did not exist in Belize. Part of the strategy the executive producer Denvor Fairweather employed relied on DVD sales in Belize, which were undermined by piracy at home and abroad. Despite efforts to fight piracy by contracting with distributors in Belize, the Caribbean, and the United States, pirating of episodes ultimately led to the cancellation of the series after an abbreviated third season (Berry, 2009).

The first season's episodes of *Noh Matta Wat* began with brief history lessons from Miss Tomasa, signaling the importance of history, education, and elders in Belizean society. In the premiere episode, for instance, we meet Miss Tomasa in the kitchen cooking, when a young child arrives and scatters a folder of pictures and newspaper clippings on the ground. After scolding the child, Miss Tomasa beckons to him and shows him her "granny archives," which include a funeral announcement for Philip Stanley Wilberforce Goldson, a Belizean politician and nationalist from the days of British colonialism, leading to an extended remembrance of his historical importance and famous sayings. This framing device not only offers viewers lessons about Belize, but also distinguishes the series from the mostly American television programming that floods Belize's airwaves. In other words, the series was both thematically and aesthetically uniquely Belizean.

A range of other textual and thematic features identifies the series as distinctively Belizean. Narratively, the series is structured around a series of tensions between different sectors of Belizean society. Though not distinct to Belize, these tensions do manifest themselves with specific reference to that nation's society, history, politics, and culture. Gender differences provide a good deal of the narrative tension in the series. In fact, one of the narrative arcs that spans the entire first season involves Lisani's father, Steve, who left Margaret to find his fortune in the United States, and returns in the first episode to unwittingly try to seduce his own daughter; he is shot to death in the second episode. Infidelity and incest are recurring melodramatic themes, particularly in serialized television narratives, but the character of the rich American immigrant (or, in this case, the recently returned Belizean expatriate) who tries to seduce young women by extravagant spending gives a distinctly local flavor to this long-standing human conflict.

Not surprisingly, the dangers of seduction loom large for the young women of *Noh Matta Wat*, both threatening and intriguing them. But again, these dangers appear in distinctly local ways. Lisani, for instance, is an excellent student with dreams of attending an American university on scholarship. Margaret, the ever-vigilant mother, sees passion as the primary barrier to Lisani's fulfillment of those dreams, and enforces strict rules and curfews. Of course, worries about the chastity of young women are rampant around the world, but in this instance they threaten Lisani's education, rather than notions such as her virginity or family honor, as might be the case in other cultures. These issues do not come into play in concerns about Lisani's sexuality; in fact, Lisani's best friend, Rosana Ramirez, a Spanish immigrant, does act more aggressively on her sexuality, and the only criticism that she endures is that she is too immature and self-indulgent. Chastity, then, is not treated as an end in itself in *Noh Matta Wat*, but as a means of staying focused on one's goals.

Still, tensions between Margaret and her children are distinguishable along gender lines, and the dangers facing young men are portrayed as quite different from those that threaten young women like Lisani. Margaret's son, Randy, is a teenager with obvious musical talents but limited commitment to school. In the premiere episode, for instance, he skips school to get performance tips at a local recording studio from Dan Man, a popular Belizean performer. Later that day he continues playing hooky with a couple of young men in the courtyard of a dilapidated building, improvising drum lyrics and drum beats on an old pail. Randy's truancy enrages his mother, which Miss Tomasa tries hard to soothe by explaining that Randy has talent, that he is studying and participating in the cultural heritage of his nation, and that he is not doing drugs or committing crimes. Again, concerns about young boys, especially boys of color in urban surroundings, falling into crime and drugs are pervasive. However, whereas black popular music is often treated as an entrée to that world, while education is presented as salvation, *Noh Matta Wat* insists on the importance and integrity of cultural expression for the Belizean people. This endorsement of Randy's musical pursuits comes across most strongly in the arguments between Miss Tomasa and Margaret, where Miss Tomasa's belief that Randy should follow his heart is treated as more rational than Margaret's insistence that he succeed in school. Put another way, Randy's musical dreams are treated as just as appropriate as Lisani's educational dreams. The presence of Dan Man playing himself in the series demonstrates both the appropriateness and respectability of such popular musical endeavors.

The tension between Margaret and her children represents a more general tension within the series between tradition and modernity. Again, this tension draws on local issues to stage the conflict, specifically rural-urban and generational divides. *Noh Matta Wat* takes place in Belize City, the largest urban center in the country. Miss Tomasa emigrated to Belize City from Punta Gordo, a fishing village of six thousand, when she was young, and she retains much of the wisdom and ways of rural Belizean life. Margaret, by contrast, is a city dweller, as are her children. However, the family represents an effort to negotiate the traditional values of the village in the urban setting of the modern city, and the primary tension between rural and urban pits the family against outsiders. In some ways, this structure can be read as a conservative endorsement of traditional family values, but it is important to note that the family that is privileged is multigenerational, matriarchal, and anything but idealized. The three women of the Diego family represent the clash between rural and urban, tradition and modernity. Miss Tomasa represents the traditional rural, Lisani the modern urban, and Margaret a halfway point between the two, trying to reconcile traditional values with modern life. While Miss Tomasa is the guardian of history, tradition, and Belizean folk culture, Lisani is the future, thoroughly modern in her dress, her dreams, and her independence. Neither Tomasa nor Lisani, however, is the main character: Margaret is. Margaret lives in the modern, urban world, trying to raise two children on her own and maintain her own small business, a lunch and snack shack, while clinging to her mother's values. She values the modern institution of education over the traditional institutions of folk culture, but reverts to traditional forms of corporal punishment when her son forsakes the former for the latter. She is an independent businesswoman, but committed first and foremost to her family, including her mother and children. Her life was, in essence, nearly ruined by modernity when Steve left her with child and went to the United States, but circumstances require that she

Figure 6.2. A transition shot in *Noh Matta Wat* utilizes Belize's natural beauty in between scenes.

remain in the modern world. This tension between tradition and modernity is, of course, common throughout the world, but it manifests in *Noh Matta Wat* in ways that are specific to Belize and similar societies.

A number of other elements in the series also identify the series as distinctly Belizean. First, *Noh Matta Wat* is shot in Belizean Creole, which is difficult to understand not only for North Americans, but also for other nearby cultures who speak different Creoles. Second, politics plays an important backdrop for the series' storylines, as a corrupt, fictional party comes to power in the country. Political corruption has become commonplace in Belize, and, despite the series' efforts to fictionalize the corrupt party, the series still drew the ire of the ruling government when it was aired. Finally, two subtle elements of Belizean culture also mark this series: the presence of Belizean food, including chirmole soup, rice and beans, and coconut milk; and extensive use of sky and sea shots to transition between scenes (see fig. 6.2).

Noh Matta Wat was an expensive program by Belizean standards. Production costs for season 1, which included one one-hour and four half-hour episodes, ran about $30,000, while advertising rates at the time were about $300 for a thirty-second spot. To break even, then, the series would have needed to include about fifty minutes of advertising time, or nearly one-third of total air time. One strategy that executive producer Denvor Fairweather employed to help defray these costs was to broadcast the series initially on Monday evening on Channel 5, the main broadcaster in Belize City, then rebroadcast later in the week on Channel 7 and KREM TV, both of which are smaller in viewership and reach. While this arrangement helped generate revenues beyond the first broadcast window, the size of the channels and the fact that episodes were rebroadcast meant that advertising revenues were far below $300 per spot. Given the fact that these broadcasters primarily reach Belize City and the surrounding areas, broadcasters and cable channels in the north and south of the country would have also made good prospects, but Fairweather was concerned that releasing broadcast-quality copies to these outlets might have led to piracy and cut into eventual DVD profits (Berry, 2009).

Fairweather, then, knew from the outset that some form of foreign revenue would be necessary to fund production, but he seems to have relied primarily on DVD sales—a decision that would come back to haunt him. Still, few efforts seem to have been made to take foreign viewers into consideration during production. Most obviously, despite the idiosyncrasies of Belizean Creole, Fairweather and writers insisted on shooting exclusively in the local language without subtitles. Nevertheless, *Noh Matta Wat* found a willing market in the Caribbean. The series was sold to the transnational satellite channel Caribvision, which is broadcast throughout the Caribbean and, until 2008, the United States via DirecTV. It also appeared on Jamaican Public Television. The alternative broadcaster Hama TV in Antigua and Barbados expressed interest, but never secured the series (Berry, 2009).

Bootlegged copies, meanwhile, appeared quickly in cities around Belize, the Caribbean, and the United States, and seem to have undermined Fairweather's plan to make back production costs through DVD sales. While this was a predictable scenario, and one that Fairweather could have avoided by more aggressively pursuing sales to legitimate television outlets at home and abroad, it is also a testament to the challenges of developing an effective business plan for a transnational television series in the contemporary era. Regardless, these bootlegged copies drastically reduced legitimate sales. In fact, vendors began selling bootlegged copies of season 2 before Studio 13 Productions released the official DVD. The producers managed to release a third season of the series, with the number of episodes drastically scaled back from their original plans, but *Noh Matta Wat* disappeared thereafter from Belizean television, despite the fact that it remained a popular show.

The case of *Noh Matta Wat* demonstrates the viability of television programming developed within and circulated throughout the African diaspora and beyond. Certainly the cultural basis for such exchanges has been well established by other forms of popular culture, by scholars, and by programs such as *Noh Matta Wat*. The possibilities for distinct portrayals of racial identity and blackness to develop through such exchanges, and their potential impact on industry lore and production practices beyond the diaspora are exciting. Ironically, the vast parallel markets in audiovisual culture that have propelled Nollywood videofilms to global prominence have diminished the prospects for such exchanges to develop more broadly.

Conclusion

While African American television is undoubtedly the dominant form of black television globally, it is far from the only type that gets produced and distributed around the world. In fact, as we have seen, a range of technological and institutional developments since the turn of the millennium has encouraged the production and circulation of non-American programming that addresses the cultural specificities of the world's minorities. Among these changes are the fragmenting of audiences and channels, especially the rise of channels targeting ethnic minorities or nonwhite audiences in the Global South; the spread of cheap production and postproduction video equipment; and the growth of commercial television in nearly every corner of the globe. These developments have diversified the types of institutional labors that black television can perform for broadcasters around the world, as well as the forms of industry lore that derive from and sustain those labors. In particular, there may be emerging a discourse about television viewing as a cultural journey that embraces cultural difference, as opposed to earlier forms of industry lore that denied difference and instead appealed to universal themes. At the same time, such embracing of cultural difference does not guarantee respect; instead, as we have seen, it can replicate the same kinds of titillation and sense of privilege that have long marked relationships between white Westerners and others.

Despite the greater openness to ethnic, cultural, and linguistic diversity among the world's television programmers, even in North America, standardized representations of audience makeup among advertisers and standardized global channel brands designed for those audiences work to homogenize certain elements of content, particularly elements of genre and content associated with "edginess." In fact, the similarities between the New Zealand minority series bro'Town and the U.S. series South Park are quite stunning, and certainly are the product of contemporary industrial practices. Black television programming that bucks these conventions can certainly cultivate popularity and cultural significance around the world, but rampant digital piracy makes it all but impossible to develop transnational business models that make such programming viable. Instead, program producers must find ways to make their industry sustainable through domestic sales only, and hope for the day when the popularity of their programming might attract legitimate foreign buyers, as is the case with Nollywood videofilms. This analysis does not deny the political and cultural significance of these illegitimate programming flows, but it does suggest that those flows cannot significantly influence more dominant flows without the kinds of institutional backing that dominant flows enjoy.

Conclusion

Transnational Televisual Aesthetics and Global Discourses of Race

The circulation of culture predates the formation of nations, and probably only a small fragment of the world's cultural exchanges ever travels through the formal circuits of commercial media institutions. The other, unsanctioned, spontaneous exchanges originate in highly localized and communitarian impressions of cultural similarity and difference, allure and repulsion. Though undoubtedly shaped by the forces of history, xenophobia, and the bloody rivalries between nations, the exchanges initiated outside the formal logics of modern institutions tend to be more idiosyncratic, more impressionistic, and less consciously theorized than the kinds of exchanges that emanate from commercial institutions.

The exchanges in black and African American television we have considered here constitute highly institutionalized exchanges. The argument of this volume is not that these are the most interesting or even, politically, the most important exchanges. They are, however, distinct from the more idiosyncratic kinds of exchanges that less organized and less formalized exchanges give rise to. They are also dominant practices: much as the circulation of white European culture and Christendom during the eighteenth century did not *determine* non-European identities, perceptions, and cultures, but did nevertheless *confront* those people and cultures, so the commercial media exchanges of today produce representations of distant and nearby cultures that confront viewers everywhere, participating in shaping worldwide perceptions of self, other, and the planet we inhabit.

Industry Lore and/as Racial Discourse

The argument that has underwritten all of the chapters of this book is the belief that television trade includes more than the circulation of programs, genres, and formats: it also entails the sharing of ideas, strategies, textual readings, perceptions of viewers, and perspectives on the medium, the world, and humanity at large that together form what we might call institutionalized discourse—or institutionalized *discourses*—of race in the contemporary world. These discourses emanate from the institutional labors that programming accomplishes for broadcasters around the world, and proliferate at the

three moments of interface that we have examined here: between producers and executives, between international buyers and sellers, and between
broadcasters and viewers.

We have referred throughout this volume to the discourses that circulate
among industry insiders as industry lore, a term that means to call attention to the status of these discourses as knowledge that produces real material effects in the industry, even as it is primarily a product of the collective
imaginations of television executives, which are nevertheless shaped by the
material conditions within which they work and the historical processes that
influence their perspectives. Industry lore does not form in a vacuum, nor
is it independent of the material processes of the industry; instead, it is part
and parcel of those processes, as much a material force as patterns of transnational channel ownership or international intellectual property regimes.
It is at the intersection of regulatory, macroeconomic, microeconomic, and
cultural forces that industry lore forms and gathers its authority to shape
television's worldwide circulation patterns and representational politics.

Industry lore works as an interpretive frame that makes the chaos of global
cultural interactions appear manageable and predictable, identifying which
genres, programs, actors, ideologies, and aesthetics have the capacity to
overcome differences of nation and language and appeal to foreign viewers.
Consequently, industry lore is a carrier of other discourses that are embedded within the representational regimes of specific television shows. While
only theoretically distinguishable from the popular discourses that also drive
the global circulation, meaning, and uptake of televisual representations of
blackness, industry lore selects from and processes popular phenomena in
ways that are institutionally useful. Thus, a study such as this, which centers
on the development, circulation, and consequences of industry lore, cannot
hope to account for the complex and diverse impact of globally traded black
television. Instead, what I have intended to do in this volume is to sketch out
some of the dominant ways the industry lore arising from popular practices
shapes the flows, uses, representations, and markets for contemporary black
and African American television.

Industry lore is, as we have seen, a consequence of a very particular form
of textual exegesis, one designed to minimize risks and increase profits. Brokers, buyers, and programmers around the world engage in such exegeses as
they try to leverage foreign cultural expressions into local cultural contexts
in ways that not only make sense, but will also prove compelling enough to
draw and hold viewers' interests. We have referred to the ways foreign buyers bend imported television to their own needs as the institutional labors of
those programs. In the 1970s and 1980s, these labors had at least as much to

do with the immediate local political and cultural landscape as they did with the properties of the texts themselves or aims of distributors. Thus, the Hungarian public broadcaster could use the imported television miniseries *Roots* to navigate its conflicting status as a public service broadcaster and a party mouthpiece, while the antigovernment Bop-TV in South Africa could use integrated American situation comedies to cobble together segments of the viewing public in ways that challenged conventional apartheid-era divisions.

As the transnationalization of television program markets, channels, and organizational configurations began to grow in the late 1980s, so did the business culture of global television, through shared industry gatherings, trade journals, training courses, and the like. The result of this continuing globalization has been the production of a transnational interpretive community of industry insiders who now look to one another to produce industry lore about what audiences find appealing in television and why. This does not mean that transnational industry lore is monolithic; rather, it means that broadcasters and producers of all kinds today look beyond national boundaries for their understandings of television trends, audiences, and pleasures.

The institutional labors of imported television programs emphasize particular textual potentialities over others. While those labors cannot limit the variety of ways local viewers read and get pleasure from imported programs, they do encourage certain kinds of meanings and pleasures and discourage others. Scheduling and promoting *The Cosby Show* as a children's program in the United Kingdom, for instance, worked to de-emphasize the romance between Cliff and Clair Huxtable, which remains a rare and prominent example of a dignified romantic relationship between a black man and a black woman on television. Similarly, airing *bro'Town* in Canada on the Aboriginal People's Television Network, surrounded by animation from indigenous minorities from around the world, encourages viewers to read the program as an expression of a similarly situated ethnic minority, rather than just another iteration of the global adult animation genre.

The model that these pages have uncovered about how media globalization influences televisual representations of blackness can be summarized as follows: importers identify and exploit particular elements of imported programming, based upon their perceptions of audience tastes and which programs meet those tastes in which ways; some of these practices find their way back to exporters, depending upon the degree of globalization of the exporters' business models, their integration into larger transnational corporate structures, and how important specific markets are for the exporter's bottom line; those institutional labors that do find their way back to exporters have the ability to influence the exporters' future catalogs, promotional and pricing practices, and, ultimately, the representational strategies of producers, depending upon the relationship between the exporter and the producer.

In practice, of course, none of the three interface sites is solely responsible for initiating industry lore; instead, the lore circulates among the sites. Exporters, for instance, work hard to convince buyers to use their programs in particular ways, and importers derive a substantial portion of their textual exegeses and institutional labor plans from ideas that originate with distributors, as well as programmers in other territories and executives elsewhere in the organization. Furthermore, industry lore does not develop independently of the kinds of historical discourses that structure reception. Rather, industry lore, much like reception, is the result of historical discourses filtering through particular fields of human knowledge and activity.

If we view it in this manner, we can begin to see that globalization does not homogenize television content or block diverse portrayals of blacks and African Americans. Rather, the institutional structures of television produce conditions where certain kinds of representations are more likely than others. In today's world, those institutional structures almost always include foreign markets. The commercial nature of global television exchanges, the multiplication of channels and fragmentation of audiences due to cable and digitization, and worldwide disparities in per-capita GDPs among nations have led to dominant representational practices in the United States that favor integrationist portraits of African American men and women at work, multicultural portraits centered around young African American male experiences in the home, hyperrealist "quality" programs that center around black criminality and drug use, and satirical portraits that travesty both minority and majority cultures at the same time that they tend toward juvenile humor. While the institutional structures in different nations, such as those attending Nollywood videofilms, do permit different kinds of representational practices, the *transnational* institutional structures that would permit these practices to become widespread and a concomitant industry lore to develop that consciously works to define cross-cultural black linkages do not yet exist. Hence, something like the Belizean serial drama *Noh Matta Wat* can find audiences in many countries, but cannot sustain itself financially because it lacks transnational institutional status and backing.

Industry lore, then, arises from a combination of sociohistorical and institutional forces, and derives its power from its status as an institutional discourse. These institutionalized discourses are a prominent feature of modernity, and are what distinguish institutionalized cultural flows from noninstitutionalized ones, particularly the ways they provide the intellectual scaffolding upon which choices about the production and distribution of culture get made. Perhaps most prominently for my concerns, the institutionalized discourses about race that circulate within the global television industries are conscious efforts to articulate understandings of race to the needs and priorities of these powerful institutions, much as powerful economic interests, governments, and churches articulated race to their own institutional needs in the eighteenth and nineteenth centuries.

The articulation of race to the institutional needs of transnational capitalist media can, ironically, produce progressive portrayals of blackness. For example, the need to find cheap imported programming for its Cartoon Network Latin America lineup that would speak to the perceived interests of young, middle-class viewers led Time Warner executives to endorse the metaphor of watching *bro'Town* as a "cultural journey" in order to embed edgy programming designed for an audience segment in one culture into the lineup of a niche channel in a very different culture. Meanwhile, industry lore about "quality" programming facilitated the worldwide circulation of *The Wire*, which exhibits a wider range of African American character types and cultural allusions than any series in recent history. In this instance, black masculinity becomes articulated to an aesthetic of gritty realism, the crime drama genre, and the needs of subscription-based cable channels in the United States and Europe, specifically through the trope of inner-city drug culture. Industry lore about quality television, then, operates as both a limiter, in that the portrayal of black men as street criminals is quite conventional, and an expander, in that it permits the very different generic, aesthetic, narrative, and ideological features of *The Wire*.

Blackness and Transnational Televisual Aesthetics

In concluding, I want to focus on the aesthetic dimensions of African American television and how different kinds of institutional practices encourage different kinds of aesthetics. In particular, I want to advance an aesthetic argument that, since television's inception, its institutional formations in most locales encouraged the use of realist aesthetics. Ironically, today's global, digital, post-network era supports highly *localized* aesthetics of hyperrealism and travesty, though the institutional forms and aesthetics of the prior era are still with us. Thus, the institutional labors of narrowcasters targeting transnational or subnational audience segments give rise to industry lore about viewers embarking on cultural journeys, viewers who are comfortable with—and even seek out—cultural difference and ambiguity.

For the moment, I want to largely bracket questions of ideology in addressing aesthetics, though of course both of these textual features are interwoven and only theoretically separable. In concluding, I will bring back in questions of ideology in order to argue that what is distinct about contemporary commercial flows of black culture is precisely their adherence to aesthetic consistency over ideological consistency, even as their aesthetic practices encourage certain ideological orientations.

Before moving on, let me reiterate my argument in general: since its earliest days, the institutional labors of television programs in most nations—and the labors of imported programs in particular—gave rise to industry lore about audience tastes that encouraged realist aesthetics. These labors were anchored by the institutional forms of television, which generally operated as nationwide broadcasters, as well as the technology of broadcasting, which could be made to conform more or less to national boundaries.

Increasingly, current television channels aim to reach ever-shrinking audience niches and sub-niches, either across or within nations, and require consistent interaction with the circuits of global television in order to operate. This set of conditions gives rise to institutional labors and industry lore that transcend national boundaries and privilege aesthetics of hyperrealism and travesty that give programming and programmers the "edge" they need to reach their viewers. This is particularly true of Internet-delivered television, where distribution is inherently transnational and viewer attention is highly furtive and fragmented. At the same time, these aesthetic practices also connect with the histories and institutional needs of minority broadcasters around the world seeking relevant entertainment at affordable prices.

Broadcast Realism, 1950–1990s

In the early decades of television, when terrestrial broadcasting was the main delivery technology and most commercial and public service broadcasting institutions centered on homogeneous national audiences, the global circulation of television culture was sporadic and disorganized. Certainly broadcasters in the United States and beyond made substantial use of internationally traded programs, but most imports tended to be used as filler and most foreign syndication revenues were merely icing on the cake. However, as was the case with the miniseries genre, when opportunities for foreign syndication did appear, they quickly became central to producers' and distributors' business models. In such a climate, portrayals of African American suffering and nobility could serve a range of institutional labors, particularly when they were contained within a twelve-hour format such as *Roots* that fit the scheduling practices of European public service broadcasters. As perhaps the most egregious example of the exploitation of nonwhite people during colonialism, slavery, as portrayed in *Roots*, provided an effective way of thinking through issues of white guilt, minority exploitation, the difference between commercial and public service broadcasting models, and the history of Western capitalism. While black history and contemporary struggles were central to the institutional labors that *Roots* performed abroad, it was easy for both exporters and importers of the miniseries to ignore or overlook those labors and focus instead on the supposed universal themes of family struggle and European history. In other words, given the institutional arrangements and the technology of broadcasting at the time, which could be made more or less to respect national borders and favored a small number of channels, it was easy for television executives to hold universalizing perspectives on global cultural flows: little economic or institutional incentive existed at the time to try to think through the complexities of transnational cultural appeal.

The institutional and technological arrangements of broadcasting made realism the primary televisual aesthetic of the network era, at least among most Western national broadcasters, who were the main producers and suppliers of the world's television fiction at the time. Realism helped both public service and commercial broadcasters smooth over subnational differences among viewers by focusing on settings, locations, and ideologies familiar to their primary audiences. While in public service nations, such as the United Kingdom, broadcasters' prime audiences may have sometimes been working-class families, rather than the middle-class families that commercial U.S. broadcasters targeted, both emphasized domestic settings, ordinary characters, and a hierarchy of ideological perspectives, where the dominant ideology was represented as the norm (Fiske, 1987; Jordan, 1981). These practices of broadcast realism served both institutional needs—privileging dominant ideological perspectives helped guarantee that most viewers would accept the program's perspective as natural—and technological ones—locating series in domestic settings made production easier and less expensive, and fit the small screen size and poor image quality of broadcast television. Thus, the U.K. working-class serial *Coronation Street* privileged moral perspectives familiar to the working class, while *The Cosby Show* privileged perspectives much closer to the middle class, but both relied on realist aesthetics to create their worldviews.

In the seventies and eighties, television series featuring African Americans that aired in the United States and abroad utilized realist aesthetics almost exclusively, a practice that permitted those series to speak to the realities of nonblacks within and beyond the nation in a universal—or at least, Western—language. At the same time, while African American series, especially, integrated other aesthetic traditions, such as vaudeville-inspired camp, sat-ire, and popular music, the variety of subgenres of realism they incorporated was significantly smaller than white series. Not only were African Ameri-can portrayals limited primarily to the situation comedy, but also to the subgenres of social realism (*Good Times, Sanford and Son*) and bourgeois realism (*Benson, The Jeffersons, The Cosby Show*). Meanwhile, white series encompassed these subgenres as well as magical realism (*I Dream of Jeanie, Wonder Woman*), documentary realism (*American Family, Candid Camera*), historical realism (westerns, historical miniseries), soap-opera realism (Jor-dan, 1981), and more. While *Roots* added diversity to the repertoire of Afri-can American television stories in terms of both programming genre and subgenres of realist aesthetics, the majority of African American portrayals in historical realist settings remained marginal to the story, designed mainly as backdrops that lent visual accuracy to scenes.

As this litany of the various subgenres of broadcast realism suggests, the specific aesthetics of realism differ among programming genres. Similarly, because cultures, genres, histories, and target audiences differed among broadcasters in different nations, the aesthetic practices of one national sys-tem did not necessarily fit comfortably with those of another system. Nev-ertheless, shared investments in realism as an aesthetic capable of smooth-ing over internal national differences did permit broadcasters in Europe, the United States, and elsewhere to exchange programming with compara-tively minor aesthetic dissonance. Thus, while *Roots* incorporated elements of historical and social realism that sat uncomfortably alongside the series' melodramatic programming genre for European broadcasters, the practice of programming panel discussions on historical and contemporary realities effectively dampened that dissonance, at least to broadcasters' satisfactions.

If broadcast realism requires fidelity to both the everyday surroundings *and* the dominant ideological perspectives of a majority of audience mem-bers (Fiske, 1987; Jordan, 1981), we can understand how industry lore during the network era had difficulty recognizing and admitting the possible appeal of African American television abroad, given that both the lived experi-ences and the ideological orientations of African Americans were assumed to be radically different from those of their fellow countrypersons, much less viewers abroad. As one major Hollywood executive put it, "Typically, a black American experience is dissimilar to a black experience anywhere else in the world. Certainly, a great many other countries in the world *have* a black pop-ulation, but they don't have the same experience as black Americans. They don't have the same history" (interview with the author, 1999). Here we can see how the assumption that viewers need to identify with characters and situations in order to get pleasure from television is rooted in the belief that the medium is inherently realist, presenting "experiences" that either enable or block identification.

Again, a confluence of institutional arrangements, technological properties, historical and cultural forces, microeconomic practices, and macroeconomic structures worked together to articulate television as a realist medium and to restrict the diversity of realist subgenres within which African American characters and themes were likely to appear. And, though realism was far from the only aesthetic option on television, especially among experimental public broadcasters such as "second" channels throughout Europe, it thoroughly dominated commercial television trade during the network era due to the institutional labors that imports were called upon to perform, namely, appealing to an undifferentiated national audience. It is not surprising, in such an environment, that the most popular African American export of the network era was *The Cosby Show*, which presented both surroundings and ideological perspectives that were aggressively middle- to upper-middleclass. After all, these were the worlds and the worldviews that viewers around much of the world were thought to share.

Of course the broadcast aesthetics of African American television did not determine their potential ideological functions abroad. Bophuthatswana Television in South Africa, for instance, programmed integrated African American imports in a way that essentially collapsed their "simulacral" and "mimetic" realist elements (Harper, 1998). In other words, while these series portrayed a version of reality *as it ideally should be*, rather than a version that mimicked the realities of African American life, Bop-TV's consistent, back-to-back scheduling of integrated imports reinforced the impression that the ideal *was* the reality in the United States.

The aesthetics of broadcast realism worked hand-in-glove with the universalizing tendencies of industry lore and the institutional priorities of nationwide broadcasters seeking to reach undifferentiated audiences. It is not that other forms of television were incapable of international appeal at the time, but rather that the institutional, technological, and cultural forces that worked to propel television across national borders could accommodate only realist aesthetic practices.

Things began to change with the introduction of cable and satellite broadcasting to more and more areas of the world in the late 1980s and early 1990s. As terrestrial broadcasters and cable operators began to program more time for youth audiences, especially in Europe, they were confronted with the question of what those viewers would watch and how to provide them relevant programming in the cheapest possible manner. They began to realize that realism was not the only, or even the best, vehicle for reaching those viewers. Instead, program brokers involved with niche channels began to talk about street slang, irreverent humor, and satirical references to popular culture as textual features that could draw, rather than alienate, viewers. This set of conditions led to forms of industry lore that extolled the virtues of African American exceptionalism, particularly male exceptionalism, in reaching fickle viewers worldwide.

The dominance of broadcasting and network models of television has continued to erode in the twenty-first century, as have the easy assumptions among industry insiders about the universal character of globally popular television programs. As cable and satellite channels have carved up the viewing public into smaller and smaller niches, production houses have followed suit, splintering into boutique operations that specialize in particular genres and audiences. Institutionally, transnationalization has taken on three major forms: transnational ownership and investment practices, a heavy reliance on international syndication revenues, and the construction of similar or identical channel brands targeting the same demographics in almost every competitive television market. All of these developments have forced television producers, syndicators, and programmers around the world to think more consciously about, and work more actively on, articulating what cultural similarities might exist among audience niches in different parts of the world who, though they may be demographically identical, are nevertheless historically, culturally, and linguistically distinct.

The need for far more nuanced understandings—one might say, theories —of race, ethnicity, and other forms of difference among industry insiders has been exacerbated by ongoing technological changes. As broadband Internet access expands and digital video coder-decoder (codec) software becomes more sophisticated and interoperable, the Internet has increasingly become an important new video delivery technology. Much of the video material on the Internet is directly accessed by users, perhaps most famously the website YouTube, which permits users to upload, view, and share amateur video and short professional clips. Many of these sites are free, including those that feature "catch-up" episodes that allow fans to watch recently aired episodes they may have missed. However, as commercial media organizations become more and more involved in Internet television, they are looking to develop a variety of business models, including pay-per-view and subscription options, as well as a variety of "channels" to help users navigate the potentially vast number of choices online. We see the beginnings of this emerging model in content aggregation services such as Netflix and Hulu that stream content over the Internet directly to home and mobile screens.

Michael Curtin and Jane Shattuc (2009) have referred to this evolving world of digital television as the "matrix" era, in an effort to distinguish the contemporary media environment from both the network and post-network eras. The changes associated with the matrix era of television have led to programming practices that favor the immediate cultural sensibilities of viewers, practices that "seek less to homogenize popular culture than to organize and exploit diverse forms of creativity" (Curtin, 1996, 197). Often these more relevant, edgy programs integrate aesthetic forms other than conventional broadcast realism, in particular the aesthetics of hyperrealism and travesty.

Hyperrealist and Travestied Aesthetics, 2000–Present

If different kinds of aesthetic practices are to become popular in a global matrix era of television, different forms of industry lore need to evolve that imagine audience pleasure and identity differently than the lore of "universal themes" that dominated Western television in the era of national broadcast realism. We see the beginnings of this sensibility in the industry lore of cultural journeys, which we discussed in chapter 6, and which permits thinking about the irreverent, nonrealist aesthetics of global animation as transnationally appealing. I would argue that industry lore within the television industry will need to continue to evolve more and more models of transnational cultural alliance and interaction in the years to come, as white media consumers become more and more of a minority both at home and globally. Much like many other industries that have long taken minority consumers for granted, Western television industries will need to change decades of conventional practice and thinking in order to compete in an increasingly global capitalist world.

Hyperrealist aesthetics are articulated with industry lore about quality television, and are not limited to televisual portrayals of blackness, but can be found in popular film, music, and literature as well. It is perhaps not surprising to find such practices dominating portrayals of African Americans today, as the variety of claims on blackness in general, and black masculinity in particular, have multiplied in recent decades as various political factions concerned with black masculinity have flourished along with new channels of communication. Under such conditions, where reality becomes a political football, concerns about identifying, representing, and recognizing reality become all the more urgent.

I want to distinguish my fairly narrow use of the term "hyperrealist" from more general theories of hyperrealism associated with postmodern theory: I mean to refer *not* to the processes whereby representation comes to dominate and ultimately subsume lived reality, but rather the aesthetic practices of extreme detail in reproducing the look, feel, and atmosphere of specific locales, events, and people. When it comes to televisual portrayals of African Americans, hyperrealist aesthetics are primarily deployed in revealing the lives and experiences of the urban poor, specifically through imagery of blighted cityscapes, drug use, violent crime, and the sex industries. I affix the prefix "hyper" to these aesthetic practices to signal how these cultural forms move beyond fidelity to realism to a fixation on, and even a fetishization of, the real. Put another way, while earlier televisual forms required *ideological* realism in order to orient the viewer to the world of the text, hyperrealism invests considerable effort and expense in creating the *look* of reality. Importantly, while broadcast realism favored familiar settings and stories, hyperrealism tends to concentrate on the lives and milieus of characters who are quite distant from the target viewers.

Beyond the social roots of this turn toward hyperrealist aesthetics in African American television portrayals, technological and industrial developments are also responsible. The shift toward hyperrealist aesthetics is part of a broader aesthetic development in television dating back to the introduction of digital editing techniques and cable competition. In particular, as competition between traditional networks and cable outlets intensified in the 1990s, the networks have increasingly turned to expensive, filmic aesthetics to try to distinguish themselves from cable (Caldwell, 1995). Some of these filmic elements include location shooting and the kinds of hyperrealist aesthetics that television had tended to shun because of its traditionally poor image quality. In the past few years, as HDTVs and high-definition delivery technologies (BluRay DVD, HD Internet videos) have become more and more common, televisual image quality has begun to rival the image quality of film screens, making hyperrealist imagery more prevalent on television. Of course today it is not the traditional networks but the premium channels that take the lead in these kinds of aesthetic developments due to their ability to spend heavily on programming and their need to distinguish themselves from competitors in order to retain subscribers. In addition, due to legal regulations on broadcasters and industry restrictions on basic cable channels, premium channels try to distinguish themselves through graphic depictions of sex and violence, which shape the kinds of realities that contemporary quality television tends to depict.

Regardless of the broader social and technological developments that have aided the spread of hyperrealist treatments of African American life, in all forms of popular culture, they tend to incorporate themes of sexism, heterosexism, criminality, and deviant sexuality. Film and music lead the global circulation of hyperrealist black aesthetics, but the specific articulation of these aesthetics to broader social and political themes differs depending on the medium. With regard to episodic television, the aesthetics of hyperrealism as they relate to African Americans guarantee that the police genre is the dominant representational form, due to the genre's conventional interest in criminality, realistic settings, and adult storylines and imagery. Episodic television tends to highlight character development over narrative development, facilitating complex portraits of criminals as well as the police officers and other institutional actors who pursue them (Anderson, 2000). The resulting combination of fetishized black bodies engaged in street drug use, violence, and sex, and complex character portrayals of criminals, the police, and institutional authorities is what leads me to define hyperrealism as a distinct form of multicultural televisual discourse (Gray, 1995).

Let me hasten to add that, simply because I identify hyperrealism as multicultural does not mean that I find it unproblematic or even laudatory. As I suggested in chapter 5, shows like *The Wire* perpetuate some fairly common and disturbing images of African American men that can too easily be deployed as backdrops for racist, homophobic, sexist—and just plain bad —television programming. However, such series certainly do not offer us a singular version of what it means to be an African American man. Nor do they portray black criminality from a white, middle-class vantage point, but often identify such criminality as only the most visible symptom of a corrupt and collapsing political, economic, and social system. Hyperrealist televisual discourses of blackness, then, are politically conflicted: they perpetuate the ugliest stereotypes while simultaneously airing ideologies and perspectives rarely seen on television. They perpetuate the idea that black male bodies are out of control in many ways—sexually, violently, and mentally—but rather than marking these excesses as racial inferiority, they identify them as indexes of the failures of capitalist modernity.

Televisual aesthetics of hyperreal blackness, then, depart significantly from traditional transnational portrayals over the centuries, in which similar stereotypes supported the ideology that blacks were uncivilized and uncivilizable, forever incapable of joining in the project of modernity. By contrast, hyperreal television represents African Americans as thoroughly urban, as the most vulnerable members of a crumbling modern world. In this way, the portrayals of blackness in such series parallel the portrayals of blackness in Nollywood films as both urban and abject.

Hyperrealist representations of blackness are not widespread in contemporary television. Before *The Wire*, the most prominent example was Charles Dutton's HBO miniseries *The Corner* (2000). Nevertheless, similar kinds of imagery have begun to seep into other television series that focus predominantly on street crime, despite the fact that this trend also conflicts with dominant industry practices of avoiding portraying African Americans as street criminals due to potential political fallout.[1] *The Sopranos* (1999–2007), the NBC series *The Black Donnellys* (2007), about a group of Irish brothers turned mobsters who live in Hell's Kitchen, and *Detroit 1-8-7* (2010), focusing on police detectives working at Detroit Homicide, for instance, occasionally featured African American criminals peopling their re-creation of contemporary urban landscapes. Given the critical and economic success of *The Wire* and its subsequent incorporation into industry lore about quality, we should expect an increase in quality television series that place African American street criminals close to the center of their stories.

The televisual aesthetic of travesty, meanwhile, gets articulated through industry lore about "edgy" programming, and tends to appear on low-rent specialty channels, particularly those carried by digital cable and satellite. These channels share similar audience profiles and identities across multiple nations and regions, and their heavy reliance on transnational television imports places these channels center stage when it comes to trying to deal with the complexities of cultural difference. Televisual travesties sometimes exhibit multiculturalism in that they derive from a decidedly black or minority perspective on race, politics, society, and the media. In their engagement with contemporary trends and debates in each of these areas, such programs offer a range of black perspectives, even as they tend quietly to endorse sexism, masculinity, homophobia, heterosexism, and, to some degree, classism.

I use the term "travesty" to refer to these kinds of television programs because of their tendency to ridicule—or, at least, their reputation for ridiculing—all groups and issues, particularly sensitive issues that are considered off-limits in polite society. Like literary travesties, which date back at least to the Greek classical period, televisual travesties entail an "undignified or trivializing treatment of a dignified subject" (Baldick, 2009, 340). Of course, in practice, such programs inevitably exhibit blind spots, or groups and attitudes that are not ridiculed, such as heterosexuals and sexism, as well as others that are frequent targets of ridicule, such as women and the poor (Gray, 1995). Herman Gray (1995) develops a reading strategy to analyze the cultural politics of such programs that focuses on identifying common targets of ridicule, and uses this strategy to argue that one of the progenitors of the sketch comedy genre, *In Living Color* (1990–1994), exhibits a sexist and anti-poor bias. In addition, travesties typically include scatological and ribald material that offends adult, bourgeois sensibilities. These "carnivalesque" features of television may be read as moments when the hierarchies of society are suspended or brought down by the "bodiliness" that all human beings share. As John Fiske (1987) argues, television's carnivalesque tendencies enact "the bringing down of all to the equality of the bodily principle" (243). At the same time, these bodily functions, at least in the series and episodes I've screened and analyzed for this book, typically do not refer specifically to female bodies: for example, menstruation is almost never a subject of humor, while erections and tinea cruris (jock itch) are. Regardless of how we read these bodily jokes—or what Daniel Lennard (2004), director of animation for the Cartoon Network, Toonami, and Boomerang channels in Europe, calls "farting and fighting"—in the lore of the industry, they help account for the global appeal of edgy programs among young men and boys worldwide.

While televisual travesties incorporate references to male bodily functions as well as several of the aesthetic practices of globally popular genres, such as allusions to anime in *The Boondocks*, those that are staged from a black or ethnic minority perspective also tend to show reverence for indigenous cultural practices and to draw on a longer tradition of satire within postcolonial cultures. This celebration and ridicule of the ethnic, combined with ridicule of the dominant local and global order of things, are what mark these programs as distinctly local in orientation and require industry insiders to revise their conventional notions about the universality of particular cultural practices and themes. As I have already suggested, the aesthetic of satire or travesty is common among the world's nonwhite and minority populations (Bhabha, 1994; Buell, 1994; Gates, 1989; Watkins, 1994). However, these satirical aesthetics have been adapted specifically to the audiovisual medium, and as such they mock not only dominant and minority cultures, but dominant, global media institutions and practices as well.

Despite their political blind spots and shortcomings, I believe that travestied televisual aesthetics constitute a global discourse of race that is quite distinct from racialized discourses that have come before, and are intimately tied into the medium of television. Specifically, although these kinds of discourses have been around in minority culture for centuries, they now enjoy an institutional status and a concomitant carrier discourse, in the form of industry lore about cultural journeys, that facilitate their worldwide circulation.

Satirical animation and sketch comedy are primarily limited to television, and are also ideally suited to the migration of television to online environments, due to their tendency to provide brief scene "bites" that do not require additional narrative material or knowledge to appreciate. Their articulation of minority aesthetics, global generic elements, and the carnivalesque shape the cultural politics of these programs. Unlike globally distributed satirical discourses of race that have been around since the sixteenth century, which emphasize the ridiculousness of nonwhite, non-Western people in order to secure the superiority and normalcy of white Westerners, these new, travestied televisual discourses ridicule both whites and nonwhites, locals and foreigners, even as they tend to reserve their most scathing critiques for white culture and the institutions of capitalist modernity, such as colonialism, the church, and the media. These aesthetics serve to introduce and exemplify shared historical, political, and aesthetic interests among minority cultures around the globe. At the same time, they also harness shared biases against women, gays, and the poor in an effort to cobble together transnational audience segments around shared identities of gender and age.

Hyperreal and travestied aesthetics can accommodate both progressive and regressive ideologies. In fact, while modernist discourses of race emanating from the state and the church emphasized *ideological* consistency across *aesthetic* differences, postmodern televisual flows emphasize *aesthetic* consistency across *ideological* differences. That is, popular culture, church doctrine, laws, and European philosophy all shared similar ideological positions on the racial superiority of whites in the eighteenth century, while in the twentieth and twenty-first centuries, the television series *The Corner* and *The Wire* shared striking aesthetic similarities, but the former promoted an ideology of individual responsibility and boot-strapping and the latter critiqued the excesses of global capitalism.

At the same time, both hyperrealism and travesty possess ideological tendencies that tilt toward conservative and progressive ends, respectively. Thus hyperrealism, much like realism, leaves viewers with the impression that the images they see are accurate and unmediated, and this impression radiates onto the ideological perspective of the particular program. Additionally, because hyperrealist texts tend to focus on life experiences that are quite unfamiliar to the viewer, they have a tendency to recapitulate the same kinds of voyeuristic curiosity and racial superiority that early anthropological films did among viewers. Travesty, as I have already suggested, is an aesthetic of disorientation that puts viewers on unfamiliar and uncomfortable footing, requiring them to ferret out the viewpoint of each individual sketch and position themselves in relation to that viewpoint. This disorientation makes travesty a risky aesthetic gambit for creators as well as critics. However, these aesthetics and their disorientations have long been a part of the cultural weaponry of oppressed minorities fighting white, Western domination.

In the final analysis then, media globalization has, at least temporarily, expanded the range of aesthetic and ideological diversity in African American television, the types and locations of viewers who watch African

American and black television, and the industry lore that underwrites the worldwide flow of African American television. We can now see poor and rich African Americans populating conventional dramas, quality programs, sitcoms, and sketch comedies, as well as black and black-identified groups from around the world on television screens everywhere. At the same time, African American women remain largely typecast as the bearers of a deracinated middle-class ideology, while elderly, gay, and rural African Americans and non-American blacks remain largely absent from the world's screens. The commercial logics of global television, in other words, favor a limited range of aesthetic practices primarily centered on the lives and sensibilities of young African American men. But these aesthetic limitations do not determine the ideological practices of the series, many of which are produced by creative individuals and teams intent on telling progressive new stories about African American life.

To return to the question of whether commercial globalization envisions African American culture as worthy of attention and preservation, which began this volume, the answer we have discovered is ambiguous. For some African Americans and minorities around the world, television promises to intensify the opportunities for cross-cultural dialogue and multiply the sites of creative expression and struggle. For others, however, the opportunities to speak to and with similarly situated people about their specific life experiences, in ways that are aesthetically true to those experiences, have only grown more rare. If channels continue to expand, if Internet delivery becomes more and more widespread, and if audience niches continue to fragment, we may see greater opportunities for these other kinds of stories as well. However, the political economy of global television, as it currently stands, militates against the worldwide circulation and recognition of these other more complicated, oppressed, and less profitable forms of difference, primarily because of the range of industry lore about the pleasures associated with transnational minority cultural circulation. Put slightly differently, the carrier discourse of industry lore has not kept pace with some of the most prevalent and promising popular discourses by and about African American programming that are currently traversing the globe. To the extent that industry can and must change to accommodate these contemporary black television travels, it will produce the necessary conditions for the production of less domineering and more culturally relevant minority television programming flows.

Notes

INTRODUCTION

1. Throughout this volume I use the terms "global" and "transnational" somewhat interchangeably, although I understand "global" to refer to a range of institutional and cultural developments that include both super- and subnational configurations. By contrast, "transnational" refers to cultures and industries that span national boundaries.

2. I use the term "African American" to refer to people and cultures of Black African descent living in the United States. By contrast, the term "black" refers to all people and cultures of Black African descent. As I hope becomes clear throughout these pages, I define blackness as a *political* identity rather than an essentialist racial identity, which exhibits significant differences from dominant political identities due to radically different historical and contemporary experiences. At the same time that I recognize that blackness is cross-cut by countless forms of difference as well, I believe that the maintenance of struggle against all forms of oppression is a key, shared feature of black communities everywhere. Consequently I also use the term "black" to refer to oppressed minorities who are not of Black African descent but who have chosen to call themselves black as a means of expressing resistance and solidarity with minority groups elsewhere.

3. I do not substantially attend here to processes of decoding, or the meanings that viewers derive from African American television imports, except that I see programming as a constant process of encoding and decoding among multiple interpretive communities, only one of which is the audience. While studies of audience decoding are undoubtedly vital for understanding the overall cultural significance of African American imports in specific locales, *Black Television Travels* investigates how industry professionals around the world act as cultural mediators in selecting and scheduling African American television and how those decisions shape worldwide circulation patterns and production practices. Consequently issues of audience reception primarily come into play in the analysis only when industry insiders recognize them and allow them to influence their decisions, or as contrasts to the ways insiders understand the cultural processes of African American television trade.

4. Black Entertainment Television (BET) International operates several low-rent transnational channels. While it does employ local programmers and content in the United Kingdom, its status as one of hundreds of digital channels offered on the Sky satellite service minimizes the channel's cultural impact. Beyond the United Kingdom, the service is offered on similar kinds of satellite services that target viewers across multiple territories. For this reason, I do not attend to BET International in this study; instead, I concentrate on dominant trends in programming and industry lore in various decades, with the exception of chapter 6, which addresses non-U.S. black television trade.

5. This limitation exists because local television stations, which are the primary syndication buyers, strip reruns five or six days per week, while networks air new episodes

only weekly. In other words, local stations burn through episodes much more quickly than the networks do. In order to minimize the frequency of repeating episodes, which might turn viewers off, most local programmers believe that they need a run of at least sixty-six episodes, or three seasons.

6. For the first three years, as much as 70 percent of syndication revenues for Hollywood television shows can come from abroad, but that number starts to decline steeply thereafter.

CHAPTER 1

1. By comparison, overall production costs for network television series in 1980 had risen an average of only 40 percent since the 1977–1978 television season ("On the Rise," 1980; Russell, 1975).

2. As evidence of the competing and often contradictory discourses and cultural currents that *Roots* unleashed, Herman Gray gives two related but quite different readings of the impact of the miniseries. In *Color Adjustment* (Riggs, 1991), Gray argues that *Roots* was largely focused on criticizing personal, rather than institutional, forms of racism. In *Watching Race* (1995), he writes that the miniseries "opened—enabled, really—a discursive space in mass media and popular culture within which contemporary discourses of blackness developed and circulated" (78). In particular, Gray credits *Roots* with helping to create the conditions for the 1980s Afrocentric movement and the popularity of black studies within the academy.

3. It has long been assumed that Africans brought to the New World were stripped of their names and rechristened with Western names, though more recent research contradicts this assumption (Thornton, 1993). Nevertheless, the idea that African Americans had lost their names was prevalent even among African Americans at the time of *Roots*' broadcast. Perhaps the most famous incidence of this assumption was Malcolm Little's decision in 1953 to rename himself Malcolm X, in an attempt to both escape the influence of the slave master's last name and mark the absence of his true, African name (Haley, 1966).

4. Indeed, the miniseries itself was a product of transnational television exchanges. Beginning its life when PBS stations imported such limited-installment BBC series as *The Forsythe Saga* (1967) and *The Six Wives of Henry VIII* (1970) in the early 1970s, the miniseries was first adapted to U.S. television in 1974, when ABC aired an adaptation of Leon Uris's novel *QB VII* in two three-hour installments during prime time. The American version of the limited-installment series subsequently found agreeable buyers in overseas markets.

5. These different programming strategies reflected the different remits of the two systems: the Western European system favored diversity by creating space for a larger number of different television shows to be aired, while the commercial system favored predictability of viewer behavior, which weekly series encouraged, in order to deliver consistent audience numbers to advertisers. In addition, most public service broadcasters at the time had formal or informal quotas on the percentage of imported programming they could air, and a weekly series with no clear ending could eat up a lot of that time. Consequently, conventional American series were a hard sell in Western Europe and much of the rest of the world.

6. International coproductions bring together producers from more than one country, with the idea that the final program will air in all partners' markets, and perhaps get

sold elsewhere as well. It has become a dominant form of television production funding in an era of globalization, particularly for public broadcasters and cable networks. The arrangement offers foreign broadcasters who are partners to the deal a significant amount of leverage over the final product.

CHAPTER 2

1. As with every axiom of industry lore, the belief that sitcoms featuring African American characters did not sell abroad had its detractors. Ron V. Brown, senior vice president of international sales for Embassy Telecommunications, claimed to have sold the integrated sitcom *Diff'rent Strokes* (1978–1986) to broadcasters in more than seventy territories, including the French commercial channel TF1 ("U.S. Programmers Converge," 1986). While such widespread international syndication is impressive, some comparison with other programs and companies can help put it in perspective. The following year, the dramatic series *Little House on the Prairie* (1974–1983) sold in more than a hundred markets and *Dallas* (1978–1991) in more than ninety. What is more, Embassy's sitcom-heavy program catalog garnered only about 10 percent of overall revenues from international sales, running well behind more drama-heavy distributors such as Metromedia, which earned 35 percent of its syndication revenues abroad. Obviously, then, Brown's insistence that his sitcoms sold well abroad must be taken with a grain of salt. In fact, the article placed Brown's comments at the end of a section about the consensus among industry insiders about the poor performance of sitcoms abroad, clearly marking them as a minority viewpoint. Nevertheless, Brown's comments remind us that industry lore is not uncontested, but rather consists of competing ideas and interests.

2. While most English-speaking whites were far from antiracist, support for apartheid at the time among English speakers was significantly lower than among Afrikaans speakers, though a slight majority of English-speaking whites did support most apartheid policies (Rhoodie, de Kock, and Couper, 1985, 331).

3. The linguistic breakdown on TV2 and TV3 is less clear, as several of the titles are given only in English.

4. In fact, the SABC channels provided more locally produced programs in South African languages, so under most current scholarly definitions, we would consider them more domestically relevant than Bop-TV. Domestic relevance, however, may come as much from how television channels imagine and address viewers in relation to one another as it does from the total amount of domestically produced programming that they air.

5. It is interesting, though by no means surprising, that even the contemporary American programs focused on traditional white folk culture rather than modern, multicultural musical or entertainment programs.

6. Of course, the same may be said of TV1's Afrikaans programming, except that ballet, classical music, and Christianity are all arguably more organic to Afrikaner culture.

7. Of course, the channel's status as a commercial venture designed primarily to advertise Sowetan businesses to Sowetan consumers helped guarantee this privileging of black viewers.

8. To some degree *Project UFO* (1978–1979), which aired against TV3's showing of *Good Times*, also reflected the integrationist identity of Bop-TV, as the show's regular cast included the African American actress Aldine King as a secretary working for white

male Air Force officers investigating UFO sightings (http://www.imdb.com/title/
tt0077065/). Just as importantly, as an imported drama, *Project UFO* drew attention
to the limited nature of the SABC's program imports. That is, because the only all-
black American series at the time were older situation comedies, TV2 and TV3 were
restricted to imports in this genre. Bop-TV, by contrast, could import a wider range
of genres, including science fiction, and the juxtaposition of the two imports at the
same time reinforced this fact. Consequently, even when airing U.S. imports, the black
South African channels came across as comparatively restrictive. The made-for-TV
movie *The Jesse Owens Story* (1984), which tells the story of an African American ath-
lete overcoming racial bias to become an Olympic champion, airs at 8:30 on Bop-TV,
and works similarly (http://www.imdb.com/title/tt0087501/).

CHAPTER 3

1. It is difficult to say with certainty the precise revenues that Viacom received from selling rights to *The Cosby Show* internationally, but a close examination of the company's
financial reports from the time gives us a good sense of how profitable the show was.
In the first two years of the show's run, revenues from foreign exports remained steady
or fell slightly, but from 1986 until 1989, exports grew between 12.2 percent and 29.3
percent, totaling more than $20 million by decade's end. Of course, not all of these
revenues can be attributed to sales of *The Cosby Show*, but the series was certainly the
most popular international property owned by Viacom at the time (Viacom, 1985b,
1987, 1991).
2. In fact, in 1987 Viacom reported $770 million in unfulfilled domestic distribution
contracts, owing chiefly to revenues from *The Cosby Show* that it was unable to collect
because, although the contracts had been signed, the show had not yet reached a sufficient number of episodes to be released into syndication (Viacom, 1987).
3. Still, the main significance of the series' international popularity for Viacom probably
had less to do with direct revenues and more to do with increasing the company's
reputation as a successful international distributor at a time when global program
markets were growing more lucrative.

CHAPTER 4

1. What is more, according to Cohen, the popularity of Moesha with teenagers allowed
him to "platform" his sales or sell first to a smaller channel and, based on that success,
sell to a larger channel. In this way, African American youth series such as Moesha
and Fresh Prince allowed for more flexible sales approaches than earlier African
American shows.
2. Durán's claim that there is no black population in Mexico is inaccurate. See, for
example, Mitchell, 2008.

CHAPTER 5

1. This distinction within the African American community was popularized by the
comedian Chris Rock's stand-up routine "Niggas vs. Black People," which aired in
1996 on the HBO special *Bring the Pain*.
2. Fox's *Cleveland Show* (2009–present) offers another contemporary example of "edgy"
animation featuring African American characters traveling overseas. A spin-off of
Family Guy (1999–present), created by Seth MacFarlane, *The Cleveland Show* focuses

on Cleveland Brown's return to his hometown and his struggles to make his second marriage work, as well as the challenges of integrating stepfamilies. The show's "edginess" comes from its gross-out humor, especially long-take vomit gags and sex jokes, as well as random references to eighties black styles, music, and popular culture. The show does not use the word "nigger" as liberally as does *The Boondocks* or *Chappelle's Show*, perhaps because the character who voices the main character is white, but the word does show up with some frequency. *The Cleveland Show* has appeared on Comedy Central branded channels and comedy channels across Europe, Asia, and Latin America.

3. I do not mean to suggest that all web series, or all web series produced by or addressing African Americans, are derivative of televisual aesthetics. Certainly a number of creative and smart web series are currently being produced. Aymar Jean Christian maintains a list of these series on his blog at http://blog.ajchristian.org/. However, the web has been inundated recently with television writers and producers seeking to get their series picked up by creating online buzz (Alemoru, 2010), and given their career aspirations and privileged access to wider distribution on television, the industry lore about how best to reach desirable viewers tends to transfer over from cable.

CONCLUSION

1. The narratives of these shows tend to deal with the political complexities of representing African Americans as street criminals by identifying potential black suspects, but exonerating them at the end, usually by arresting a corrupt white businessman, politician, etc.

References

Acham, Christine (2004) *Revolution Televised: Prime Time and the Struggle for Black Power.* Minneapolis: University of Minnesota Press.

——(2007) "'I'm Rich, Bitch!!!' The Comedy of *Chappelle's Show.*" In *Cable Visions: Television beyond Broadcasting*, ed. Sarah Banet-Weiser, Cynthia Chris, and Anthony Freitas, 319–37. New York: New York University Press.

Adejunmobi, Moradewun A. (2007) "Nigerian Video Film as Minor Transnational Practice." *Postcolonial Text* 3 (2): 1–16.

Alemoru, Olu (2010) "Showcasing Talent on a Smaller Screen." *Los Angeles Wave*, 24 February. Accessed 1 July 2011. http://www.wavenewspapers.com/entertainment/85296392 .html.

Al-Mugaiseeb, Khalid (1998) Interview by the author with CEO, Kuwait TV 2.

Alvarado, Manuel, and Edward Buscombe (1978) *Hazell: The Making of a TV Series.* London: British Film Institute.

Alvey, Mark (2004) "'Too Many Kids and Old Ladies': Quality Demographics and 1960s U.S. Television." *Screen* 45: 40–62.

Anderson, Christopher (2000) "The Weeping Detective." Paper presented at the Telecommunications Colloquium, University of Wisconsin–Madison.

Anderson, Christopher, and Michael Curtin (1997) "Mapping the Ethereal City: Chicago Television, the FCC, and the Politics of Place." *Quarterly Review of Film and Video* 16: 289–305.

Ang, Ien (1991) *Desperately Seeking the Audience.* London: Routledge.

Appadurai, Arjun (1996) *Modernity at Large: Cultural Dimensions of Globalization.* Minneapolis: University of Minnesota Press.

Bagdikian, Ben (2000) *The Media Monopoly.* Boston: Beacon.

Baldick, Chris (2009) *The Oxford Dictionary of Literary Terms.* 3rd ed. Oxford: Oxford University Press.

Barnett, Clive (1995) "The Limits of Media Democratization in South Africa: Politics, Privatization and Regulation." *Media, Culture and Society* 21: 649–71.

Barns, Lawrence (1981) "TV's Drive on Spiraling Costs." *Business Week*, 26 October, 199.

Barthes, Roland (1972) "The Great Family of Man." In *Mythologies*, trans. Annette Lavers, 100–116. New York: Hill and Wang.

Becker, Ron (2006) *Gay TV and Straight America.* Piscataway: Rutgers University Press.

"Belgian Parliament Adopts TV Law as Flanders Socialists Withdraw Ban" (1986) *New Media Markets*, 26 November. Accessed 4 January 2007. http://web.lexis-nexis.com.

Berry, S. Torriano (2009) Interview by the author with director, *Noh Matta Wat.*

Bhabha, Homi (1994) *The Location of Culture.* London: Routledge.

Bielby, Denise, and C. Lee Harrington (2008) *Global TV: Exporting Television and Culture in the World Market.* New York: New York University Press.

"Big Brother Not Watching Bop-TV" (1984) *Rand Daily Mail*, 23 August, 10.

Birchall, Clare (2007) "How Gay Sex Changed the World." *Guardian*, 21 July, 75.

Bleicher, Joan (2004) "Germany." In *Encyclopedia of Television*, 2d ed., ed. Horace Newcomb, 588–91. New York: Fitzroy Dearborn.

Bodroghkozy, Aniko (1992) "'Is This What You Mean by Color TV?': Race, Gender and Conflicted Meanings in NBC's *Julia*." In *Private Screenings: Television and the Female Consumer*, ed. Lynn Spigel and Denise Mann, 143–67. Minneapolis: University of Minnesota Press.

"Bop-TV Blackout Angers Viewers" (1984) *Rand Daily Mail*, 16 July, 1.

"Bop-TV Issue: You Don't Kid Us, Pik Is Told" (1984) *Rand Daily Mail*, 16 August, 4.

"Bop-TV Petition Fails" (1984) *TV World*, December, 8.

"Bop-TV's Fare Just Excellent" (1984) *Rand Daily Mail*, 10 August, 8.

Boskin, Joseph (1986) *Sambo: The Rise and Demise of an American Jester*. New York: Oxford University Press.

Botha, Martin (2006) Personal communication with the author, 14 January.

Boyd, Todd (2001) *The New H.N.I.C.: The Death of Civil Rights and the Reign of Hip Hop*. New York: New York University Press.

Boyer, Peter J. (1986) "Production Cost Dispute Perils Hour TV Dramas." *New York Times*, 6 March, C26.

Brennan, Steve (2005) "International Markets Like *Chris* at TV's MIPCOM." Accessed 2 July. http://www.backstage.com/bso/esearch/article_display.jsp?vnu_content_id=1001308155.

Brunsdon, Charlotte (1990) "Problems with Quality." *Screen* 31: 67–90.

Buell, Frederick (1994) *National Culture and the New Global System*. Baltimore: Johns Hopkins University Press.

"But 'Closed Skies' over South Africa?" (1984) *Rand Daily Mail*, 18 August, 8.

Buxton, James (1985) "Italy's Private Television Networks Become Legal." *Television Business International*, 6 February, I2.

Caldwell, John Thornton (1995) *Televisuality: Style, Crisis, and Authority in American Television*. New Brunswick: Rutgers University Press.

——— (2008) *Production Culture: Industrial Reflexivity and Critical Practice in Film and Television*. Durham: Duke University Press.

Cartell, Philip (2007) "Nollywood Comes to the Caribbean." *Film International* 5 (4): 112–14.

Cassidy, Marsha, and Mimi White (2002) "Innovating Women's Television in Local and National Networks: Ruth Lyons and Arlene Francis." *Camera Obscura* 17: 31–69.

Caughie, John (1990) "Playing at Being American: Games and Tactics." In *Logics of Television: Essays in Cultural Criticism*, ed. Patricia Mellencamp, 44–58. Bloomington: Indiana University Press.

Chapman, William (1977) "*Roots* Becomes Japan's Latest Fad." *Washington Post*, 23 October, A1+.

Christian, Aymar Jean (2009) "Orlando's Joint: Urban, Stoned and Running a Business." Televisual Blog. Accessed 1 July 2011. http://blog.ajchristian.org/2009/12/11/orlandos-joint-urban-stoned-and-running-a-business/.

Clark, Bob (1999) Interview by the author with president, Story First Communications (Russia).

Clarke, Kamari Maxine, and Deborah A. Thomas (2008) *Globalization and Race: Transformations in the Cultural Production of Blackness*. Durham: Duke University Press.

Cloud, Dana (1996) "Hegemony or Concordance? The Rhetoric of Tokenism in 'Oprah' Winfrey's Rags-to-Riches Biography." *Critical Studies in Mass Communication* 13: 115–38.

Cohen, Bert (1999) Interview by the author with CEO, Worldvision.

Coleman, Robin R. Means (1998) *African American Viewers and the Black Situation Comedy: Situating Racial Humor*. New York: Garland.

comScore (2007) "'Primetime' U.S. Video Streaming Activity Occurs on Weekdays between 5–8 P.M." Accessed 20 September 2009. http://www.comscore.com/Press_Events/Press_Releases/2007/03/Primetime_US_Online_Video.

Correia, J. Manuel (1984a) "Jam as They Like, Bop-TV Wins." *Rand Daily Mail*, 25 August, 3.

—— (1984b) "TV1 Gain Leaves Its Black Rivals Behind." *Rand Daily Mail*, 31 August, 5.

—— (1984c) "TV4 Will Be Launched in March." *Rand Daily Mail*, 6 December, 1.

Correia, J. Manuel, and Sue Faulkner (1984) "Fight's On to Watch Bop-TV." *Rand Daily Mail*, 2 August, 1.

Cowell, Alan (1984) "South Africa Whites See Black TV." *New York Times*, 1 August, C22.

Cunningham, Stuart, and Elizabeth Jacka (1996) *Australian Television and International Mediascapes*. Cambridge: Cambridge University Press.

Curtin, Michael (1996) "On Edge: Culture Industries in the Neo-Network Era." In *Making and Selling Culture*, ed. Richard Ohmann, 181–202. Hanover, NH: Wesleyan University Press.

—— (1999) "Feminine Desire in the Age of Satellite Television." *Journal of Communication* 44 (2): 55–70.

—— (2008) *Playing to the World's Biggest Audience: The Globalization of Chinese Film and TV*. Berkeley: University of California Press.

Curtin, Michael, and Jane Shattuc (2009) *The American Television Industry*. New York: Palgrave Macmillan.

Curtis, Hillary (1997) "Have Comedy, Will Travel?" *TV World*, August–September, 31–36.

De Bens, Els, and Hedwig de Smaele (2001) "The Inflow of American Television Fictions on European Broadcasting Channels Revisited." *European Journal of Communication* 16: 51–76.

Deeb, Gary (1977) "Black Presence of TV Limited to Comedy." *News and Courier Charleston Evening Post*, 17 June, 15C.

Deeken, Aimee (2006) "Second Lap for Adult Swim's *Boondocks*." *Mediaweek*, 20 January, 5. Accessed June 10, 2009. ABI/INFORM Global.

Dewi, Torsten (1999) Interview by the author with commissioning producer of international coproductions, Prosieben (Germany).

Diamond, Malcolm (1977) "*Roots*." *RAIN* 21: 6–7.

Dinerman, Ann S., and Dom Serafini (1997) "The World's 95 Power TV Buyers." *Video Age International*, 16 June, 1.

Dixon, Kathleen (2001) "The Dialogic Genres of Oprah Winfrey's 'Crying Shame.'" *Journal of Popular Culture* 35: 171–91.

Dixon, Travis (2000) "A Social Cognitive Approach to Studying Racial Stereotyping in the Mass Media." *African American Research Perspectives* 6 (1). Accessed 15 July 2009. http://www.rcgd.isr.umich.edu/prba/perspectives/winter2000/tdixon1.pdf.

Downing, John (1988) "*The Cosby Show* and American Racial Discourse." In *Discourse and Discrimination*, ed. G. Smitherman-Donaldson and T. A. Van Dijk. Detroit: Wayne State University Press.

Dudziak, Mary (2000) *Cold War Civil Rights: Race and the Image of American Democracy*. Princeton: Princeton University Press.

Durán, Ignacio (1999) Interview by the author with vice president of international affairs, TV Azteca.

Eastman, Susan Tyler, and Douglas A. Ferguson (2006) *Media Programming: Strategies and Practices*. 7th ed. Belmont, CA: Thomson/Wadsworth.

Elam, Harry J., Jr., and Kennell Jackson (2005) *Black Cultural Traffic: Crossroads in Global Performance and Popular Culture*. Ann Arbor: University of Michigan Press.

Ellis, John (2000) "Scheduling: The Last Creative Act in Television?" *Media, Culture and Society* 22: 25–38.

Ely, Melvin Patrick (1991) *The Adventures of* Amos 'n' Andy: *A Social History of an American Phenomenon*. New York and Toronto: Maxwell Macmillan.

Entman, Robert M., and Andrew Rojecki (2000) *The Black Image in the White Mind: Media and Race in America*. Chicago: University of Chicago Press.

"Europe's 'Other' Channels: Numbers Double Every Three Years" (1997) *Screen Digest*, 1 March, 57–64.

Fabre, Michel (1979) "The Reception of *Roots* in France." *American Studies International* 17 (3): 36–39.

Falaiye, Muyiwa (1999) "Africa versus the West in the Court of Reparations." *African Studies Quarterly* 3: 23–28.

Feuer, Jane, Paul Kerr, and Tise Vahimagi (1983) *MTM: Quality Television*. London: British Film Institute Publishing.

Firehorse Films (2003) "Go Home, Stay Home." Television script.

Fiske, John (1987) *Television Culture*. New York: Routledge.

—— (1996) *Media Matters: Race and Gender in U.S. Politics*. Rev. ed. Chicago: University of Chicago Press.

Flanigan, James (1987) "The American Dream Is Best Export U.S. Has." *Los Angeles Times*, 9 September, sec. 4, p. 1.

Flint, Joe (2005) "As Critics Carp, HBO Confronts Ratings Decline." *Wall Street Journal*, 8 June, B1.

Ford, Jeff (1999) Interview by the author with controller of acquisitions, Channel 5 Broadcasting (United Kingdom).

Foucault, Michel (1979) *Discipline and Punish: The Birth of the Prison*. Trans. Alan Sheridan. New York: Random House.

—— (1980) *The History of Sexuality*. Vol. 1, *An Introduction*. Trans. Robert Hurley. New York: Vintage.

"Freedom of the Air" (1984) *Rand Daily Mail*, 23 August, 10.

Fuller, Linda (1992) The Cosby Show: *Audiences, Impact, and Implications*. Westport, CT: Greenwood.

Funt, Peter (1979) "Where Did All the Miniseries Go?" *New York Times*, 18 November, D43, 46.

Games, Dianna (1984) "SABC's Bottom Line Is Respectability." *Rand Daily Mail*, 17 July, 1.

Gandy, Oscar (1998) *Communication and Race*. London: Arnold Press.

Garcia-Cuesta, Paloma (1999) Interview by the author with acquisitions director, Antena 3 (Spain).

Gates, Henry Louis, Jr. (1989) *The Signifying Monkey: A Theory of African-American Literary Criticism*. Oxford: Oxford University Press.

Geissler, Michael (1992) "The Disposal of Memory: Fascism and Holocaust on West German Television." In *Framing the Past: The Historiography of German Film and Television*, ed. Bruce Murray and Chris Wickham, 220–60. Carbondale: Southern Illinois University Press.

Gilroy, Paul (1993) *The Black Atlantic: Modernity and Double-Consciousness.* Cambridge: Harvard University Press.

Gitlin, Todd (1983) *Inside Prime Time.* London: Routledge.

Goldberg, David Theo (1993) *Racist Culture: Philosophy and the Politics of Meaning.* Malden, MA: Blackwell.

——— (2002) *The Racial State.* Malden, MA: Blackwell.

Gomez, Michael, ed. (2006) *Diasporic Africa: A Reader.* New York: New York University Press.

Gray, Herman (1986) "Television and the New Black Man: Black Male Images in Prime-Time Situation Comedy." *Media, Culture and Society* 8: 223–42.

——— (1995) *Watching Race: Television and the Struggle for "Blackness."* Minneapolis: University of Minnesota Press.

——— (2005) *Cultural Moves: African Americans and the Politics of Representation.* Berkeley: University of California Press.

"Gyökerek és Emberek" (1980) *Magyar Nemzet,* 20 February, 4.

"A Győkerek Győkerei" (1980) *Népszava,* 5 February, 5.

Haag, Laurie L. (1993) "Oprah Winfrey: The Construction of Intimacy in the Talk Show Setting." *Journal of Popular Culture* 26: 115–21.

Hairman, Robit (1987) "Television by Apartheid." *Village Voice,* 3 May, 8.

Hajjawi, Bassam (1999) Interview by the author with president and CEO, International Distribution Agency (Jordan).

Haley, Alex (1966) *The Autobiography of Malcolm X.* New York: Grove.

Hall, Carla, Victoria Dawson, Jacqueline Trescott, Desson Howe, and Megan Rosenfeld (1986) "Thursday Night at the Huxtables." *Washington Post,* 6 November, D1.

Hall, Stuart (1993a) "Encoding/Decoding." In *The Cultural Studies Reader,* ed. S. During, 90–103. New York: Routledge.

——— (1993b) "What Is This 'Black' in Black Popular Culture?" *Social Justice* 20: 104–15.

——— (1996) "New Ethnicities." In *Stuart Hall: Critical Dialogues in Cultural Studies,* ed. David Morley and Kuan-Hsing Chen, 442–51. London: Routledge.

Harper, Phillip Brian (1998) "Extra-Special Effects: Televisual Representation and the Claims of 'the Black Experience.'" In *Living Color: Race and Television in the United States,* ed. Sasha Torres, 62–81. Durham: Duke University Press.

Harrison, James (2004) "FX289 Lines Up HBO Drama Hit." *Channel 21,* 21 September. Accessed 20 September 2009. http://www.c21media.net/news/detail.asp?area=4&article=21820.

Havens, Timothy (2000) "'The Biggest Show in the World': Race and the Global Popularity of *The Cosby Show.*" *Media, Culture and Society* 22: 371–91.

——— (2006) *Global Television Marketplace.* London: British Film Institute Publishing.

——— (2008) "The Hybrid Grid: Globalization, Cultural Power, and Hungarian Television Schedules." *Media, Culture and Society* 29: 219–39.

Havens, Timothy, Amanda D. Lotz, and Serra Tinic (2009) "Critical Media Industry Studies: A Research Approach." *Communication, Culture, Critique* 2: 234–53.

Henderson, Felicia D. (2010) Interview by the author with executive producer, *Soul Food.*

Henry, Greg (1986) "Why Is It That a Show Which Pulls a Massive 51 Per Cent Following in Its Home Country Can Only Muster a Measly Three Million Viewers Here?" *Televisuality,* 21 April, 33–34.

Herman, Edward, and Robert McChesney (1997) *The Global Media: The New Missionaries of Global Capitalism.* London: Cassell.

Hesmondhalgh, David (2000) *The Cultural Industries*. London: Sage.

Heuton, Cheryl (1990) "An Enviable Situation: The Format Once Declared Dead Now Rules Syndication." *Channels*, 17 December, 36–38.

Hilmes, Michelle (2003) "Who We Are, Who We Are Not." In *Planet TV: A Global Television Reader*, ed. Lisa Parks and Shanti Kumar, 94–110. New York: New York University Press.

Hirsch, Paul (1972) "Processing Fads and Fashions: An Organization-Set Analysis of Cultural Industry Systems." *American Journal of Sociology* 77: 639–59.

hooks, bell (1981) *Ain't I a Woman? Black Women and Feminism*. Boston: South End.

——(1992) *"Eating the Other: Desire and Resistance."* In *Black Looks: Race and Representation*, 21–39. Boston: South End.

——(1995) "Performance Practice as a Site of Opposition." In *Let's Get It On: The Politics of Black Performance*, ed. C. Ugwu, 210–21. Seattle: Bay Press.

Hoskins, Colin, Stuart McFadyen, and Adam Finn (1997) *Global Television and Film: An Introduction to the Economics of the Business*. New York: Oxford University Press.

Houston, Marsha (2000) "Multiple Perspectives: African American Women Conceive Their Talk." *Women and Language* 23: 11–17.

Huff, Richard (1996) "Sharing the Joke." *Television Business International*, October, 52.

IDATE Consulting and Research (2010) *TV 2010: Markets and Trends, Facts and Figures*. Montpelier, France. Accessed 11 June 2010. http://www.idate.org/2009/pages/download .php?id=124&t=f_telech_actu&fic=White_Paper_TV.pdf&repertoire=news/508_ TV_2010.

Jackson, Kennell (2005) Introduction to *Black Cultural Traffic: Crossroads in Global Performance and Popular Culture*, ed. H. Elam and K. Jackson, 1–39. Ann Arbor: University of Michigan Press.

JanMohammed, Abdul R., and David Lloyd (1990) "Toward a Theory of Minority Discourse: What Is to Be Done?" In *The Nature and Context of Minority Discourse*, ed. A. R. JanMohammed and D. Lloyd. Oxford: Oxford University Press.

Jenkinson, David (2006) "Sky Bar Set High." *Channel 21*, 25 May. Accessed 20 September 2009. http://www.c21media.net/news/detail.asp?area=4&article=30618.

Jhally, Sut, and Justin Lewis (1992) *Enlightened Racism*. San Francisco: Westview.

Jordan, Marion (1981) "Realism and Convention." In *Coronation Street*, ed. Richard Dyer, 27–39. London: British Film Institute Publishing.

Kaner, Mark (1999) Interview by the author with president of international, Twentieth Century Fox Television Distribution.

Keown, Michelle (2005) *Postcolonial Pacific Writing: Representations of the Body*. New York: Routledge.

Kinging, Glen (1976) Letter to David Wolper from program manager, Channel 7 Sydney, 11 October. David L. Wolper Archives, 282-016. University of Southern California, Los Angeles.

Kochman, Thomas (1983) *Black and White Styles in Conflict*. Chicago: University of Chicago Press.

Kover, Amy (1998) "The After-School Specialist." *Fortune*, 13 April, 32.

"La Cinq and M6 Still Not Meeting Obligations" (1989) *New Media Markets*, 24 May. Accessed 4 January 2007. http://web.lexis-nexis.com.

Lampel, Joseph (2011) "Converting Values into Other Values: Fairs and Festivals as Resource Valuation and Trading Events." In *Negotiating Values in the Creative Industries: Fairs,*

Festivals, and Competitive Events, ed. Brian Morean and Jesper Strandgaard Pedersen, 334–47. Cambridge: Cambridge University Press.

Lander, Richard (1984) "South Africa in a Jam as Bop Hops Color Line." *Globe and Mail*, 28 February, 21.

Larkin, Brian (2008) *Signal and Noise: Media, Infrastructure, and Urban Culture in Nigeria.* Durham: Duke University Press.

Lazarus, Herb (1999) Interview by the author with president, Carsey-Warner International.

Leavy, Suzan (1990) "Performers Cash In on S.A. Sales." *Stage and Television Today*, 11 October (*Archive: 1959–1994*). Accessed 25 August 2012. http://www.proquest.com.

Lennard, Daniel (2004) "United States of Animation." *Channel 21*, 18 May. Accessed 18 April 2007: http://www.c21media.net/features/detail.asp?area=2&article=20435.

Levin, Gary (2004) "HBO Met Its Match in Itself." *USA Today*, 28 September, D1.

Levine, Elana (2001) "Toward a Paradigm for Media Production Research: Behind the Scenes at *General Hospital*." *Critical Studies in Media Communication* 18: 66–83.

——— (2007) *Wallowing in Sex: The New Sexual Culture of 1970s American Television.* Durham: Duke University Press.

Lippman, John (1992) "Banking on the Huxtables." *Los Angeles Times*, 30 April, D1.

Lipsitz, George (1994) *Dangerous Crossroads: Popular Music, Postmodernism and the Poetics of Place.* London: Verso.

Loader, J. A. (1985) "Church, Theology and Change in South Africa." In *South Africa: A Plural Society in Transition*, ed. D. J. van Vuuren, N. E. Wiehahn, J. A. Lomard, and N. J. Rhoodie, 272–302. Durban, South Africa: Butterworth.

Lócsey, Gabriella (1980) "Gyökerek és az Emberek." *Magyar Nemzet*, 20 February, 4.

Lott, Eric (1993) *Love and Theft: Blackface Minstrelsy and the American Working Class.* New York: Oxford University Press.

Lotz, Amanda (2004) "Textual (Im)Possibilities in the U.S. Post-Network Era: Negotiating Production and Promotion Processes on Lifetime's *Any Day Now*." *Critical Studies in Media Communication* 21: 22–43.

——— (2006) *Redesigning Women: Television after the Network Era.* Urbana: University of Illinois Press.

——— (2007) *The Television Will Be Revolutionized.* New York: New York University Press.

Luscombe, Belinda (2009) "Making New Mileys: Disney's Teen-Star Factory." *Time*, October 22, http://www.time.com/time/magazine/article/0,9171,1931732,00.html. Accessed August 31, 2012.

Lustyik, Katalin, and Philippa K. Smith (2010) "From *The Simpsons* to '*The Simpsons* of the South Pacific': New Zealand's First Primetime Animation, *bro'Town*." *Television and New Media* 11: 331–49.

Mahlati, Cawe (1999) Interview by the author with CEO, Bophuthatswana Television.

Mahler, Richard (1990) "What Sells Best Overseas." *Electronic Media*, 15 January, 82.

Marenzi, Gary (2008) Interview by the author with co-president for worldwide television, Metro-Goldwyn-Mayer.

Martin, Neil A. (1980) "Miniseries Are Getting Maxi Again." *New York Times*, 14 December, D36.

Mayne, Jane (2007) "The Colour Maroon." *Cape Times*, 23 November, 8.

McCabe, Janet, and Kim Akass, eds. (2007) *Quality TV: Contemporary American Television and Beyond.* London: I. B. Tauris.

McGregor, Charles (1977) "The *Roots* Phenomenon." *Warner World*, 3+.

Michell, John (1984) "SA Miles Ahead of SABC-TV Oxwagon." *Rand Daily Mail*, 15 August, 10.

Miller, Toby, et al. (2005) *Global Hollywood 2*. London: BFI Publishing.

Mitchell, Elizabeth (2009) Interview by the author with executive producer, Firehorse Films.

Mitchell, John L. (2008) "Mexico's Black History Is Often Ignored." *Los Angeles Times*, 13 April.

Mitchell, Tony, ed. (2001) *Global Noise: Rap and Hip-Hop outside the USA*. Middletown, CT: Wesleyan University Press.

"Mit Látunk—Mit Hallunk" (1980) *Népszava*, 12 February.

Morris, David Z. (2010) "Minzoku Madness: Hip Hop and Japanese National Subjectivity." Ph.D. diss., University of Iowa.

Mufson, Steve (1986) "The 'Cosby Plan' for South Africa." *Wall Street Journal*, 30 July, sec. 1, p. 17.

Mulder, Frank (1999) Interview by the author with director of program acquisition and sales, Nederlandse Omroep Stichting.

NCTA (2011) "History of Cable." Accessed 1 July 2011. http://www.ncta.com/About/About/HistoryofCableTelevision.aspx.

Nederveen Pieterse, Jan (1992) *White on Black: Images of Africa and Blacks in Western Popular Culture*. New Haven: Yale University Press.

Newcomb, Horace (2000) "Television and the Present Climate of Criticism." In *Television: The Critical View*, 6th ed., ed. Horace Newcomb, 1–16. Oxford: Oxford University Press.

Newcomb, Horace, and Robert S. Alley (1983) *The Producer's Medium: Conversations with Creators of American TV*. New York: Oxford University Press.

Newcomb, Horace, and Paul Hirsch (1983) "Television as a Cultural Forum." *Quarterly Review of Film* 8: 45–55.

Nielsen Media (2007) "Nielsen Begins Including College Students Away from Home in Its National People Meter Sample." Accessed July 15, 2010. http://www.prnewswire.com/news-releases/nielsen-begins-including-college-students-away-from-home-in-its-national-people-meter-sample-53799402.html.

Nippert, Matt (2004) "*The Simpsons* of the South Pacific." *New Zealand Listener*, 25 September. Accessed 18 September 2009. http://www.listener.co.nz/issue/3359/features/2630/the_simpsons_of_the_south_pacific.html.

Nixon, Rob (1994) *Homelands, Harlem and Hollywood: South African Culture and the World Beyond*. London: Routledge.

"No SABC Monopoly" (1984) *Rand Daily Mail*, 20 July, 8.

Ogunnaike, Lola (2005) "The Comic-Strip Revolution Will Be Televised." *New York Times*, 30 October, 29.

Okome, Onookome (2007) "Nollywood: Africa at the Movies." *Film International* 5 (4): 4–9.

Omi, Michael, and Howard Winant (1994). *Racial Formations in the United States from the 1960s to the 1990s*. New York: Routledge.

"On the Rise in Network TV: Costs and Independents" (1980) *Broadcasting*, 30 June, 28–43.

Owen, Bruce M., and Steven S. Wildman (1992) *Video Economics*. Cambridge: Harvard University Press.

Owens-Ibie, Nosa (2000) "Programmed for Domination: U.S. Television Broadcasting and Its Effects on Nigerian Culture." In *"Here, There, and Everywhere": The Foreign Politics of American Popular Culture*, ed. R. Wagenleitner and E. T. May. Hanover: University Press of New England.

Papathanassopoulos, Stylianos (1989) *The Deregulation of Television and Policies for New Media Development: A Comparative Study of the United Kingdom, France, Luxembourg and the Broadcasting Policy of the European Community during 1981–86.* London: City University.

Payne, Monica (1994) "The 'Ideal' Black Family? A Caribbean View of *The Cosby Show.*" *Journal of Black Studies* 25: 231–49.

Peck, Janice (1994) "Talk about Racism: Framing a Popular Discourse of Race on Oprah Winfrey." *Cultural Critique* 27: 89–126.

Peterson, Richard A., and N. Anand (2004) "The Production of Culture Perspective." *Annual Review of Sociology* 30: 311–34.

Pfister, Roger (2005) *Apartheid South Africa and African States: From Pariah to Middle Power.* London: I. B. Tauris.

Poindexter, Paula M., and Carolyn A. Stroman (1981) "Blacks and Television: A Review of the Research Literature." *Journal of Broadcasting* 25: 103–22.

Poussaint, Alvin (1998) Foreword to *African American Viewers and the Black Situation Comedy: Situating Racial Humor,* ed. R. R. Means Coleman, xi–xiv. New York: Garland.

Pratt, Andy (2004) "The Cultural Economy." *International Journal of Cultural Studies* 7: 117–28.

Quinlan, Sterling (1979) *Inside ABC: American Broadcasting Company's Rise to Power.* Winter Park, FL: Hasting House.

Raphel, David (1976) Letter to David Wolper from president, Twentieth Century Fox International Corporation. David L. Wolper Archives, 282-016. University of Southern California, Los Angeles.

Raschka, Marilyn (1988) "Hold Your Fire, It's *Cosby* Time: TV Show's Popularity Cuts across All Factions in Beirut." *Chicago Tribune,* 19 June, sec. 5, p. 16.

Reid, Robert H. (1978) "*Roots* Is on German TV." *News Free-Press,* 9 March.

Reynolds, Debbie (1984) "New TV Station Sparks Fresh Row." *Rand Daily Mail,* 19 November, 3.

Rhoodie, Nic J., C. P. de Kock, and M. P. Couper (1985) "White Perceptions of Socio-Political Change in South Africa." In *South Africa: A Plural Society in Transition,* ed. D. J. van Vuuren, N. E. Wiehahn, J. A. Lomard, and N. J. Rhoodie, 303–34. Durban, South Africa: Butterworth.

Richter, Paul (1985) "Viacom Quietly Becomes a Major Force in TV." *Los Angeles Times,* 22 September, sec. 5, p. 1.

——— (1986) "Networks Get the Picture of Cost-Cutting." *New York Times,* 26 October, sec. 5, p. 1.

Riggs, Marlon (1991) *Color Adjustment.* San Francisco: California Newsreel Distributing.

Roeder, Bill (1978) "*Roots* in South Africa." *Newsweek,* 15 May, 27.

"*Roots* a Hit in Australia" (1977) *Daily Variety,* 13 January. David L. Wolper Archives, 283-015. University of Southern California, Los Angeles.

"Roots Sets TV Records in Italy" (1978) *San Diego Union,* 30 September. David L. Wolper Archives, 283-015. University of Southern California, Los Angeles.

Ross, Karen (1996) *Black and White Media: Black Images in Popular Film and Television.* Cambridge: Polity Press.

Ruggie, John (1993) "Territoriality and Beyond: Problematizing Modernity in International Relations." *International Organization* 47: 139–74.

Russell, Irwin E. (1975) "Memo to All Involved ABC Personnel," 14 November. David L. Wolper Archives, 104-003. University of Southern California, Los Angeles.

Sacchi, Franco, and Robert Caputo (2009) *This Is Nollywood.* San Francisco: California Newsreel Distributing.

Saenz, Michael (2004) "Programming." In *Encyclopedia of Television*, 2d ed., ed. Horace Newcomb, 1833–42. New York: Fitzroy Dearborn.

Scannell, Paddy (1988) "Radio Times: The Temporal Arrangement of Broadcasting in the Modern World." In *Television and Its Audiences: International Research Perspectives*, ed. P. Drummond and R. Patterson. London: BFI Publishing.

Schapiro, Mark (1991) "Lust-Greed-Sex-Power: Translatable Anywhere." *New York Times*, 2 June, B29.

Schnedecker, Gary (1999) Interview by the author with director of acquisitions, Disney Channel España.

Seeger, Murray (1978) "*Roots* Successful in W. Germany." *Jackson Daily News*, 16 March. David L. Wolper Archives, 283-015. University of Southern California, Los Angeles.

Seiler, John (1999) *Transforming Mangope's Bophuthatswana: Towards Democracy in the North West Province.* Accessed 15 September 2001. http://www.mg.co.za/mg/projects/bop/.

Shattuc, Jane (1997) *The Talking Cure: TV Talk Shows and Women.* London: Routledge.

Sherwood, Rick (1992) "For Whom the 'Bell' Tolls." *Hollywood Reporter*, 3 November, S1.

Shohat, Ella, and Robert Stam (1994) *Unthinking Eurocentrism: Multiculturalism and the Media.* London: Routledge.

Silverstone, Roger (1994) *Television and Everyday Life.* London: Routledge.

Simpson, Peter R. (1976) Letter to David L. Wolper from president, Simcom International, 27 August. David L. Wolper Archives, 282-016. University of Southern California, Los Angeles.

Smith-Shomade, Beretta (2007) *Pimpin' Ain't Easy: Selling Black Entertainment Television.* London: Routledge.

Sofley, Kris (2005) "Comic Strip Series Fans Controversy." *Channel 21*, 3 November. Accessed 20 September 2009. http://www.c21media.net/news/detail.asp?area=4&article=27345.

Sollors, Werner (1979) "The Reception of *Roots* in Germany." *American Studies International* 17 (3): 40–44.

Somerset-Ward, Richard (1976) Letter to David Wolper from director–United States, British Broadcasting Corporation, 28 September. David L. Wolper Archives, 282-016. University of Southern California, Los Angeles.

South African Truth and Reconciliation Committee (1997) *Media Hearing.* September 15–17. Accessed August 24, 2012.

Spiller, Nancy (1990) "Bop-TV Is Free from S. African Censorship." *Chicago Tribune*, 18 June, C5.

Spring, Greg (1998) "Why Some U.S. Sitcoms Can Conquer Europe." *Electronic Media*, 5 October, 6.

Squire, Corinne (1994) "Empowering Women? *The Oprah Winfrey Show.*" *Feminism and Psychology* 4 (1): 63–79.

Stevenson, Richard W. (1987) "TV Boom in Europe Is Aiding Hollywood." *New York Times*, 28 December, D1.

Stoler, Ann Laura (1995) *Race and the Education of Desire: Foucault's History of Sexuality and the Colonial Order of Things.* Durham: Duke University Press.

Stone, Merv (1976) Letter to Milton W. Krasny, Wolper Television Sales, from manager of program purchasing, Canadian Broadcasting Corporation, 5 August. David L. Wolper Archives, 282-016. University of Southern California, Los Angeles.

Story, Louise (2007) "At Last, Television Ratings Go to College." *New York Times*, 29 January. Accessed 22 January 2009. http://www.nytimes.com/2007/01/29/business/media/29nielsen.html?pagewanted=all.

Stovall, Taylor (2005) "Black Community, Black Spectacle: Performance and Race in Transatlantic Perspective." In *Black Cultural Traffic: Crossroads in Global Performance and Popular Culture*, ed. H. Elam and K. Jackson, 221–41. Ann Arbor: University of Michigan Press.

Straubhaar, Joseph (1991) "Asymmetrical Interdependence and Cultural Proximity." *Critical Studies in Mass Communication* 8: 39–59.

———(2007) "Região, Raça, e Clase Social: Recepcão de TV na Salvador, Bahia." *Flow TV*. Accessed 21 June 2011. http://flowtv.org/2007/04/place-race-and-class-watching-brazilian-tv-in-salvador-bahia/.

Taylor, Charles, and Amy Guttmann (1992) *Multiculturalism: Examining the Politics of Recognition*. Princeton: Princeton University Press.

Taylor, Ella (1989) *Prime-Time Families in Post-War America*. Berkeley: University of California Press.

Thorburn, David (1987) "Television Melodrama." In *Television: The Critical View,* 4th ed., ed. Horace Newcomb, 628–47. New York: Oxford University Press.

Thornton, John (1993) "Central African Names and African-American Naming Patterns." *William and Mary Quarterly*, 3rd series, 50: 727–42.

Tinic, Serra (2005) *On Location: Canada's Television Industry in a Global Market*. Toronto: University of Toronto Press.

Tobin, Betsy (1990) "The Language of Laughs." *TV World*, October, 29.

Tomaselli, Ruth, Keyan Tomaselli, and Johan Muller (1989) *Broadcasting in South Africa*. New York: St. Martin's.

"Top Import Moves Mover for New Magazine Show" (1998) *New Media Markets*, 2 July. Accessed 20 September 2009. *Factiva*.

"Top Series by Country" (1999) *Media and Marketing Europe*, 31 May, 49.

Torre, Paul (2009) "Block Booking Migrates to Television: The Rise and Fall of the International Output Deal." *Journal of Television and New Media* 10 (6): 501–20.

Torres, Sasha (2003) *Black, White, and in Color: Television and Black Civil Rights*. Princeton: Princeton University Press.

"Transformation Scene in World Television" (1992) *Screen Digest*, February, 33–40.

Tucker, Ken (1992) "TV Review: *The Fresh Prince of Bel-Air*." *Entertainment Weekly*, 17 April. Accessed 1 July 2011. http://www.ew.com/ew/article/0,,310235,00.html.

Tulloch, John, and Manuel Alvarado (1983) *Doctor Who: The Unfolding Text*. London: St. Martin's.

Turow, Joseph (1981) "Unconventional Programs on Commercial Television: An Organizational Perspective." In *Individuals in Mass Media Organizations*, ed. C. Whitney and J. Ettema, 107–30. Beverly Hills: Sage.

———(1996) *Media Systems in Society: Understanding Industries, Strategies, and Power*. 2d ed. New York: Longman.

———(1997) *Breaking Up America: Advertisers and the New Media World*. Chicago: University of Chicago Press.

Turow, Joseph (2005) *Niche Envy: Marketing Discrimination in the Digital Age*. Cambridge: MIT Press.

TVB (2010) *TV Basics*. Television Bureau of Advertising Inc. http://www.tvb.org.

Tyrer, Thomas (1994) "Syndicators Get In on Teen Business." *Electronic Media* 14 November.

Umbach, Klaus (1978) "Der Dschungel Hebt." *Der Spiegel*, 20 February, 184.

"The U.S. as TV Programmer to the World" (1977) *Broadcasting*, 18 April, 48–54.

"U.S. Programmers Converge in Cannes" (1986) *Broadcasting*, 21 April, 89.

Van Slambrouck, Paul (1984) "South African Whites Clamor to Tune In Black TV." *Christian Science Monitor*, 3 February, 7.

Viacom (1985a) Advertisement. *TV World*, February, 116.

——(1985b) *National Automated Accounting Research System Annual Report*. Accessed 4 January 2007. http://web.lexis-nexis.com.

——(1986) Advertisement. *TV World*, February, 25.

——(1987) *Securities and Exchange Commission Form 10-K*. Accessed 4 January 2007. http://web.lexis-nexis.com.

——(1991) *Securities and Exchange Commission Form 10-K*. Accessed 4 January 2007. http://web.lexis-nexis.com.

VT4 (2008) Program Schedule. Accessed 18 November 2008. http://www.vt4.be/tvgids.php?dag=1.

Waller, Ed (2006) "Cowell's Duets Find Canadian Partner." *Channel 21*, 5 June. Accessed 20 September 2009. http://www.c21media.net/news/detail.asp?area=4&article=30698.

Walt Disney Company Inc. (2003) Form 10-K. Filed December 12, 2003. Accessed August 31, 2012. http://www.sec.gov/Archives/edgar/data/1001039/000095014803002883/v95088e10vk.htm.

——(2007) Form 10-K. Filed November 21, 2007. Accessed August 31, 2012. http://www.sec.gov/Archives/edgar/data/1001039/000119312507252227/d10k.htm.

Warner Brothers (1994) "Cumulative Gross Receipts for *Roots II*." 30 September. David L. Wolper Archives, 298-043. University of Southern California, Los Angeles.

——(n.d., a) Promotional materials. David L. Wolper Archives, 300-002. University of Southern California, Los Angeles.

——(n.d., b) Promotional kit. David L. Wolper Archives, 282-027. University of Southern California, Los Angeles.

Watkins, Mel (1994) *On the Real Side: Laughing, Lying, and Signifying—The Underground Tradition of African American Humor That Transformed American Culture from Slavery to Richard Pryor*. New York: Simon and Schuster.

"West Germans Tune In *Roots* by Millions" (1978) *Birmingham News*, 9 March, 21.

Whaley, Deborah E. (forthcoming) "Graphic Blackness/Anime Noir: Aaron McGruder's *The Boondocks* and the Adult Swim." In *Watching While Black: Centering the Television of Black Audiences*, ed. Beretta Smith-Shomade. New Brunswick: Rutgers University Press.

"What's Hot on TV Worldwide" (1986) *Advertising Age*, 1 December, Global Media section, p. 60.

White, Shane, and Graham White (1998) *Stylin': African American Expressive Culture from Its Beginnings to the Zoot Suit*. Ithaca: Cornell University Press.

Williams, Raymond (1974) *Television: Technology and Cultural Form*. Glasgow: Fontana.

——(1980/2006) "Base and Superstructure in Marxist Cultural Theory." In *Media and Cultural Studies KeyWorks*, rev. ed., ed. Meenakshi Gigi Durham and Douglas Kellner, 130–43. Oxford: Blackwell.

"With a 'Dish,' America Watches the World's TV" (1984) *Rand Daily Mail*, 18 August, 8.

Wolper, David (1976) Letter to David Raphel, president, Twentieth Century Fox International Corporation, 18 February. David L. Wolper Archives, 282-016. University of Southern California, Los Angeles.

Wolper, David, with David Fisher (2003) *Producer: A Memoir*. New York: Lisa Drew Books/ Scribner.

Zook, Kristal Brent (1995) "Warner Bruthas." *Village Voice*, 17 January, 36–37.

——— (1999) *Color by Fox: The Fox Network and the Revolution in Black Television*. New York: Oxford University Press.

——— (2008) *I See Black People: The Rise and Fall of African American–Owned Television and Radio*. New York: Nation Books.

Index

About the Author

Timothy Havens is an associate professor of communication studies, African American studies, and international studies at the University of Iowa.